Reflection
in Learning & Professional Development

Theory & Practice

Jennifer A Moon

KOGAN
PAGE

First published in 1999

Kogan Page Limited
120 Pentonville Road
London
N1 9JN
UK

Stylus Publishing Inc.
22883 Quicksilver Drive
Sterling
VA 20166-2012
USA

British Library Cataloguing in Publication Data

A CIP record for this book is available from the British Library.

ISBN 0 7494 2864 3

Typeset by JS Typesetting, Wellingborough, Northants.
Printed and bound by Biddles Ltd, Guildford and King's Lynn.

Dedication

To Kyla and Shelley for whom this book must represent a deprivation of my attention and to Peter for depriving the book of my attention and preserving my sanity rather well. To those others whose reflections, in their minglings with my own, have contributed to this book.

Contents

Preface

The study of reflection

The ramifications of the literature that refers to reflection and to what it seems to be could well lead you to doubt that it exists as a subject in its own right. You might well then doubt the case for the study of reflection. However, the rate of growth of literature on this subject, particularly in the last 20 years, and its apparent face value and broad practical application, provide due justification for its study, despite the difficulties that surround its identity. It is a term that, at the least, has meaning for many, even if it is not well acknowledged in formal psychological terms.

This book is an attempt to take an overview of reflection – in terms of the literature, the common meanings of the word and its value in practical ways of improving learning and professional practice. What follows here is a look at the book as a whole with indications of some of the difficulties faced in making sense of the activity of reflection, which will provide a rationale for the structure of the book.

One of the difficulties of studying the literature on reflection is that it emanates from many different sources. Some of the sources are distinct disciplines, such as education, psychology, philosophy, and sociology; and, although other sources cross disciplines, they have a particular focus, such as experiential learning, reflective practice and the training of the reflective practitioner. Studies on reflection in experiential learning are often unrelated to studies of reflection in other contexts, or else only related via common reference to work such as that of Dewey or Habermas. As in many cross-disciplinary topics, there has been little integration of similar work, perhaps because researchers tend to develop within the cultures of their own disciplines and to cross boundaries is often to face a relatively alien culture. Indeed the differences in cultures can be very evident in professional practice. The work on reflection in the context of practice – reflective practice – originated mainly in the professions of teaching and nursing, but there is little integration of these two sources, and relatively few professional educators have crossed boundaries, even if they have been attempting to develop similar attributes in their novices or their trained professionals. It is as if reflection has been viewed through a series of narrow frames of reference, with little overlap.

Similarly, difficulties arise in the study of particular topics in reflection, such as reflective judgement. There are many implications of this work for educational situations and yet it is scarcely applied there. Furthermore, there are areas of human activity in which reflection would seem to play a large part, such as counselling, therapy and personal development, but in books about these substantial applications, it is hard to find any detailed reference to reflection, Additionally, in counselling, the term can have a different connotation to that implied in other contexts.

There are few accounts of reflection that attempt to cut across professional boundaries. Boud, Keogh and Walker (1985) is, perhaps, the main one, though this book largely preceded the output of Schön (1983) on reflection in professional practice, and the further work that Schön's book inspired. Other work that crosses boundaries includes Mezirow (1990), Atkins and Murphy (1993), Calderhead and Gates (1993), Barnett (1994, 1997) and Hatton and Smith (1995), but in these the summarizing accounts are mostly introductions to their own research or reasoning and are not extensive.

A further complication to the discussion of reflection and other cognitive activities arises from problems of vocabulary. The ability to be precise in academic reasoning on cognitive activities, such as knowledge, knowing, teaching and learning – and reflection – is itself marred by a vocabulary that is either overly extensive or not extensive enough. For example, the following words can apparently be synonymous with reflection – reasoning, thinking, reviewing, problem solving, inquiry, reflective judgement, reflective thinking, critical reflection, reflective practice (Kitchener, 1983). A term such as 'critical thinking' may either be allied with reflection or reflective thinking (Barnett, 1997; Dewey, 1933) or defined separately, as in King and Kitchener (1994). The problem may be rooted in the relatively few efforts of those engaged in these studies to move outside their disciplines to see how others have applied the terms.

While in general there may be too many words and meanings floating around the idea of reflection, in some areas of its study there are distinct deficiencies in vocabulary, and this is particularly the case in the study of reflection in learning. When words are missing, concepts tend to be missing and the absence of concepts may distort understandings. This will be discussed further in Chapter 9 where it has been necessary to invent vocabulary in order to progress understanding.

The modern psychology literature is relatively unhelpful in the study of reflection in that there are few references to such activity and it is mostly unclear how it might be distinguished from cognition or, more precisely, how it coincides with, or differs from, the process of thinking. In the same way that the relationship of reflection to thinking is vague, so are the interrelationships between reflection, thinking and emotion.

For the thesis of this book, perhaps the most noticeable gap in the literature is that on reflection in the process of learning, even though most of the applied references to reflection can be interpreted as involving learning of some form or other. The existence of this gap between an identification of the nature of reflection and the processes of learning means that the many applications of reflection in educational and professional situations are guided by assumption or guesswork. It is this gap that the book largely attempts to address. Nevertheless, in attempting to draw reflection even slightly from the realms of intuition and instinct, it is important not simply to abandon its common-sense meanings, but to ground theory in these. The application of reflection to improve learning and practice would not be served well by abstracting a theoretical term that loses its common meaning for practitioners. We are mindful, therefore, of the common-sense understandings of reflection just as much as the specialized meaning attributed to it in other areas of the literature.

The aim and structure of this study of reflection

We have so far talked of the complexities of the literature of reflection and pointed out the direction that this book will take. However, it is not the intention here to pull the ideas in the literature into one precise definition as this could only pretend to be accurate because different people have intentionally defined reflection differently. Rather, the view taken here is that there is more in common between the different uses of the term than might at first appear and that at least boundaries can be placed around the term to provide it with greater coherency.

The chapters of Part I of this book review the literature of reflection. This mainly consists of a consideration of the variety of contexts in which the term has been described or in which work has been done on it or with it. Chapter 1 lays some groundwork for the study of reflection in discussing the common understanding of the word in everyday speech and goes on to look at research that provides a developmental context for reflection. Another element of the background of the study of reflection is its frequent reference to the work of Dewey and Habermas, which here is seen as a 'backbone' of theory. Chapter 2 reviews the contributions of these two authors and some work that is closely related. Chapter 3 deals with reflection in experiential learning and Chapters 4, 5 and 6 consider its role in professional practice, initially reviewing the work of Donald Schön. Chapter 7 looks at reflection in counselling, therapy and personal development.

The first chapter in Part II – Chapter 8 on reflection and learning – takes stock of the conclusions of previous chapters, cutting through the different terminologies and applications to seek the common elements among the work done in this are and gain a more coherent understanding of its nature in all of its different contexts.

With a more coherent understanding of reflection, there is an opportunity to relate reflection more closely than hitherto to the process of learning, thereby addressing the gap identified earlier. Unfortunately, the literature on learning does not provide a coherent view of the real world of academic learning within which the role of reflection can meaningfully be explored. To further this review of learning, the chapters in Part II take a detour from the topic of reflection and seek to develop a useful overview of higher level learning to which it can be related. In this context, Chapters 9 and 10 provide relevant background material to the study of learning and Chapter 11 demonstrates the development of a speculative a map of learning and representation of it that will enable hypotheses to be developed about the role of reflection in learning in Chapter 12.

Part III represents the practical side of the book – the use of reflection to improve learning and practice. Chapter 13 considers the conditions of the learning environment that encourage reflection. Chapter 14 is a description of two case studies in professional development and practice where deliberate and carefully designed exercises involving reflection contributed to the greater impact of short courses and to effective decision making. The last two chapters detail practical activities and exercises that encourage learners to reflect on their learning or practice. Chapter 15 specifically concerns the use of learning journals and Chapter 16 consists of a range of other activities that use reflection to improve processes in learning and practice.

Part I

The literature of reflection

Chapter 1

Some background to the study of reflection

Introduction

This chapter provides some background to the discussions of reflection in its
different contexts. First, the lay or common-sense view of the term is considered
because, if there is to be an improvement in reflective processes, it will be most
effective if the idea is clearly related to the general understanding of the word.
This view of the term is used as a basis for comparison with the more technical
views of reflection.

The chapter moves on to lay another foundation for reflection that tends to
be neglected. Part of the common understanding of the term is that reflective
capacity varies among individuals and develops with age but also within an
educationally stimulating environment. The discussion considers several studies
that have viewed aspects of reflection as an evolving capacity within individuals.

Common-sense views of reflection

Writing in the literature of teacher training, Morrison (1996) refers to reflection
as a 'conceptual and methodological portmanteau'. As has already been intimated,
the literature contains many interpretations of the word and, immersed within
this chaotic catalogue of meanings, it can be difficult to recall that there are
common-sense meanings of reflection as well. As this book provides practical
support to those encouraging reflection, it is necessary to take into account
the understandings of the word that people bring to a learning situation and
clarify where these understandings differ from theoretical interpretations. For

example, there are some theoretical definitions of the term that are narrow, in effect honing off parts of the commonly understood activity by denoting particular purposes or conditions under which reflection occurs. Reflective judgement (described later in this chapter), is one such example (King and Kitchener, 1994). While this makes it more manageable for research or application purposes, it can have the effect of dissociating it from common-place experience. This contributes to a split between theory, theorizing and practice.

The way in which the word 'reflection' is commonly used suggests several understandings. First, that reflection seems to lie somewhere around the process of learning and the representation of that learning. We reflect on something in order to consider it in more detail ('Let me reflect on what you are saying') or to re-represent it in oral or written form. Second, to be of significance for study, we have to regard reflection as implying purpose (Dewey, 1933; Hullfish and Smith, 1961). Generally, we reflect for a purpose, although conclusions to complicated issues can just 'pop up' without our being conscious of there having been a reflective process. This last situation could imply that reflection has occurred unconsciously and might then overlap with intuition. An alternative to the notion of processing with purpose, therefore, is processing that leads to a useful outcome.

The third understanding of the word is that it involves complicated mental processing of issues for which there is no obvious solution (Dewey, 1933; King and Kitchener, 1994). For example, people do not use the word reflection to describe their processing of simple mental arithmetic or their mental processes en route to a known place. They are more likely to use the words 'think' or 'recall'. Rather, reflection appears to suggest more processing than would occur when simply recalling something.

These considerations indicate that common usage of the word imply a form of mental processing with a purpose and/or an anticipated outcome that is applied to relatively complicated or unstructured ideas for which there is not an obvious solution. This suggests close association with, or involvement in, learning and the representation of learning.

As well as developing tight definitions of the term itself, some writers have elaborated forms, levels and other categorizations of the process. Examples are Van Manen's levels of reflection (Van Manen, 1977) and Schön's reflection in- and on-action (Schön, 1983). While, again, these categorizations may be helpful in trying to 'capture' reflection for academic use, they do not seem to be represented in common language. They may, indeed, represent different forms of reflection – or else the forms may appear to differ because they have been initiated or guided differently or used for different purposes. For example, reflection is interpreted as a specialized tool for professional practice and interpreted differently from its involvement in learning from experience. The mental act, however, may be the same in both and perhaps no different than if applied by a child who reflects on what she did when she last played with her favourite toy. Reflection may, therefore, be a much more simple activity than the contents of the portmanteau mentioned above might seem to indicate.

The distinctions may be in how it is guided, used or treated theoretically.

In the common-sense meaning of reflection, there can be an overlap between the use of words such as 'reflection' and 'thinking'. These words can refer to the same activity – for example, the notion of the 'reflective practitioner' (Schön, 1983), is largely captured in the colloquial phrase 'thinking on your feet'. Similarly, phrases such as 'let me think about this one . . .' and 'let me ponder or reflect on this' appear to have the same meaning.

In another sense, the term is used to pull together a broad range of previous thinking or knowledge in order to make greater sense of it for another purpose that may transcend the previous bounds of personal knowledge or thought. An example is where the sense of it is that of taking an overview or 'sitting back' from a situation to review it. The notions of critical thinking or critical reflection come into this usage of the term (Barnett, 1994), and this connotation also relates to the idea of being wise or having wisdom in the sense of 'being reflective'. 'Being reflective' itself has broader connotations as it is more like a long-term characteristic of a person's behaviour, rather than the description of a mental activity. A person who is reflective seems to be someone who comfortably and successfully engages in the mental activity of reflection and would make decisions that are well considered. This accords with the reflective learning style (Honey and Mumford, 1986). In the literature, the term 'reflective practitioner' often seems to relate more strongly to the characteristics of the person than to the habitual use of reflection as a mental tool, though, in some cases, both meanings are implied in the term.

From these various considerations, more common views of reflection emerge. It is seen as a means of transcending more usual patterns of thought to enable the taking of a critical stance or an overview. There is also the idea of 'being reflective', which says something about the type of person and their manner of behaving and engagement in the mental activity of reflection. The word is applied here with the sense of saying something not so much about what a person does as what they are.

We begin to get a picture of a common idea that has a variety of different connotations. This picture is developed more strongly over subsequent chapters. The question is, do these different ways in which reflection is viewed describe different mental activities or one activity with different interpretations? The different ways of using the word have significance for theoretical writing about reflection as well as practical applications or evaluations of it in education or practice (Newell, 1994; Fitzgerald, 1994). The suggestion that is set up for testing in subsequent chapters is that reflection itself is a mental process with purpose and/or outcome. It is applied in situations where material is ill-structured or uncertain in that it has no obvious solutions, a mental process that seems to be related to thinking and to learning. It is suggested that the apparent differences in reflection are not due to different types of reflection – in other words, to differences in the process itself, but to differences in the way that it is used, applied or guided. The term 'framework' is applied to these uses or applications or means of guiding the activity.

If reflection is a relatively simple mental process, another set of concerns in this part of the book is to disentangle the basic activity from the surrounding frameworks.

Developmental stage approaches to reflection

There are some hints of a hierarchical, if not a developmental, approach to reflection in the work of a number of writers. For example, Habermas and Van Manen's work, which is discussed in the next chapter, suggests an organization of knowledge that moves from capacity for interpretation of relatively structured information towards the need to interpret in situations of uncertain ideas.

The individual's progression from dealing with basic 'certain' knowledge to working with uncertainty is one of the strands that underlies the developmental stage approaches to reflection and the development of thinking (Belenky, Clinchy, Goldberger and Tarule, 1986; King and Kitchener, 1994). The feature of these studies clearly common to them all is that the highest stage of development is characterized again by an awareness of, and the ability to work with, provisional or uncertain knowledge.

The studies of reflective thinking of King and Kitchener

In contrast to much of the literature on reflection, which has applied reflection or its interpretation, King and Kitchener base their construct on a substantial volume of empirical work that focuses on the quality of cognitive activity involved in reflective thinking (King and Kitchener, 1994). 'Reflective judgement' is the term that they apply to the most advanced stage of the reflective judgement model, and the model is a description of the development of reflective thinking in their terminology. They are not, therefore, concerned with the whole idea of reflection, but with a derived construct that is defined for experimental purposes. Their findings, however, elaborate our understanding as a whole.

In their model of reflective judgement, seven stages are described, but the first three are seen as 'pre-reflective thinking', with the subject viewing knowledge as almost always stable and certain. Only the final two stages are designated as being truly reflective. The ability to make reflective judgements is the most advanced stage. The implication is that the advanced stages are not attained by everyone.

The authors note that reflective judgement is identified as a more advanced form of thinking than the 'top' stage identified in Perry's classic study of (male) students' intellectual and ethical development (Perry, 1970). The ability to make reflective judgements, therefore, is characteristically adult and appears to result from a developmental progression. Knowledge and reasoning skills are involved in the lower stages of the model. However, the capacity to make reflective judgements is taken to indicate that individuals have reached an understanding that enables them to cope in situations of uncertain information. In these situations, the subject can acknowledge that there is no 'right answer' and can accept that experts may disagree as to the 'best solution' of a dilemma. In this respect, King and Kitchener note the similarity between their model and that of moral judgement (Kohlberg, 1963), in that the most advanced stages both rely on a person's ability to cope with uncertain knowledge.

It is also in respect of a person's understanding of the uncertainty of knowledge that King and Kitchener distinguish between reflective thinking and critical thinking. In their view, critical thinking is aligned with problem-solving skills where a set of techniques, which can be learned, will facilitate the process of solution. It is suggested that the ability to reach the higher stages of reflective thinking may require these problem-solving skills, but that a capacity to cope with uncertainty is required in addition.

The King and Kitchener reflective judgement model is supported by sub-stantial experimental work over more than 10 years, with 1700 subjects in 33 studies. Given its experimental basis, it is worth remembering that while the aim might have been to measure 'epistemological cognition', there was inevitably influence from variables affecting the ability to express or represent the cognitions, whether orally or in written tasks. The difficulty of distinguishing the processes of learning from the representation of that learning is common to many studies of reflection and learning.

Studies of 'women's ways of knowing'

The work of Belenky, Clinchy, Goldberger and Tarule (1986) demonstrates some findings in common with those of King and Kitchener. They describe their work as research on the problems of learning and knowing and, like King and Kitchener, refer to the work of Perry (1970). However, they distinguish their approach sharply from that of Perry because their subjects were a selected and not socially representative group of women of a mixed age group while Perry worked with male students. Like Perry, but unlike the more experimental approach of King, et al., Belenky, et al., used a loose interview structure as the research tool and organized the observed patterns of thinking and attitudes into a series of stages of development of knowledge.

Underlying the work of Belenky, et al., is the contention that there is gender bias in many studies of thinking, with the bias being perpetuated within the structure of a male-managed educational system. They question the assumption that men function cognitively in the same way as women or that the genders share similar needs when it comes to the support they need for their learning. They make proposals for the types of educational provision that might fit the particular development needs of women.

The interpretation of the interviews of the women in the Belenky study distinguishes seven groups that were characterized by epistemological under-standing and the relationship of their views of themselves to their knowing.

While the categories are not presented as stages of a developmental process, there is an implication that they do represent progression and the suggestion is made that women who were not challenging themselves educationally or were unable to move from disadvantaged backgrounds would not progress beyond the earlier categories.

While there is a broad similarity between the King, *et al.*, and Belenky, *et al.*, schemes, most striking is the match between the stage of reflective judgement of the former and Belenky's 'position of constructed knowledge', which is also the highest category in the latter research. Women in this group understood that knowledge is provisional and that the knower is part of the construction of the knowledge. One of the women in this group reflected that she could be mislead by her subjective world and was still concerned about the judgements of others, but now recognized an inner sense that enabled her to reason and use intuition in a balanced manner.

The Belenky, *et al.*, study is not explicit about the role of reflection in the development of knowledge, but it is implied strongly in the nature of comments such as that above. In addition, this comment demonstrates how the search for self and inner confidence is central in enabling women to transform their 'way of knowing'. Although this style of response may, in part, be an artefact of the style of the interviewing, reflective interaction is the basis of the teaching and learning ('connected teaching') that is suggested by the study to facilitate development in women's thinking.

It is of interest that, like the King and Kitchener stages of development, knowledge in the least developed groups of the Belenky, *et al.*, research seems to have involved little reflection. The women in these groups are described as unable to speak for themselves and as simply the receivers of knowledge from others. King and Kitchener describe the assumptions of their lowest group as being characterized by the view that 'there is assumed to be an absolute correspondence between what is believed to be true and what is true', and that 'knowledge can be obtained with certainty by direct observation'. Such views imply a belief that knowledge is 'given' and there is no place for reflective activity that could develop that knowledge independently.

Other evidence of development in the capacity to reflect

There is further support for the notion that, in a relatively advanced state of development, reflection is involved in working with 'ill-structured' material. Holm and Stephenson (1994) have contributed to a book on reflection in nursing (Palmer, Burns and Bulman 1994). They write as student nurses who have been inducted into habits of reflection on their course, and they consider their experiences of this process in the chapter. By means of written examples, they note a number of stages of development in their ability. The penultimate stage is one in which they observe themselves to be 'questioning the given'. In the last stage, which seems to relate to aspects of King and Kitchener and Belenky, *et al.*'s stages, they were able to use reflection to bring clarity to unclear situations.

It is interesting to note that in the act of writing their chapter, Holm and Stephenson are demonstrating capable meta-cognitive reflection on their own process of learning, as further evidence of the developed state of their abilities. It would be interesting to know how much their development is due to direct educational guidance and how much to self-development.

A particularly important observation that emerges from the chapter by Holm and Stephenson is that learning to reflect was a difficult process and entailed the use of skills that by no means all of the students possessed at the beginning of their nursing education. That reflection is a difficult process, particularly when it supports changes of behaviour, is a theme that will be returned to later in the book on several occasions. For many, it appears that the capacity to reflect purposefully needs to be fostered or coached. Those who can engage in such activity may promote it without appreciating the difficulties others have when trying to do this.

Wisdom and reflection

The stage of reflective judgement identified by King and Kitchener and, in respect of its similarity, the work of Belenky, *et al.*, meets many of the criteria of the notion of 'wisdom' (Kitchener and Brenner, 1990). In its common form of understanding, wisdom is the culmination of the development of a group of qualities that, generally, are seen to include reflection (Arlin, 1990; Birren and Fisher, 1990, and others in Sternberg, 1990; Barnett, 1994).

In the context of their discussion of wisdom, Kitchener and Brenner suggest that some of the criteria for wisdom are met at the stage of reflective judgement. These include the ability to cope with uncertain knowledge (in ill-structured questions) and the understanding of the fallibility of knowledge as it applies to themselves, and in terms of the limitations of strategies that can be applied to problem solving. They also include the ability to make astute decisions. Kitchener and Brenner note that in many, but not all, studies, wisdom is associated with older age (Meacham, 1990) and that reflective judgement is an adult (not childhood) quality. They consider that wisdom may be dependent on the development of the understandings of uncertainty that are displayed in the advanced stages in the reflective judgement model. However, they suggest that other qualities – such as breadth and depth of knowledge and good communication skills – may characterize what is commonly defined as the wise person.

While mentioning the same qualities of wisdom as those above, Barnett (1994) conceives of wisdom as encompassing action also – 'wisdom is some kind of relationship between knowing and action. "Wisdom" implies limits to both knowing and action'. Barnett thus develops a definition of wisdom that is reminiscent of many ideas of 'reflective practice' (see also Chapters 5 and 6).

Conclusion

This chapter has supplied some details of the background to the literature on reflection. The exploration of the common view of reflection provides some information about how reflection is used in everyday speech. It seems important to take this view into account in developing any theoretical view that could have practical implications.

'Reflection' seems to be seen as a basic mental process with either a purpose or an outcome or both, that is applied in situations where material is ill-structured or uncertain and where there is no obvious solution. Reflection seems to be related to thinking and learning.

The apparent differences in reflection in the literature may actually be differences in the framework of use or of guidance of reflection rather than in the process itself. This idea is set up as a model for comparison with the interpretations of later chapters.

A series of studies suggests some connotations of a developmental sequence. This can partly be interpreted in epistemological terms and there is some educational influence on the developmental process. Reference is made to the implications of both the developmental process and the common view of reflection in later chapters, particularly the next chapter.

Chapter 2

The 'backbone philosophies' of reflection – Dewey and Habermas

Introduction

It is probably true to say that most writers on reflection begin their articles with a preamble that refers to one or two of four writers whose work or models have influenced the manner in which the term is viewed. These writers are John Dewey, Jürgen Habermas, Donald Schön and David Kolb. As to which of these writers is chosen usually depends on the angle the writer is taking.

This chapter introduces the work of Dewey and Habermas and others whose stance is complementary, while Kolb and Schön are introduced in the contexts of their work in later chapters – Kolb in the context of experiential learning in Chapter 3 and Schön in the context of reflection in professional development in Chapter 4.

Dewey and Habermas described reflection in different ways and for different purposes. Dewey's purpose was for the elucidation of educational processes and the more general understanding of human function, whereas Habermas used it to clarify and develop epistemological issues in the sociology of knowledge. While the two approaches could be seen to divide the literature, yet they could also be seen to be taking complementary views that build on each other. Dewey's and Habermas' views are enlarged on in the second part of this chapter, by a consideration of how they have been applied by other significant writers, particularly within the context of education.

This chapter sets out some of the central ideas that are referred to in later parts of this book. The work of Dewey and Habermas could be described as the backbone of the study of reflection.

John Dewey's approach to reflection

Dewey is concerned with the nature of reflection and how it occurs – the skills by which we manipulate knowledge or reprocess it towards a purpose (Dewey, 1933). His approach is seen as psychological and educational, but it is clearly rooted in his observations of his own processes and those of others. Dewey (1933) allies reflection with thinking and uses a number of terms for it. He describes it as 'the kind of thinking that consists in turning a subject over in the mind and giving it serious thought'. Reflection is a chain of linked ideas that aims at a conclusion and is more than a stream of consciousness. The anticipated end to be reached determines the process of operations that lead to it. In this respect, the anticipated outcome could be said to coincide with the purpose of reflection, which is an important point also made in Chapter 8.

Although Dewey ascribes some importance to the outcome of reflection, more crucial for him is the initiation of reflective thinking in a state of doubt, uncertainty or difficulty. It is the need to solve the 'perplexity' that guides the process. He considers that a mix of skill and attitude govern the quality of the process, and that a form of testing through action on the basis of the idea appropriately concludes reflective activity.

In summary, reflective thinking for Dewey is 'Active, persistent and careful consideration of any belief or supposed form of knowledge in the light of the grounds that support it and further conclusions to which it leads . . . it includes a conscious and voluntary effort to establish belief upon a firm basis of evidence and rationality' (Dewey, 1933).

The main features of Dewey's approach to reflection and reflective thinking are the generation of the process through 'perplexity', a sense of goal directedness and the notion of testing or evaluation, which brings Dewey's approach into the realms of experiential learning (Jaworski, 1993). Dewey believes that the process can be improved by having an understanding of, and experimenting with, forms of thinking and that the motivation for improvement of these skills is initiated by formal education.

Other writers who have continued Dewey's work

In a similar manner to Dewey and building on Dewey's work, Hullfish and Smith (1961) picked up the banner for reflective thinking. They describe it as being different from 'the looser kinds of thinking primarily by virtue of being directed or controlled by a purpose – the solution of a problem'.

A distinction between the views of Hullfish and Smith and Dewey lies in the former writers' stress on the roles of imagination and emotion in knowing and then in anticipating possible solutions to problems. They say that the key to good-quality reflection is 'the controlled use of sentiency, memory and imagination in a balance that is appropriate to the particular purpose or problem at hand'.

Others also consider that Dewey neglected the role of emotion in reflective processes and make a strong case for its inclusion (Boud, Keogh and Walker, 1985). In this respect, the somewhat neglected book of Hullfish and Smith might be seen to complement that of Dewey's with its greater emphasis on skills, attitudes and emotion in reflective activity.

Rather surprisingly, the concept of reflective thinking developed by Hullfish and Smith also seems to anticipate Schön's construct of reflection-in-action (Schön, 1983), although whether or not this activity can be considered to be reflection is questioned. Hullfish and Smith say that reflective thinking can be used to draw together thought and knowledge to produce immediate action in such situation as when, to use their example, a burning log falls on to a carpet and threatens a fire. Unlike Schön, however, they do not appear to distinguish the reflection that relates to immediate action from that on a problem in the longer term.

Jürgen Habermas' approach to reflection

The philosophical stance taken by Jürgen Habermas is that reflection is a tool used in the development of particular forms of knowledge. Habermas is concerned with the nature of the knowledge that man has selected to adopt or the nature of knowledge that human beings, by reason of their human condition, have been motivated to generate (the 'knowledge constitutive interests'). Habermas focuses on the nature of the different processes that underlie the generation of these forms of knowledge, and reflection is one of these processes (Habermas, 1971).

Knowledge constitutive interests 'guide and shape' human knowledge with their characteristic processes of inquiry (Carr and Kemmis, 1986). The technical or instrumental knowledge constitutive interests are represented in a concern to understand the environment in which man lives, with a motivation, ultimately, to gain control over it via the methods of the empirical-analytical sciences. The sciences seek to objectify the world and attempt to understand it in terms of scientific explanation.

The knowledge constitutive interests in the historic hermeneutic disciplines – the social sciences and humanities – are concerned with the understanding of human beings' behaviour and forms of communication. The material of this domain cannot be reduced to scientific explanation and the development of knowledge relies on interpretation and integration of ideas in order to understand the meanings of human behaviour and communications. For example, we interpret human actions and opinions in order to develop knowledge or representations of knowledge in the arts and humanities. The social sciences operate partially as historic hermeneutic disciplines, but other aspects of the social sciences are suggested by Habermas to belong to the third form of knowledge constitutive interests – the emancipatory interests, where they should contribute to the emancipation of social groups.

Emancipatory interests rely on the development of knowledge via critical or evaluative modes of thought and enquiry so as to understand the self, the human condition and self in the human context. The acquisition of such knowledge is aimed at producing a transformation in the self, or in the personal, social or world situation or any combination of these.

It was particularly important for Habermas in his work to demonstrate that the methods of empirical analytic enquiry cannot form an adequate basis for social sciences. He argued that the interpretations in social sciences are themselves derived from subjectively influenced research and therefore a continuous evaluation of the manners in which the knowledge has been generated is required. While the basic method of the social sciences can be interpretive, critical or evaluative processes of enquiry are necessary to create a critique that can foster self-understanding and a questioning of the processes by which interpretative enquiry can be subject to distortion.

Other writers' work in relation to Habermas' writings

Such reasoning is reflexive and the literature on reflection itself justifies Habermas' view that evaluative inquiry has an important role in the enquiry of social sciences. It is noted later, for example, that constructs such as 'reflection-in-action' (Schön 1983) appear to have been accepted into established theory without substantial testing. Once ideas have been put into print, they easily became utilized as if they are fact. Social sciences that incorporate critical theory, serve emancipatory interests by generating questioning and understanding. The critical theory emerges from the processes of critique and evaluation and the social sciences that add the tendency for appropriately guided action or practice. For Carr and Kemis (1986), the action of self-reflection enables the researcher 'to expose and identify self-interests and ideological distortions . . . [by analysing] . . . the correspondences and non-correspondences between understandings, practices and the structure of educational situations'. The goal is greater emancipation within the situation and the researcher.

In terms of the role of reflection, there is some disagreement in the literature on its role in instrumental inquiry. Barnett (1994) suggests that it is implicit in Habermasian analyses that reflection does not play a large part in the physical sciences, while Morrison (1995) and Clarke, James and Kelly (1996) include it as representative of the methodology of 'efficient' but not transformative reflective practice. Reflection is involved in interpretive enquiry in the sense of a concern to clarify and interpret meaning towards a consensus of understanding, but, while it might be seen as an optional method of interpretive enquiry, it is integral to emancipatory interests. Emancipation and the resulting empowerment are brought about by reflection that enables practitioners to understand their true situations sufficiently to create the freedoms that they need for themselves (Barnett, 1997).

Common and distinctive elements of Dewey's and Habermas' writings

Dewey and Habermas have in common the notion that reflection serves to generate knowledge. Their views on this may be considered to be complementary in that Dewey considers the process, and Habermas considers the place of the process in the acquisition, development and consideration of knowledge.

There is, however, a distinction between them that is evident in their consideration of the motivation that underlies reflection. Habermas' work drives towards the ideals of empowerment and political emancipation (Morrison, 1995), towards truth, freedom and justice, whereas Dewey's more detailed analysis of reflection rests in interpretive interests, in 'making sense of the world' in the process of effective education. Perhaps because Habermas himself endeavoured to promote the emancipatory functions of knowledge, those interpreting his work in the field of reflection seem prone to imply that there is particular value and status to this form of knowing. In some writings, such as Smyth (1989) and Morrison (1995, 1996), there is some idea that reflective activity should work towards emancipatory goals. It might seem to be more appropriate to recognize the potential value of all forms of purposeful reflection (Hatton and Smith, 1995) while noting its particular use as a tool for emancipation.

The common-sense view of reflection is that it is a mental process that is couched in a framework of purpose or outcome. On this basis, reflection used for emancipatory purposes can be viewed as the operation of the basic mental process acting within a framework that encourages critique and evaluation towards an outcome that is liberating in its effect. In other words, it is the framework of intention and any guidance towards fulfilment of that intention that is significant in distinguishing one act of reflection from another. The mental process itself may not differ from one situation to another.

Developments of the views of Dewey and Habermas in the context of education

Knowledge constitutive interests applied in a vision of higher education

Barnett (1997) provides an example of the application of the knowledge constitutive interests of Habermas to higher education – particularly the emancipatory interests and the associated ideas of critical theory. His work interprets, applies and develops the ideas proposed by Habermas and, in particular, Barnett's orientation exults the use of reflection as a tool for evaluation and criticism of society in contrast to its application to knowledge in current views of higher education.

While critical thinking has been fundamental to the development of Western universities, Barnett (1997) suggests that it has not been a well-defined concept. He suggests that in its concern mainly for discourse about knowledge, it will not support the higher education for which we should aim in the next decade. This should be a system that is not only reflexively critical at levels of the nature of knowledge, self (the learner), the institution and the world, but also generates action in pursuit its beliefs. This incorporation of critique and action, he designates as a state of critical being: 'The full potential of critical being will . . . be achieved through the integration of its expression in the three domains of knowledge, self and world, and in being lived out at the highest levels of critique in each domain. Through such an integration of the critical spirit, critical but creative persons will result, capable of living effectively in the world' (Barnett 1997).

Barnett considers that, currently, the notion of reflection is superseding that of 'criticism' because it carries reflexive and self-monitoring connotations. He warns that there is a danger that it could become an ideology that requires reflection only at interpretive levels and disregards the potential for empowerment and emancipation. He comments on the current fragmented view of reflection – a view that is supported by the first chapter of this book – and sees it as another barrier to the application of reflection aimed at reaching the potential for critical being.

Barnett (1997) suggests that, in order to bring about the state of critical being, the frame of reference in higher education must be changed towards a focus on the student as a developing person. He identifies understanding, self-reflection and action as three domains that need to be part of the work of the university and argues that space needs to be given in order for these capacities to become established. Students need the right space, time and support in order to develop in these domains and put their learning into action.

In his analysis of higher education in the present time and visions for change, Barnett applies Habermasian ideas in a real situation and demonstrates the role of reflection in the generation of change and political empowerment. While he describes how reflection can operate within an educational system in a theoretical context, like Habermas, Barnett assumes the nature of reflection and only in relatively global terms does he describe the conditions in the classroom that will facilitate the changes towards his vision.

Emancipatory ideals and classroom pedagogy – a synthesis

Part of Van Manen's work in education is similar to that of Barnett, but it considers the effects of an element of the educational process – curriculum development – rather than an entire stage of education (Van Manen, 1977). In a second publication 14 years later, Van Manen tackles the analysis of reflection in the context of teaching (Van Manen, 1991) in a manner more akin to Dewey's work. In this sense, Van Manen relates his work to both Habermas and Dewey and demonstrates their complementarity.

In his work on the curriculum, Van Manen (1977) uses the Habermasian scheme of knowledge constitutive interests to analyse the current state of curriculum development and envisage the development of it. He bases the three levels of his scheme on the quality of reflective activity and questioning that underpins curriculum development. His argument is that the curriculum should be developed by using motives that support emancipatory ideals, which is level 3 in his model. In terms of the first two of Van Manen's levels, curriculum development is either instrumental and concerned about ' "best choice" . . . in accordance with the principles of technological progress – economy, efficiency and effectiveness' or with the values, assumptions and presuppositions that underlie curriculum development. On level three, curriculum development processes should question and analyse these assumptions as a means of interpreting the 'nature and quality of the educational experience'. The worth of the values, assumptions and presuppositions in their contribution to social wisdom and justice is assessed by continuous critique.

As in the writings of Barnet and Habermas, reflection is central to the third of Van Manen's levels of critique and evaluation. It is important at the second level, but deals directly with social interpretation. At the first level, the decisions for the curriculum are instrumental and are deliberative rather than reflective.

In the work described, Van Manen, like Habermas, was concerned with reflection as a tool that could be applied to a task – in this case, that of constructing a curriculum. However, in his later work, reflection is applied to pedagogical processes (Van Manen, 1991) in a style of writing that is, in itself designed to engage reflection on the essence of teaching and learning in novice teachers. Van Manen's analysis here is more akin to that of Dewey – indeed his book has a similar tone to Dewey's (1933). Here, Van Manen defines reflection in terms of a means of mental action that distances the person from events in order that they may be viewed in a more objective manner.

Van Manen suggests that there are different conditions in which reflection is applied. The model that he develops is applied quite widely in the literature (Van Manen, 1991) and there are other references to it later in this book. The first level of the application of reflection is thinking and acting on an everyday basis. The second level is more specific reflection on incidents or events. The third and fourth levels appear to match the employment of reflection implied in the second and third knowledge constitutive interest described by Habermas (1971) and Van Manen himself with reference to curriculum development above (1977). The third is the development of understanding through interpretation. This is gained by reflection on personal experience and that of others. The fourth is reflection on the way we reflect, which leads towards an understanding of knowledge and its nature. This leads to the possibilities of emancipation. In these levels, Van Manen is distinguishing between reflection on experience and reflection on the conditions that shape experience.

Van Manen also talks about a form of reflection similar to the state of 'being reflective' described in Chapter 1 – an ongoing awareness or thoughtfulness, a 'mindfulness' in (in this case) pedagogical situations.

Revisiting the development of reflection

While the work of Habermas in terms of reflection is not directed towards the processes of the individual, there are some implications of a hierarchy of processes in the knowledge constitutive interests. For example, the reflection involved in interpretation is a basis for the interpretations themselves, which lead towards emancipation. In other words, knowledge must be developed first by interpretive or instrumental means before it is possible to take a critical overview of that knowledge and the processes that have led to its generation. Educational processes tend to deal with facts in a discipline before they deal with interpretive issues concerning those facts.

In the model of reflective judgement, there is a close resemblance between the criteria for reflective judgement and the activities of evaluative and critical enquiry that underlie the development of knowledge towards emancipatory ends in the work of Habermas (1971) and, later, Van Manen's writings. Kitchener says 'Despite the fact that our knowledge of reality is subject to our own perceptions and interpretations, it is nevertheless possible, through the process of critical enquiry and evaluation, to determine that some judgements about reality are more correct than other judgements' (Kitchener, 1983).

Like King and Kitchener, the Belenky, *et al.*, study (1986) relates to the Habermasian scheme. This is particularly evident in the epistemological understanding achieved by the women in the 'constructed knowledge' position, but, additionally, the case studies provide a strong flavour of emancipation in their description of women who achieved change in their lives as a result of a critical understanding of their social and personal positions. Rather akin to the writings of Habermas and Barnett, there is a sense of an emancipatory 'driving force', which values emancipation as an ultimate goal. This is displayed throughout the writing, but whether this force emanates from the subjects or is a value of the writers is hard to determine.

Conclusion

The approaches of the stage development theorists, Dewey, Habermas and the others mentioned all bear some basic relationship to a common-sense view of reflection in which it is seen not as clearly different from thinking, but as having added connotations of purposiveness. Sometimes the achievement of an outcome implied by all of the writers mentioned in this chapter is the idea that reflection characteristically operates on ill-structured material. As before, it is suggested that what may appear to be very different views in the literature may only in fact differ in terms of the nature of the framework of purposes and outcomes of reflection rather than the process itself. The discussion so far has added some conditions to this view of reflection. The work of Habermas, Barnett and Van Manen suggest that reflection has different enabling roles depending on the material towards which it is directed. Interpretive enquiry reflection works towards the identification of the best solution and, by means of critical reflection and overview, it both evaluates the status of the knowledge and builds theory. Furthermore, it can be used to enable the attainment of states of emancipation. In all of these roles, reflection is the tool for service rather than being part of the service itself.

Chapter 3

Reflection in experiential learning

Introduction

This is the first of several chapters that review the manner in which reflection has been considered in fields of professional education and development.

The literature of experiential learning has largely evolved in the training and professional development fields and, to a lesser extent, that of adult education. It increasingly impinges on formal education in its application to placements, fieldwork and accredited work-based learning. The development of this field was boosted by the publication of the Kolb cycle of experiential learning in the 1980s, although forms of this cycle are evident in earlier literature, including the work of Dewey in 1933.

In general terms, the distinguishing features of experiential learning are that it refers to the organizing and construction of learning from observations that have been made in some practical situation, with the implication that the learning can then lead to action (or improved action). A factor that is noticeable in many studies is the evangelical presentation of experiential learning, or 'learning by doing' (Gibbs, 1988). It would appear that this approach is often used in order to press the contrast to its favour, with classroom or book-based learning. Kolb says: 'experiential learning is not just a series of techniques to be applied in current practice, but a program for profoundly re-creating our personal lives and social systems' (Kolb, 1984).

The field of experiential learning is characterized by contradiction and Eraut's definition of experiential learning focuses on the nature of the 'experiential' rather than the element of 'doing':

> To avoid the truism that all learning is experiential, . . . I propose to restrict the term 'experiential learning' to situations where experience is initially apprehended

at the level of impressions, thus requiring a further period of reflective thinking before it is either assimilated into existing schemes of experience or induces those schemes to change in order to accommodate to it.

(Eraut, 1994)

Reflection is presumed to have a key role either in experiential learning or in enabling experiential learning. This role is explored in this chapter in the context of the studies that tend to identify themselves with experiential learning. The range of what is interpreted as experiential learning is very broad, as is illustrated in publications such as Boud and Miller (1996) and Warner Weil and McGill (1989). While later chapters in this book deal with learning that is not so directly associated with experience, the distinction is hard to draw while the definition of 'experience' is itself so vague. Adding to this complicated situation, some writers contend that, as adults, we cannot learn from experience without reflection (Pearson and Smith, 1985; Burnard, 1991). This begs further questions about the nature of learning as well as learning and reflection.

The reflective element of experiential learning seems to be similar to the discussions that emanate from professional development literature. While the emphasis on reflection in the experiential cycle tends to concern it as a way of making sense of experience, reflection in such activities as reflection in- and on-action tends to be focused on change in the quality of the outcome – in the practice. Again, it is for simplicity rather than on the basis of logical reasoning that we retain the discussion of these interpretations of the role of reflection in different chapters.

Towards a consideration of the role of reflection in experiential learning, the first part of this chapter reviews the use of terms generally, and applies this to the well-used Kolb cycle of experiential learning, which apparently designates a clear role to reflection in the process of learning. The latter part of the chapter considers the work of four writers who have taken a more analytical approach to reflection in experiential learning. The result of this is that no consistently held view of the role of reflection can be found, but some important questions about reflection and, in particular, its role in experiential learning are raised. Some of these questions are revisited in later chapters.

The terminology of experiential learning

What has been said above has begun to demonstrate the difficulties of assessing the role of reflection when the terminology varies so much. To address this problem, the meaning of key terms and ideas in experiential learning are considered below. It is only by understanding what experiential learning might be that there is the possibility of understanding what the role of reflection in experiential learning might be. For example, it is by reflecting on experience that learning is supposed to occur – but what is 'experience'?

Experience

Eraut's definition of experiential learning (quoted above) is based on his definition of experience, but others have defined experience in different ways. Cunningham (1983) provides a summary of the historical and political circumstances in which experiential learning evolved and his account helps to put it in perspective. While in most reports experience means action, with psychomotor involvement or physical engagement (Kolb, 1984, Nyatanga, 1989, and Kelly, 1994, for example), in other reports experience is broadened to include presentation of abstract material already codified into oral or written language. An example of this might be learning from a lecture, which might be a single stream of information that leaves questions or thoughts provoked but unresolved. It might be learning from listening to or reading a range of sources where ideas might need to be integrated (see, for example, Cunningham, 1983, and Usher, 1985) or vicarious learning (Steinaker and Bell, 1979). Sometimes the interpretation of experience has to be gathered from the context of the presentation (Boyd and Fales, 1983, for example).

This lack of clarity about the nature of the experience to which reference is made, seems to be particularly characteristic of the literature where experiential learning is involved in professional development. On the basis of this observation, Burnard (1991) asked nurses and student nurses what they understood by experiential learning. He notes that most of the nurses considered that the definition of experience in experiential learning involved activity outside the classroom. If 'experience' as it is understood by Burnard's nurse students is 'outside the classroom', questions are raised as to what its distinctive criteria are and how it differs from, for example, a similar demonstration in the classroom. Learning outside and inside the classroom can hardly be different kinds of learning all together.

Because of the vagueness of definition in the literature and because of the context of this book, in which reflection is investigated in a broad range of learning, experience is taken to have a broad meaning as do, for example, Boud, Keogh and Walker (1985) who suggest that experience could mean 'a workshop, a field trip, a lecture . . . an event arising from a personal study project or a totally unplanned occurrence in daily life'. The experience may be initiated by external or personal interests and is quite likely to be made up of many elements (smaller 'experiences'). The experience could also be on a much larger scale, such as the processes underlying a curriculum (Steinaker and Bell, 1979) or that of a series of counselling sessions (Boyd and Fales, 1983).

Adopting a broad definition for experience recognizes that meaningful experience will rarely comprise one element, such as pure activity. In most placement or field trip experiences, for example, the learner is taught or told as well as 'doing'. There may have been some prior teaching that underpins observations made and needs to be integrated with new learning. The learner may be required to read about the situation. Some of the material of experience that will be subjected to reflection will be theories or knowledge already gained or the understandings from previous events. The processing of information from learning-by-doing could involve the additional cognitive work of translating the action into language or symbolic material in order that it is represented orally or in written form. A point that will be made several times in this book is that some learning will emanate from the process of representation (Eisner, 1991). Thus, few situations of learning from experience will be pure activity or absolutely distinguishable from all aspects of classroom teaching. It seems reasonable to suggest that no learner will come to a situation without any relevant prior knowledge and experience. In later chapters the idea that the nature of learning itself can be defined as the active construction of meaning by a learner building on and modifying meaning that they have arrived at in prior learning will be developed further (see particularly Chapter 9). All of this means that it is not possible to predict exactly what 'experience' is being perceived by the learner.

The learner's intention for learning

Before the nature of the intention to learn is described, it is necessary to establish that the learner should intend to learn. Experience cannot be developed into appropriate learning if the learner does not intend to learn or if the flow of experience is too fast (Eraut, 1994). This might seem to contradict those who suggest that experiential learning (usually implying 'learning by doing') is intrinsically motivating for the learner. It is an often-stated tenet of adult education that adults prefer to learn in this way (Cunningham, 1983; Kolb, 1984; Knowles, 1993). Usher suggests that this seems to be an assumption rather than an idea justified by evidence (Usher, 1985).

In a formal learning setting, the learner's intention for experiential learning may be inspired, or even ordered, by others, but they can only guide the learner by setting an objective or attempting to guide the process of reflection and its outcome. Reflection and learning are essentially private and under the control of the learner, although the nature of an objective that is assessed can be a powerful influence on the process of learning. Awareness has recently grown of how the overt nature of assessment tasks affect learners' strategies for learning (Ramsden, 1992).

Teachers' intentions for the outcomes of experiential learning may also be covert (Gore, 1993; Cunningham, 1983). Burnard's work (1991) on the understanding of experiential learning was mentioned earlier. The results of a questionnaire study on the use of experiential learning in nurse training suggested that while students thought that the aim of this type of learning was instrumental in enabling them to become better professional nurses, staff used experiential techniques with the intention of facilitating personal growth in the students as people acting within a profession. Students and staff construed the meanings differently, and these differences could have had consequences for the educational processes.

Kelly's Personal Construct Theory (Bannister and Fransella, 1974) extends the ideas underlying what was noted above about the personal construction of meaning. In suggesting that an individual's behaviour is a response to their personal construing of events (experience), Kelly implies that to facilitate the processes of the individual in, for example, interpreting a particular experience, the facilitator will need to view the experience as if they were looking at it through the learners' eyes. This 'view' will be constructed of past as well as present experiences. Kelly thus emphasizes the personal nature of the ways in which we construe and the consequences that this might have for educating and learning.

The outcome of experiential learning

The outcome or result of experiential learning is action or learning or more learning. The learning may be of any type. It can deal with emotions, the self or higher-order learning, where knowledge is developed and consolidated. While it can lead to learning of new skills, the implication of experiential learning is that observation of, or involvement in, activity is construed in cognitive terms, rather than a mimicking of the same activity. Implicit in the notion of most experiential learning theory is also perpetuation – that the learning leads to the action that is, in effect, experimentation, which leads to more experience and reflection . . . . This is expressed in Kolb's cycle of experiential learning, described in the next section.

Reflection in experiential learning – Kolb's experiential learning cycle

Although others were working on experiential learning long before Kolb, Kolb's experiential learning cycle (Kolb, 1984) created an explicit model that is cited widely in texts in the fields of education, professional development, training and elsewhere. Kolb's cycle has also been reinterpreted in different ways (by, for example, Gibbs, 1988, Warner Weil and McGill, 1989, and Dennison and Kirk, 1990). Notably, Kolb himself does not say very much about the process of reflection (Boud, et al., 1985), although the significance of his work for the activity of reflection may be that he sets it in a context in learning. He sees it as the process that develops concepts from the medium of experience. As in many other situations, the process seems to be taken as understood. Despite this lack of information about reflection as such, Kolb's learning cycle (see Figure 3.1) is a third 'root' of reflection alongside Dewey and Habermas.

Kolb's cycle of experiential learning, as originally drawn, is a circle in which 'reflective observation' is the process of bringing the 'concrete experiencing' of events or experiences to the state of 'abstract conceptualization'. Abstract

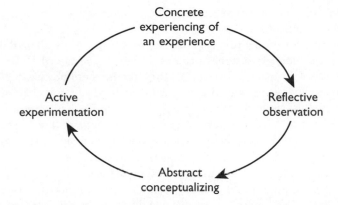

Figure 3.1 *A simplified version of the experiential learning cycle (Kolb, 1984)*

concepts, thus formed, guide a further stage of 'active experimentation' and, thence, more 'concrete experiencing'.

An important feature of Kolb's idea is that the process of learning perpetuates itself, so that the learner changes 'from actor to observer', from 'specific involvement to general analytic detachment', creating a new form of experience on which to reflect and conceptualize at each cycle. The quality of the reflection is crucial in ensuring that the learner does progress in their learning. In the rhythm between involvement and reflective detachment, Kolb relates the cycle also to Piaget's sequence of developmental stages (Piaget, 1971), which culminates in the flexible interaction between different forms of knowing that are linked by appropriate forms of learning. In Piagetian terms, this is the stage of formal operations.

Essential to the attainment of this stage is the capacity for reflective and abstract functioning with symbolically represented objects. It might be reasonable to suggest that the pre-reflective stages identified by King and Kitchener as the first two stages of their schema of reflective thinking are located before the Piagetian stage of formal operations. Similarly, relating the two schemes, it could be possible that stage of formal operations could be divisible into a number of stages that relate to the learning of more able teenagers and adults and are characterized operationally by the progressive developments in the capacity for reflective judgements.

The processes of assimilation and accommodation underpin the Piagetian stages of development and the Kolb cycle. Assimilation is the intake of information from the environment and accommodation is the modification of what is already known by the learner in the light of the new learning. These processes are fundamental to the manner in which learning will be described in Part II.

Kolb applies the cycle to a wide range of situations, such as those in which action and reflection are required to occur more or less at the same time. These might match the concept of reflection-in-action and on-action (see Chapter 4) as well as longer-term situations, such as the learning that occurs in the course of following a curriculum.

Kolb also uses his model to imply that learners may vary in their abilities to function in the different sectors of the cycle. While they need to be able to operate in all of the parts of the cycle, they might therefore have 'preferred learning styles' and so a scale to allow individuals to identify their style has been developed theoretically so as to guide their learning (Kolb and Fry, 1975). As reflection is one of the sectors of the cycle, it suggests that learners may need more or less help to reflect on what is observed at the stage of concrete experiencing (towards abstract conceptualization). Furthermore, in referring to 'abilities', Kolb might be taken to be indicating the possibility of improvement – that someone could improve their ability by means of reflective observation. The possibility of the improvement of the ability to reflect is developed in the last part of this book.

Experiential learning and reflection – the processes of reflection in experiential learning

While Kolb's experiential learning cycle does not, itself, expand on the concept of reflection, it attempts to locate it in a sequence of activities of learning from experience. A number of writers focus more directly on reflection in experiential learning, and suggest the processes that it may consist of, and it is on this work that the focus will now be. The processes that are identified have much in common. Four examples are summarized in relation to each other and to the Kolb cycle (shown in Figure 3.1). The background to the work to which reference is made is described below. All represent important work on reflection (Steinaker and Bell, 1979; Boyd and Fales, 1983; Boud, Keogh and Walker, 1985; Atkins and Murphy, 1993).

The four papers were written originally for work in different contexts. The researchers come from different backgrounds and, although they all tackle the processes of reflection, their other influences can be evident in the emphases that they impose. For example, Boud, et al., stress the importance of affective influence from humanistic psychology, while Boyd and Fales stress the importance of clarifying the problem – a need that derives particularly from the counselling context of their work. The four pieces of work are described below.

The account by Boud, Keogh and Walker is the most comprehensive of the four; indeed, it is one of the most comprehensive general accounts of reflection. In 1985, when the constituent papers were collected, it is clear that the impact of Schön's work on reflection in professional practice (see Chapter 4) had not been fully felt, and is not influential in the view presented. While the inspiration of Boud, et al., was the process of experiential learning (as was indicated above), they recognize that the process of experiential learning is applicable to formal or classroom learning. Their contention that the emotions play a significant role in the process of reflection has been mentioned and they comment on how this respect of their view differs from that of Dewey.

Steinaker and Bell (1979) describe their experiential learning taxonomy as being of value in any situation in which change or behaviour is the goal, though their references are largely to formal education settings. The taxonomy is presented as the sequence of events involved in the process of reflecting on experience after exposure to it. The required outcome can be a substantial curriculum planning exercise (Kenworthy, 1986) or, on a lesser scale, the learning of a song. The greatest value of this taxonomy might be in the way that it relates appropriate styles of guidance/teaching to the stages of learning or reflection that it identifies.

Boyd and Fales (1983) synthesize their account of 'reflective learning' from several studies of the experiences of adult educators and counsellors, not only those in educational settings. They see reflective learning as the 'key element in learning from experience', saying that it is ' the core difference between whether a person repeats the same experience several times . . . or learns from experience in such a way that he or she is cognitively changed or affectively changed'.

The task for Atkins and Murphy (1993) was to summarize the literature on reflection. For their model of 'reflective processes', they draw on the material of Boyd and Fales, and of Boud, et al., but refer, as well, to Mezirow (1983) and Schön (1983).

Table 3.1 summarizes the writers' thoughts on the stages of reflection.

Matching the analysis of these papers to the Kolb cycle, all of the accounts of the process of experiential learning start with the experience (Steinaker and Bell call it 'exposure'). The interpretation of 'experience' here means that it may be in the formal education setting. The experience might not be a single occurrence of an event, but might be continuous and varied in terms of its components. The assumption is that the general aim of reflection is to move beyond current thoughts, ideas or behaviours with regard to the experience – in other words, to learn from the it. Expressed in terms of the Kolb cycle, it is to move to a new cycle, and not to require the learner to circle through the same experience again with no change to their learning.

Boyd and Fales, and Steinaker and Bell, pick up Dewey's suggestion that reflection always begins with a problem or sense of discomfort in the learner. In fact, Dewey did suggest that his use of the word 'problem' could be interpreted too literally. The negative implications of the word and 'discomfort' do not seem always to accord with the reasons for reflecting as reflection may occur because a person decides to reflect and while this can be purposeful, it is not inspired by confusion or a problem. In a class situation, students may spontaneously reflect or do so because they have been asked a question. Boud, et al., circumvent this issue by talking about 'deliberate' reflection. In a milder, but more comprehensive manner it can be described as the existence of the 'need to resolve' or purpose, which may be inspired internally or externally.

Table 3.1 *The stages of reflection in the experiential learning cycle identified in four papers*

Summary of stages	Theorists			
	Boyd and Fales (1983)	**Atkins and Murphy (1993)**	**Boud, Keogh, Walker (1985)**	**Steinaker and Bell (1979)**
Experience	Experience	Experience	Experience	Exposure
Need to resolve	Inner discomfort	Uncomfortable feelings		('readiness')
Clarification of issue	Identification/ clarification			Identification
Reviewing, recollecting			Return to experience	Participation and return to experience or representation
Reviewing the emotional state		Critical analysis of feelings	Attend to feelings	
Processing of knowledge and ideas	Openness to new information	Critical analysis of knowledge	Association, integration, validation	Modification/ internalization
Resolution	Outcome/ integration/ acceptance	New perspective on learning	Outcome/ resolution	
Transformation	Possible transformation			Possible transformation
Possible action	Decision whether or not to act		Possible action	'Dissemination' (action)

Boyd and Fales suggest that there is a phase of 'clarification of the issue for reflection' that might be a matter of verbalizing what have been images or ideas. In informal situations, the process may not be obvious, but it is important in counselling or formal educational situations, questioning not only 'what is the purpose of this period of reflection?', but also 'what is really the issue to be resolved?'. An example of a form of this clarification is the suggestion by Moon (1996a), Harri-Augstein and Thomas (1991) and Burnard (1991). They suggest that, in order to improve the outcome of learning, the learner needs to be aware of the current practice or situation or level of knowledge so that they can conceive better the learning that is required.

Several writers (Boud, *et al.*, and Steinaker, *et al.*) suggest a stage of returning to the experience – 'reviewing', 'recollecting'. This might involve returning to notes made at the time of the experience or talking through an event with a group in a debriefing session (Van Ments, 1990; Pearson and Smith, 1985). This stage may or may not involve coding the material of the experience into language. Eisner points out that the process of codification of the experience modifies the perception of the experience (Eisner, 1991). Describing an experience is not a direct translation because of the limitations of words and the reinterpretation (or reconstruing) that is involved in the process. The subsequent reflection may thus be on the verbalized version of the experience, not the experience itself.

In the processes of clarification of the issue for reflection and that of recollecting and reviewing, it would appear likely that the processes interact. To clarify the issue requires recollection, and to recollect is probably to clarify. In the overarching schema, these stages are combined.

Boud, *et al.* (and following them, Atkins and Murphy) stress the importance of emotion at this stage. As was mentioned previously, the role of emotion in reflection is not clear. Thus, although the subject matter at issue for reflection may be personal emotional reactions to an event, Boud, *et al.*, are more concerned with the role that emotion plays in facilitating or blocking reflective processes. Given that it is essentially a private process (Usher, 1985), emotional influences – such as avoidance of an area of thought – can steer the process of reflection more strongly than any other influence. Indeed, in counselling, the emotional attitude towards an area of consideration can make the difference between moving towards new behaviours or remaining stuck with old patterns.

While its importance should not be diminished, reviewing the emotional state might not be an automatic part of the reflective process and people might need to be guided or encouraged to undertake this phase. Atkins, *et al.*, describe the process as one of critical analysis of feelings alongside knowledge components. In a different sense of 'emotional involvement', Steinaker and Bell (1979) describe how 'the participant becomes emotionally identified with the experience. It becomes 'my experience'. The relationship between emotion and reflection is discussed later in other contexts, particularly in Chapter 8.

Boyd and Fales' stage of 'openness to new information' ('acquiring a broad perspective', 'gathering more information') could be combined with the next phase of processing of knowledge and ideas. They suggest that it has particular significance in the formal educational setting as 'we believe it is the [stage] most available to intervention on the part of educators and counsellors' (Boyd and Fales, 1983). Boyd and Fales observe that learners can 'often lose much of the information available at this stage because of inadequate means of "capturing" or fixing the new information' and that training in 'reflective strategies' can help. They describe a particular 'openness or receptivity to information' and a 'conscious or unconscious laterality of perspective' as significant and facilitative qualities of this stage.

The next phase is one in which there is a 'processing of knowledge and ideas'. It could be seen as central to the whole process of reflection and its relationship to learning, but in most of the papers reviewed, not a great deal of attention is paid to it except by Boud, *et al.* For Kolb, this stage is, or is apparently approaching, that of 'abstract conceptualization'. For Boud, *et al.*, it is 're-evaluating experience' and they analyse it using a series of 'elements' that may not occur in sequence. They are:

- 'association, that is, relating new data to that which is already known;
- integration, which is seeking relationships among the data;
- validation to determine the authenticity of the ideas and feelings which have resulted; and
- appropriation, that is, making knowledge one's own' (Boud, *et al.*, 1985).

Boud, *et al.*, relate this sequence of processes to that suggested to occur in learning on the constructivist view of learning, which is described in Chapter 9.

A stage of 'resolution' or outcome is recognized in all of the papers. It is the attainment of the purpose of the reflection.

Some carry their notion of reflection into a further phase. Boyd and Fales and Steinaker and Bell suggest that the learner can re-evaluate other areas of cognition or, on a major basis, other aspects of their life in view of the new learning. This stage of 'possible transformation' begins to approach the notions of emancipation and criticality that have featured in the discussion of reflection in frames of reference discussed earlier (Habermas and Barnett, in particular). The idea of transformation is also closely bound up with the notion of reflective judgement (King and Kitchener, 1994). It is noticeable that the possibility of transformation is relatively rare in the literature on reflection in learning from experience, even when the rhetoric of the accounts indicates that the 'experience' in experiential learning can refer to major life events for the learner. This is another example of the degree to which the notion of reflection has been regarded through a series of narrow frames of reference with few overlaps.

There seems to be some variation regarding the end point of reflection in these four views. While it is singled out for discussion concerning its role in learning from experience, it is not clear where reflection ends and other aspects of learning from experience take over. For example, some writers have added a further phase of action – 'possible action'. Boud, *et al.*, indicate that action may or may not happen, but the impact of the learning from reflection may be increased by the involvement in some action. Boyd and Fales leave the learner with a 'decision whether to act'. Whether or not 'action' is designated as an end point in the experiential learning process can be determined to some extent by the context in which the researchers have worked. In work that is associated with professional practice (see Chapter 6), a stage of action is more likely to be posited. Action is clearly defined in the Kolb cycle as active experimentation that leads to new experience and the stage at which the cycle is ready to begin again. The assumption is, however, that the new experience represents a progression from the first.

Experiential learning and reflection – further implications

Table 3.1 demonstrated that a number of experiential learning theorists generally agree on the characteristics of the phases of reflective activity in the experiential learning cycle. These phases follow how the experience is experienced.

- development of a need to resolve something;
- clarification of the issue;
- review and recollection;
- review of the emotional state;
- processing of knowledge and ideas;
- eventual resolution and possible action and transformation.

On looking in more detail at any aspect of experiential learning, an important factor tends to become lost – that of the recycling of the cycle, which is when the learning and action can provide new forms of experience that is itself the subject of reflection and so on.

The sequence of stages in a cycle of learning could provide an identity for reflection, but there are other issues to consider. These other issues imply that, while this sequence may be helpful in shedding light on reflection and its relationship to learning, it is far from the whole picture. There appears to be much more interaction between the phases than is suggested above and the concept of a cycle itself may be misleading. What we have considered so far raises many questions, some of which are revisited after the review of the broader field of reflection in learning in Chapter 13.

What is the relationship between reflection and learning?

The identification of the phases that the four papers imply to be reflection beg a number of questions about the cycle of experiential learning and the nature of reflection, including the following.

- If these phases are 'reflection', where does actual learning occur?
- The phases themselves might represent learning but then where does reflection fit in?

Only Boud, et al., seem to indicate a process of mental processing that might accord with learning (re-evaluating experience) and that is then intimately linked with reflection.

Reflection and recycling – is reflection on raw experience the same as reflection on already learnt material?

In the experiential learning cycle, the same set of processes is suggested to occur in a first cycle from experience to experimentation as in subsequent cycles. The discussion of the meaning of experience proposes that experience can be interpreted as a physical involvement in a situation ('raw experience') or as conceptual material that has been learnt, but acknowledges that, in the real world, any experience is likely to be made up of both of these elements. In a model situation, where one could distinguish between raw and previously learnt material, according to the Kolb cycle, the learner may at first be reflecting on the real-life events of a situation, but, in a subsequent cycle, might be reflecting on the images and thoughts they have developed about the events. It seems possible that what is called 'reflection' in the cycle might involve different mental processes in these two situations. In the first situation, it might seem that the learner is 'making sense' of the raw experience in order to learn from it. This seems to be more like a simple view of learning than reflection, though. In the second situation, the process of reflection is applied to what has already been learnt and this use of the term does seem to be more in accord with the views of reflection expressed earlier. The prefix 're' might also be taken to imply a secondary rather than a primary process – a form of reprocessing rather than an initial processing. This is to the definition of reflection and might be taken to question the very use of the term 'reflection' in the Kolb cycle where it refers to experience as 'raw' experience. To summarize the issue in a question:

- is the reflection on material already learnt the same as, or different from, that which the Kolb cycle suggests occurs in the direct processing of raw experience (in an initial cycle of experiential learning)?

Reflection and the construction of experience – can reflection be distinguished from experiencing an abstract conceptualization?

Eisner (1991) talks of learning in terms of the learner's involvement in the construction of meaning. The constructivist view of learning has been alluded to by Boud, *et al.*, and mentioned earlier in this chapter. It is widely accepted in the study of learning, but does not seem to have been applied to the phases of reflection described above or more generally in the literature of experiential learning. Eisner says 'I came to believe that humans do not simply have experience; they have a hand in its creation, and the quality of the creation depends on the ways they employ their minds'.

In particular, Eisner emphasizes the selectivity of sensory perception, suggesting that 'perception is a cognitive event and . . . construal, not discovery, is critical'. In other words, meaning is already being created in the manner in which a learner perceives an experience. Eisner describes the development of concepts from this process that are related to the manner in which the material of learning has been perceived.

Boud and Walker (1990) acknowledge that learners construct what they experience and consider the manner in which experience is interpreted (and presumably learned) according to cultural determinants. However the authors do not substantially link this with their previous work on reflection, which tends to view the process more objectively. Boud and Walker (1993) reviewed the model of reflection that they developed in 1985 (Boud, *et al.*, 1985) and emphasized the role of the learner in a new diagram. In this, for example, the learner determines the experiences that they choose to notice and further process. While this implies a shift towards a learner-based constructivist view of experiential learning, these more recent views are cited less often than those of the 1985 paper.

It seems reasonable to ask if reflection, as viewed in the context of experiential learning, is being seen as learner information processing or the description of a series of phases of guidance for the learner? In the latter case, these phases may or may not correspond to mental events, but are assumed to facilitate the reflective phases of learning from experience.

Reflection and experiencing – how does a learner know what to reflect on?

There are several other issues that are raised by Eisner's paper (1991). The first follows from the notion that the learner constructs their own experience and concerns the form of guidance needed by learners. If learners do not learn from experience, but from their perceptions of experience, there are implications for the nature of guidance required by learners in order to make sense of experience. As learners will be at different points in their perception of the experience, more concern needs to be given to the starting point of learners. Learners are then helped to focus on the appropriate elements of the experience from which to learn in order to reach the required outcomes of the learning. This further implies the need to pay more attention to the prior experiences of the learner that will affect their initial perceptions of the experience. For example, as noted earlier in this chapter, the ways in which emotional experiences can modify the learner's ability to approach certain types of learning.

There is another implication of the suggestion that the learner does not learn 'the experience', but what they perceive to be the experience, perception being consciously or unconsciously subject to direction by past experience. Usher (1985) questions how the educator should guide the selection of perceptions of the experience so that the learning may (possibly) match that anticipated by the educator. The Kolb cycle does not account for this.

In a related point, Usher suggests that learners may not be willing to draw on the range of experiences required by the teacher's anticipations of the learning. He reports that adult learners (with whom he is mainly concerned) are often reluctant to draw on their personal experiences – or else, if they do so, develop them into anecdotes, rather than objectified ideas in a suitable form for reflection and development of ideas. He argues that learners need to learn how to reflect – how to select from current external experiences and draw on their own (internal) experiences in order to learn and then to move beyond the given.

To summarize the implications of this section as a question:

- what does experiential learning look like if the qualities of the experience that are involved are those determined by the learner's perception rather than outside influence?

There would appear to be implications from this for the guidance of the process of learning from experience.

Is the process of learning from the representation of learning appropriately depicted by the cycle of experiential learning?

Eisner's suggestion about the role of representation of learning in the promotion of learning implies that while we develop meaning in the process of learning, we may continue to explore meaning and develop it further in the process of representation. The implication of this is that, for example, the writing of a report that results from reflection on experience is another way in which we develop meaning and not simply an outcome of reflection. Furthermore, Eisner suggests that we choose 'different forms of representation to construct meanings that otherwise elude us'. On this basis, if a learner is asked to represent their learning in a particular manner, the required form of representation is likely to influence the form of the learning. The representation could be in the form of an assessment task, and the process of assessment in formal education has strong effects on the nature of learning (Ramsden, 1992).

The point that Eisner makes about representation suggests further modifications for the idea of experiential learning. First, that the notion of a specific 'outcome' to experiential learning is misleading as the outcome can be construed differently by the learner or the observer. This concern is satisfied by the possibility of re-cycling, and learning from the representation of learning could be depicted as a second cycle where 'experience' is the experience of representation. On the other hand, learning from representation might better be depicted as a subcycle between reflection, abstract conceptualization and representation or active experimentation. An alternative depiction would show the cycle in reverse, with representation being the source of learning. The greater question is whether or not the very wide use of the cycle of experiential learning drawn as a circle is facilitative or generally leads us to oversimplify our views of learning and constituent reflective processes. Perhaps a network of interconnections in the events of experiential learning might depict reality more appropriately.

The implications of the discussion thus far

The discussion raises questions about experiential learning and reflection rather than gives answers. The questions suggest that the cycle of experiential learning is simplistic and while simplicity is to be valued, it can mislead. On this basis, the layout of the phases derived from the work of Boud, *et al.*, Atkins, *et al.*, Boyd, *et al.*, and Steinaker, *et al.*, is too simple. The notion of the 'outcome' of experiential learning requires that constructivist learning theory or comments like those of Eisner about learning from the process of representing learning be taken into account. Learning and the role of reflection in learning do not seem to be as tidy as the experiential learning cycle suggest.

There is another possibility. Although the term 'experiential learning cycle' is regularly used, it is generally in the context of guiding learners. In other words, it is actually used to structure teaching, training or the guidance of learning. There seems to be an assumption that the cycle used for guiding learning would be the same as that which might describe the information processing events of learning. On the same basis, the description of reflection in terms of phases might be useful for facilitating reflection, while not necessarily being representative of what goes on in the brain. For example, 'returning to the event' is clearly described in terms of a form of physical activity in some of the accounts – such as involvement in discussion. The stage of 'returning to the event' in that context is a form of guidance to the learner as to how to learn, not a direct description of the form of information processing.

The lack of definition in the experiential learning cycle and clarity as to whether the processes described are teaching or learning or the guidance of learning provides an example of the confusions that exist about the basic processes of education. It is not surprising that the assumptions still persist that what is taught is what is learnt.

The discussion has also illustrated a danger of splitting up a process into stages, whether this be the Kolb cycle as a whole with its identified stages or the more detailed analysis that focuses on reflection in the cycle of experiential learning discussed earlier in this chapter. The identification of phases can seem to 'tidy up' a process that appears to be far from a neat sequence of discrete stages. However, even a simple application in a practical situation will indicate that, in reality, the process is 'messy', with stages re-cycling and interweaving as meaning is created and recreated.

Reflection in experiential learning and action research

Kolb viewed the experiential learning cycle as an aspect of the holistic relation-ship between man and the environment – a 'transaction' that is capable of having much wider implications than simply for learning. The Kolb cycle mirrors processes of problem solving, creativity and research and the sequence has become closely associated with the process of action research. The aim of action research is to bring about well-founded educational development (for example, in the improvement of teaching) and while action research is not focused specifically on reflection and learning, they are involved in the cycle.

The cycle of action research is considered at the end of this chapter on experiential learning for several reasons. First, the cycle is closely associated with experiential learning, but demonstrates a different sequence of activities that includes reflection. In this way, action learning provides another viewpoint on reflection. Second, while it is closely related in terminology and pattern to experiential learning, action research clearly refers to the actions of individuals, not to the sequence of mental processes of just one person. A third reason for taking a brief look at action research at this point is that it provides a bridge between experiential learning and reflection in professional practice. This is because its sequence suggests the manner in which a practitioner might recognize that their practice is in need of change and so plan, execute and evaluate the change. Last, as will be demonstrated below, action research is seen by some in the political context of bringing about transformation with the aim of emancipation – a dimension of reflection that was introduced in Chapter 2. –

Action research is normally seen as the practical activity of a practitioner within the environment in which they work. The basic form of action research is described as a 'self-reflective spiral of cycles of planning, acting, observing, reflecting then replanning, further action, further observation and further reflection' (Carr and Kemmis, 1986). This implies a process of action planned on the basis of reflection on a particular situation, followed by the implementation of the planned action, observation of its effects on all aspects of the environment, then reflective evaluation of the action in relation to the evaluative evidence. This is followed by re-cycling processes as indicated by the first cycle (Kemmis, 1985).

Jaworski (1993) applies this cycle of action research to classroom teaching. A classroom event triggers a process of reflection 'accounting for' the event. There is then a critical analysis of the event, a change and subsequent reflection to observe that change and so on. She describes the stage of critical reflection as a stage that is 'hard to achieve alone' and suggests that it is useful to collaborate with others at this point. She says, 'Needing to express my own analysis of an event and to account for it to someone else enabled me to be more critical of my own thinking. This put me into a better position for future action'.

The notion of expressing oneself is a form of representation of learning and illustrates the points made by Eisner (1991) described above. The expression of views can be seen as a mini-cycle between reflection and learning within the greater cycle of action research.

Jaworski's form of interpretation of action research neglects what for some is seen as the political essence of the process (such as Gore, 1993). Carr and Kemmis (1986) related Lewin's original work to Habermasian knowledge constitutive interests and the implied forms of action. For them, real action research aims towards, or results in, emancipation.

The literature on the politicized interpretation of action research tends to focus on the potentially emancipatory outcomes rather than the practical nature of the reflective process, but Kemmis (1985) says, 'We are inclined to think of reflection as something quiet and personal. My argument here is that reflection is action oriented, social and political. Its produce is praxis [informed, committed action] the most eloquent and socially significant form of human action'.

Reflection in action research appears to have two stated roles. The first is to form the basis for the planned action, where there is reflection on the meaning of the observations of an event or a situation in order to plan the action. The second, which takes place after the action, is to evaluate the problems and effects of the action. Reflection is retrospective in both phases of the cycle. In the one it concerns the nature of the situation that stimulates the planning of action and in the second it provides the basis for evaluating action already taken, but will also form the basis for new action if more action is envisaged. In this way, it links the considered events of the past with future planning and development (Carr and Kemmis, 1986).

Returning to the Kolb cycle of experiential learning, it is possible to identify both forms of reflection in operation there, as well as the form that the Kolb cycle emphasizes – learning from experience. Kolb suggests that the new learning is tested in action or experimentation and that this results either in the planning of more experience or in more experience *per se*. The action phase of the Kolb cycle therefore mirrors the sequence of action research with the two uses made of the reflective process.

Conclusion

This chapter has reviewed the place of reflection in the body of the literature on experiential learning. It has served to raise questions about the Kolb cycle and experiential learning in general as well as achieve the primary aim of the chapter, which was to consider the role of reflection in experiential learning. There are problems of ill-defined terms as well as the lack of clarity about whether the cycle of experiential learning is really about the guidance and teaching process or learning. These questions are addressed again in Chapter 12.

The work on experiential learning is helpful in furnishing us with ideas about how to guide reflection in learners, but it does not seem to explain its relationship to learning – except to reiterate that learning or further learning or action can be an intended purpose for reflection and an outcome.

Perhaps the most important question that arises from this chapter is the somewhat academic one of whether someone reflects on 'raw experience' or what is designated as reflection by Kolb is another aspect of learning. It is tentatively suggested that the idea of reflection is more about reprocessing already learned material of learning than of learning it from direct experience, but this subject is returned to in Chapter 12.

The role of reflection in experiential learning is not clear because of the multitude of confusions about its interpretation. However, in general, the use of the term does not move away from the simple mental process described in Chapter 1 and there is emphasis on the purposes or outcomes of learning and action. Again, the simple process of reflection is characterized by the framework of use and guidance within which it resides.

Chapter 4

Reflection in professional practice – the work of Donald Schön

Introduction

The next three chapters concern the role of reflection in the professions. In this context, the term has been seen as an important element in appropriate professional practice and much of this work has been inspired by Donald Schön's book, *The Reflective Practitioner* (1983). In pursuing the role of reflection in this field of professional practice, this chapter considers Schön's work directly. It takes a critical overview of his constructs because they have been so influential on other work. The following two chapters take a wider view of reflective practice – first, from a theoretical standpoint, then from a more practical and applied standpoint.

The Reflective Practitioner had the effect of initiating interest and a considerable output of papers on the subject over the next decade and a half. However, some of those writing under the banner of 'the reflective practitioner' do not employ the terminology in the same manner as Schön and do not cover the same ground. While this other literature may seem to be outside the original meaning of the reflective practitioner, Schön's constructs have been subjected to no better testing and have no more claim to be right than the conceptions of others, except that many practitioners and their educators demonstrate enthusiasm for Schön's work.

Theory and practice – the place of reflection in Schön's view

Schön makes reference to two main processes of reflection in professional practice – reflection-in and reflection-on-action. However, it is the significance of the former in characterizing the work of professionals and influencing their professional education that is the major concern of his work. A particular concern for this account of reflection is the status and identity of reflection-in-action. If reflection-in-action was the same function as reflection-on-action, the construct could not be claimed as a special characteristic of professionals. That it might be appropriate to use a different term for reflection-in-action does not diminish Schön's work because his focus is the nature of professional action and its relationship to theory, not the nature of reflection as such. It is hard to gauge whether or not the mass of papers that were inspired by Schön's work were inspired by the notions of reflection-in-action or other features of his work. Whether or not reflection-in-action is indeed reflection and in what way it relates to reflection-on-action will be considered at several points in this chapter.

Schön's book *The Reflective Practitioner* was preceded by an earlier book (Argyris and Schön, 1974) that initiated a debate on contradictions in professional practice as it is assumed to operate and as it appears to operate in real situations. Argyris and Schön focus on two forms of theory of practice or action. Espoused theories are those that are formally seen by a profession to guide action and encompass the formal philosophy of the profession. Greenwood (1993) provides as an example, the manner in which nursing theory considers the focus of nursing to be the person, not the disease, and, in a similar way, educational theory holds that learners should be enabled to be increasingly self-directed (Brookfield, 1987). Espoused theories tend to be the theories taught to novices and held publicly to characterize the professions. Whether or not they are applied in daily practice is the matter of Argyris and Schön's debate.

Argyris and Schön say that the second form of theory – 'theories in use' – represent the patterns learned and developed in the day-to-day work of the professional and it is these that characterize the real behaviour of professionals. Brookfield describes theories in use as guiding the 'intuitively based activities' that are 'privately developed, proven ways of performing that are contextually specific, idiosyncratic and unmentioned in textbooks of professional practice' (Brookfield, 1987). For the argument that he develops later, he stresses the privacy of theories in use in contrast to the public portrayal of espoused theories.

Schön discusses the state of dissatisfaction in professions and with professionals as a 'growing crisis' (1992). He considers that the problem is associated with the failure of professions to modify their behaviour in changing social situations and cope with 'the loss of a stable institutional framework of purpose and knowledge within which professionals can live out their roles and confidently exercise their skills' (1992). Schön builds on the ideas of the previous book to suggest that there is a gap between the prepositional (espoused) knowledge and theory that supposedly underpins a professional activity and the reality of how a professional practitioner acts. He sees it essentially as a problem for educators of professionals.

Schön suggests that espoused theory does not, and cannot, guide practice and that the epistemology of professional knowledge and practice is related to the manner in which professions have developed and their beliefs about their forms of practice. Alongside Habermas (1971), Schön identifies the instrumental practice of scientists as being less of a problem for them as theory more naturally guides practice in the sciences. Medicine and engineering are examples of science-driven professions. However, in professions such as social work and education, there is not a body of secure knowledge that can be used instrumentally to guide practice and this results in a state of confusion. It is for similar reasons – the absence of a secure body of knowledge – that Habermas points to the same problem existing for the social scientists in their methods of research. Schön describes instrumental methods as the methods that are appropriate for the application of theory to practice when 'deciding is separated from doing', or when 'means are separated from ends' (1992). The decision-making process in these professions – and one might add nursing here – is not often amenable to such a positivist stance: 'real-world problems do not come well-formed. They tend to present themselves, on the contrary, as messy, indeterminate, problematic situations' (1992). They may be situations in which the concern has to be the discovery of the right questions to be asked or resolved, rather than the more easily understood professional issues of problem solving where rules are present to be followed so that the solution is assured.

Schön's discussion of 'messy' and ill-structured problems relates to King and Kitchener's work (1994) on the development of reflective judgement. The implication of the stage approach is that the ability to cope with an ill-structured problem in which the knowledge is uncertain is a more advanced stage in the development of reflective thinking than that associated with problem solving. In problem solving, rules are to be followed, though problem-solving skills may be a necessary condition for reflective judgement. This might be taken to suggest that the methods of science are more amenable to being introduced early than those of the social sciences, though this is not to denigrate the complexities of advanced reasoning.

Central to Schön's ideas is the apparently contradictory observation that in the minor professions, many practitioners do cope well with uncertain situations apparently without the guidance of espoused theory. Schön uses the term 'artistry' to describe this professional ability. 'Artistry' is 'the competence by which professionals handle the indeterminate zones of practice . . . an exercise of intelligence, a kind of knowing, though different in crucial respects from our standard model of professional knowledge. It is not inherently mysterious; it is rigorous in its own terms'(1987).

Schön distinguishes 'artistry' from the competence that arises from following professional rules. The professional rules are described by Schön as being the routine, the situations that are met in the day-to-day work of the professional.

The 'artistry', for Schön, characterizes the professional – as, for example, when a lawyer 'thinks like a lawyer'. This might not be a very sound argument as the process of thinking like a lawyer or other professional is surely characterized by dealing with the unexpected as well as the expected (Eraut, 1994).

Barnett (1992) suggests that some of the knowledge that is used in practice must be derived from espoused theory, even when much of it is 'know-how' learned in the day-to-day activities of the work situation and the knowing and the action are functioning simultaneously. Common sense suggests that there may also be some anticipatory thinking about the situation (Greenwood, 1993).

In Schön's original account (1983), 'knowing-in-action' describes the orderly response to a situation in which expectation of the effect of an action accords with the action that arises and its actual effects. Schön says that when something does not accord with expectations, when there are surprises, we might respond through the activity of reflection-in-action. He contrasts reflection-in-action with trial and error. It has 'a form, an inner logic according to which reflection on the unexpected consequences of one action influences the design of the next one' (1992). He describes the process as involving a 'making sense' of the anomaly. The reflection is on both the anomaly that is evident and the relevant knowing-in-action that has contributed to the situation. To this extent, reflection-in-action has a critical function. It involves, as well, a restructuring of the relevant understanding, a reframing of the problem and the development of a new way of performing that is enacted. Reflection-in-action occurs at the time of the action. However, as is shown later, Schön is somewhat ambiguous as to whether the time for reflection may involve a 'stop and think' or must always – for reflection-in-action – be 'smoothly embedded into performance' (1992). He contradicts himself (1987, 1992) about this detail, which is significant for the study of reflection.

Schön describes much knowing-in-action as being tacit, and, as such, it is not immediately available to the conscious mind (Polyani, 1966), nor can it be readily put into words. He also suggests that the process of reflection-in-action may not be conscious. If something cannot be described verbally, it is not as amenable to being 'taught' in the more conventional modes of professional education – herein, according to Schön, lies the major issue for professional educators (1987). In terms of establishing the veracity of Schön's constructs, it also proves difficult as a matter for researchers or for those who might wish to criticize the construct.

It seems difficult, at times, to separate knowing-in-action and reflection-in-action, both in the manner in which Schön describes them and in the manner in which they are applied to action. For example, Schön uses examples of sport where there is correction and recollection of action in order to make action effective. The interaction of acting and correcting and acting again – initially knowing-in-action and then later reflection-in-action and then knowing-in-action – would be very difficult to separate, particularly as much of the knowing is tacit.

The tacit nature of knowing-in-action, the difficulty of separating it from what Schön calls reflection-in-action and the problem of intervening in the operation of the action in order to coach it or correct it is illustrated in work directed at correcting habitual faults in, for example, aiming at a target. In the game of darts, there is a condition known as 'dartitis', which is characterized by the player starting the aim correctly in a physical and visual sense, but being unable to release the dart from their fingers at the appropriate moment. Perhaps because throwing a dart is not usually verbally mediated, trying to improve the situation by talking about the sequence of activities does not seem to be effective. It can be helpful, however, to break down the sequence into separate elements of performance and master each without attempting the whole. As or more effective is a holistic approach that, for example, might involve imagining a relaxed and successful throw. This does not easily suggest that the action is made up of separate functions of reflection-in action and knowing-in-action. Schön does not mention the role of imagination in reflection-in-action and it may be that he thereby ignores an important feature of it.

Additionally, common sense might query why reflection-in-action is seen as a process that is only characteristic of professional artistry. The same kind of messy decision making is characteristic of thoughtful parenthood, for example. It might be the actual content of the knowing-in-action and how it is used in reflection-in-action at 'the coalface' of professional activity that is important. Artistry might be a description of competence and style in which knowledge and action are sufficient to deal smoothly with situations that are unexpected or unpredictable to the individual experiencing them – at whatever level this occurs in professional or everyday situations.

There may be characteristics that define artistry in particular professions or groups of professions. Bandler and Grindler (1979), for example, studied the patterns of behaviour used by Milton Erikson, a hypnotherapist of world reputation, to identify how he was interacting with his clients so effectively. Significantly for the comments about tacit knowledge, Erikson says that Bandler and Grinder provide 'a much better explanation of how I work than I, myself can give. I know what I do, but to explain how I do it is much too difficult for me' (Bandler and Grindler, 1979). In other words, there may be specific characteristics of the functioning processes of different professions, with professionals themselves largely unconscious of them and unable to describe them.

Reflection-in-action and reflection-on-action

Here, the identities of reflection-in-action and reflection-on action are considered. Schön distinguishes the process of reflection-in-action from that of reflection-on-action: 'Clearly, it is one thing to be able to reflect in action and quite another to be able to reflect on our reflection-in-action so as to produce a good verbal description of it; and it is still another thing to be able to reflect on the resulting description [of action]' (1987). In the course of writing two accounts, he seems confused as to how these activities differ at a crucial point. There are inconsistencies in the way he treats the moment of 'stop and think', which he describes as a 'pause in the midst of action'. In 1987, he implies that the activity of 'stop and think' is reflection–on–action when reflection is not directly related to current action. In contrast, in 1992, he provides two examples of reflection–in–action where there is a pause and comments, 'In examples such as these, reflection–in–action involves a "stop and think"'.

These 'woolly edges' of the definitions of reflection–in–action and reflection–on–action contradict the notion of clear distinction implied by the quotation above. If the processes are different in quality but are both forms of reflection, then 'stop and think' time during action either is always one form of reflection or the other (and the theorizing in one of the papers is misleading) or else sometimes it is one type of reflection and sometimes the other. This might depend on how long the 'stop' is. Another possibility – which contradicts Schön's notion that they are different – is that reflection–in–action and reflection–on–action are part of a continuum, the same processes being involved that act quickly and usually unconsciously during action or, further along the continuum, act more slowly and probably more consciously.

In addition, Schön seems to make a distinction between the processes of reflecting–on–action where the reflection is reliant on making a verbal description of the content of the reflection–in–action, and where there is reflection on the resulting description (1987, 1992). He describes these as 'distinct kinds of reflection' (1992). If, as it appears from the papers cited, Schön ties the notion of reflection–on–action to the review of the material of reflection–in–action with or without the help of verbal descriptions, he is, by the tightness of his own definition, tying the practitioner to reflecting only on what has been her response to an unexpected situation or a surprise. This might not include reflection–on–action that is an evaluation, for example, of the cognitive processes that have guided an event in which an action went smoothly. Schön's position might accord here with Dewey's notion of reflection as a response to a situation of uncertainty or a problem, though Schön's concern is reflection on the practitioner's action in the situation of uncertainty, which is considerably narrower than Dewey's application of the term.

In the context of his work on theory and action, Schön identifies that the role of reflection–on–action is not only one of learning and informing action, but also the building of theory.

Reflection in professional education

The tacit nature of the process of reflection, the manner in which it guides action and the difficulties that this poses for the education of professionals has been mentioned before. With his views on reflection in professional practice established, Schön considers the conditions under which students of the professions should be educated in order that they should become reflective practitioners. He suggests that learning to practice professionally is a matter of contextualizing the professional knowing-in-action into the particular socially and institutionally structured context of that profession – that shared by 'a community of practitioners'. For this he uses the term 'knowing-in-practice' (1987). For the education of professionals, he distinguishes between learning the routine functions of the profession, and learning how to cope with situations of uncertainty where the process of reflection-in-action operates and the artistry of the profession is demonstrated.

Schön advocates the use of a 'practicum', which is like a laboratory environment in which professional action can be explored. It supports the student in moving towards increasing professionalization in their behaviour. Schön allies the inculcation of professional learning to coaching. A coach will facilitate learning by setting situations that are routine or that demand reflection-in-action, though a coach acknowledges that people may initially learn to act as a result of knowledge of rules and facts before they meet the conditions of uncertainty in which reflection-in-action operates. Schön suggests that the process of development in the practicum might, for a student, be a movement from conscious reflection on what has already been unexpected in a practical situation to the unconscious processing of this alongside the action (McKinnon and Erikson, 1988). Morrison (1996) describes how this process is presumed to underlie the education of teachers.

Summary of Schön's main points

Before considering some of the criticisms of Schön's work that will act as a means of moving on to the general conceptions of reflective practice, here is a summary of the main points he makes in his work:

- practitioners do not draw so much on espoused theory when they act, but on context-specific, idiosyncratically developed 'theories in use';
- there are two main forms of reflection used by the professional – reflection-in-action and reflection-on-action;
- reflection-in-action occurs in association with action and guides the process of action via knowledge in use, which is derived from theory in use, and makes limited contact with espoused theory and, according to Schön, reflection-in-action only occurs in situations where the action yields unexpected consequences and is not part of actions that go according to plan;
- reflection-on-action is the form of reflection that occurs after action and relates, via verbalized or non-verbalized thought, to the action that the person has taken – in other words, it is a relatively narrow concept that is

retrospective and has a role in learning, in informing action and in theory building;

- because of ambiguities in Schön's writing about 'stop and think' periods associated with action, it is not clear how reflection-in-action is distinguished from reflection-on-action, although he does stress that they are different;
- a suitable setting for the education of the reflective practitioner is the virtual world of a practicum where, in a risk-free environment, a student is coached to respond appropriately to situations posed by developing a capacity to process information during action – or, in Schön's terminology, reflection-in-action.

Criticisms of Schön's work on reflection

The effect of Schön's ideas was to provide a stimulus to rethink the relationship between theory and practice in professional practice (Smyth, 1989). Within the extensive field of professionalism, Schön's work promoted discussion in many different areas – among professionals, among the theorists on the professions and other work, among the educators of professionals, among those with interests in professional practice methods and among those whose interests lie more specifically with reflection. It is hardly surprising, therefore, that his work fails to satisfy all these different groups and, perhaps unreasonably, some of the criticisms refer to what he does not cover as well as what he does cover.

The lack of precision of Schön's terminology

There are many ways in which Schön's work is open to criticism and one is its loose use of terminology. Sometimes, as we have seen, Schön fails to hold a consistent approach to the constructs such as reflection-in-action and reflection-on-action, which, as constructs, have been taken as models of practice by many researchers and commentators. Eraut (1994) asks, for example:

> What precisely does Schön mean by reflection-in-action and is it an adequate explanation of the creative processes he seeks to describe? Finding answers is not easy because Schön proceeds mainly by example and metaphor rather than sustained argument. He also tends to stray away from his own definitions and evidence into making statements which are difficult to defend.

A general point that provides helpful background to the critical reading of Schön's work is made by Schulman (1988). He suggests that Schön makes effective use of dichotomy, which has the effect of persuading the reader to accept his theorizing more easily than might be warranted. Schulman describes dichotomy as 'a wonderful rhetorical device . . . [that] . . . captures our attention and sharpens the lines of . . . argument'.

In dichotomy, the justification of one side over the other sets up a 'one or the other' or a 'black and white' situation for the reader, so that, for example, technical rationality in professional practice is regarded in a negative light or that the reader is persuaded that reflection-in-action is more important than reflection-on-action and is distinct. Fenstermacher (1988) characterizes Schön's discussion of technical rationality and artistry as a discussion of good versus evil.

There are assertions in the literature that a proficient professional must operate in a flexible mode, which may mean engaging in technical rational methods where appropriate (Barnett, 1992, and Fenstermacher, 1988, for example). Selman (1988) suggests that Schön, himself, was probably working with both a technical rational approach and with artistry, such as when he used the example of building a gate as an example of the use of artistry. Schön's use of dichotomies promotes an awe of clarity that is not always borne out in his examples. Eraut (1994) notes the confusion of processes that arise in his examples:

> In some cases the master-professionals have set up processes for participants (in engineering or science management) to sort out a problem rather than attempt to solve it themselves: a sensible course of action no doubt but Schön describes them as setting up the conditions for reflection-in-action, implying that participative problem-solving and reflection-in-action are the same thing.

This quotation also demonstrates Schön using an example of reflection-in-action that is far from the notion of a situation of 'surprise' at the unexpected.

Lauder (1994) also questions the simplicity of Schön's constructs and how they relate to reflection. He suggests that reflection may be too simple an idea to account for the linkage between theory and practice that actually occurs. Using an example from nursing, he queries how Schön's model demonstrates that the theoretical values of caring are incorporated in an action of caring. The selection of appropriate means to reach an end by way of an action requires concern for the particular – in this case, the patient's needs for care now. There also needs to be concern for the universal – here, the principle of care contributing to the good of mankind. On this view the action is set in the context of knowledge developed by technical rational methods so that it is interwoven in a complex of theory and experience. Separating espoused theory and practice in the manner of Schön seems to be too simplistic and the role of reflection in the process comes into doubt.

Can we reflect during action?

The insecurity of the construct of reflection-in-action is expressed already in Schön's own contradictions. Court (1988) doubts that reflection can coincide with action. She suggests that reflection-in-action implies that 'time outs' or the use of 'double vision' in teaching would mean the loss of momentum of a lesson. She suggests that 'deliberation' is a preferable term for the mental process that occurs during action as it is a more focused and problem-centred activity.

'Deliberation', however, would still need to be linked with the ongoing mental process that occurs during action (Court, 1988).

Van Manen (1991) seems to be suggesting a similar idea. He considers that there is not time to reflect during action and describes reflection-in-action more as a process of making a decision where the products of reflection are competently utilized in what might be a tacit response to a situation. This appears to include both Schön's notion of knowing-in-action and reflection-in-action (which occurs in response to the unexpected) and, thus, use of the word 'absorb' suggests the smooth operation that Schön observes in professional activity. It suggests also that it may not be a reflective process that occurs during action, but the result of habitual reflective practices that guide action. Van Manen's broader and more inclusive view of how we act in a considered manner accords with the frequent, but, in fact, mistaken view of reflection-in-action, which is that it guides all action (not just cases of the 'unexpected', which was Schön's proposal). In breadth and relative simplicity, Van Manen's views seem to sit comfortably with observations of professional action and his clear view that 'stop and think' represents reflection-on-action is helpful.

There are certainly doubts about the nature of reflection-in-action as described by Schön. The doubts are not about the existence of the cognitive activity that is apparently characteristic of professionals (see below), but whether it is or is not the same as reflection-on-action, and, without access to physiological data, this must remain partly contentious. There are several possibilities that are not mutually exclusive:

- the process of reflection does occur during action and reflection-in-action and reflection-on-action exist as separate processes;
- reflection occurs during action or pauses in action and is the same brain activity as reflection-on-action, and the processes are not, therefore, distinctive;
- reflection, as such, does not occur during action, but an alternative process such as 'deliberation' (Court, 1988) occurs;
- reflection does not occur during action, but in 'stop and think' pauses, which are the same as reflection-on-action.

Eraut (1994), after an apparently frustrating attempt to make sense of Schön's writing on reflection-on and reflection-in-action, concludes that the most fruitful course is to remove the term reflection from Schon's work because of the confusion that it has caused. Eraut regards reflection-in-action as meta-cognition, which might, nevertheless, be construed as a form of reflection. As Eraut (1994) implies, Schön's thesis does not rely on the existence of reflection during action, only on the notion that some form of distinct mental process exists at the time of action that may differ from what occurs later (reflection-on-action). The issue with which Schön is mainly concerned is that the distinct process is not easily taught or learned in conventional classrooms.

From reasoning and the literature, the preferred interpretation in this book is that apparent reflection during action is more akin to a decision-making process, based, perhaps, on the rapidly accessed product of previous reflection – in effect, a meta-cognitive process, but still a form of reflection. It is suggested that reflection-on-action is reflection on already learnt material, and that it may occur during pauses in action or long after action.

The time frame of reflection – reflection-before-action?

Hatton and Smith (1995) introduce the useful notion of the 'time frame' of reflection in relation to an event. This construct helps to organize thinking about reflection during or after action and the role of 'stop and think' periods. However, some also consider that reflection is involved in the anticipation of an event and Schön has been criticized for not including this form of reflection (Greenwood, 1993). Neither reflection-in-action or reflection-on-action, as such, allow for anticipation of an event. Van Manen (1991) describes 'anticipatory reflection', which refers to considerations taken before an event, perhaps involving the planning of the event. This might be an example of the power of dichotomous thinking 'implicitly undervaluing those factors that fall outside the pair stressed (Greenwood, 1993). In support of 'reflection before action', Greenwood says, 'It is at least arguable . . . that much of the suffering in the world including that caused through nurses' errors could have been avoided if practitioners stopped to think about what they intended to do and how they intended to do it before they actually did it'. She provides the example of clinical briefings as reflection before action.

That Schön does not include a separate category of reflective practice for anticipation of events may be justified. It is suggested here that anticipation may imply a combination of reflection and imagination. In this combination, reflection-on-action – the revisiting of prior experiences of the same or similar events – is stretched into the future with the use of imagination. Imagination may work with the outcomes of reflection-on-action, but would not be considered to be a part of reflection.

Operationalizing Schön's constructs

While there has been much theoretical speculation about Schön's constructs of reflection, surprisingly few have set out on the obvious task of operationalizing them. Newell (1994) considers that reflective practice should have implications of an empirical nature 'because we are invited to pursue reflective practice *because it changes practice*' (Newell's italics). In a sceptical manner, he urges the definition and operationalization of the concept of reflection ('in Schön's Model 11 world') in order that the claims might be substantiated.

Kirby and Teddlie (1989) attempted to operationalize the notion of 'reflective teaching', which is derived from Schön's work on practice (Argyris and Schön, 1974; Schön, 1983), and failed to achieve this. They compare their instrumental approach to that of other studies that rely on comment on qualitative data such as case studies:

The applicability of the theory of reflective practice depends upon its ability to be empirically tested in a series of studies, . . . requiring operational definitions of key constructs. A theory is of little value if the major constructs are too obscure to allow development of any satisfactory operational definition. [Reflective practice] Theory has been particularly subject to this criticism.

(Kirby and Teddlie, 1989)

Kirby and Teddlie recommend further attempts to develop research instruments to test the concept of reflective practice in general terms and then with different subjects and in different teaching contexts. This might furnish the notion of reflective practice with more 'content' (Richardson, 1990) or a 'recipe' for reflective activity (Fitzgerald, 1994). As some of the content of reflection-in-action is tacit, research on the process by which it operates can only be through observation and inference. Investigation of reflective practice has thus proved problematical. Perhaps this means that the main value of Schön's work should be seen as that of stimulating thought rather than being a prescription.

Schön's constructs in other contexts

Schön's construct of reflection-on-action is not contentious, though in his main use of the term it is narrow (Clarke, James and Kelly, 1996). Practitioners need to reflect on an event and on their knowledge-in-action that has contributed to the outcome of their action, but they probably also need to draw in material from elsewhere, which may be a theory, experience, lessons or advice from others. Reflecting back on an action alone does not seem to be sufficient in professional practice, nor does it facilitate development and improvement. However, it is with respect to reflection-on-action that Schön's work is most closely related to experiential learning and action research. The notion that more material must be drawn into the process of reflection in order to facilitate better action, then further experience, then more reflection suggests the possibility of viewing reflection-on-action in cyclical terms, as in the cycle of experiential learning.

While he does refer to Habermasian ideas, Schön does not demonstrate concern for the uses of reflection that take the practitioner beyond the significance of the immediate event (Schön, 1992; Fitzgerald, 1994). Morrison (1996), for example, sees Schön's views of reflection-in-action as essentially short term. He conceives of reflection-in-action as a lens through which practice is examined, which produces 'social, political and cultural myopia in reflective practitioners'. While Morrison agrees that reflection-on-action is a 'longer lens', he remains critical of the lack of concern for the social, political and ethical awareness and the emancipation that can emanate from reflective processes as described by Schön. Smyth (1989) supports this view. He describes the vision of professionals as a concern with the 'micro aspects' of a situation, as opposed to 'macro concerns' of political and ethical issues or the wider generalizations that might be made from events in professional practice. In terms of Van Manen's model (described in Chapter 2), which records levels of reflection, Schön's reasoning about reflection resides mainly in the first two levels.

A summary of the criticisms associated with Schön's views of reflection and practice

- While Schön uses simple terms and dichotomies to emphasize the points he makes, the real world of practice may not be as clearly defined. For example, espoused theory probably has some role in guiding practice.
- While there are calls for the operationalization of terms so that research may be conducted, the tacit nature of personal theory and knowledge that guides practice make this problematical. Sometimes theoretical writing has beneficial roles in stimulating thought and research while it cannot be tested. This may be the appropriate manner in which to view Schön's work.
- Reflection-on-action is not contentious, but, in the manner in which Schön applies it, appears to be narrow. In order for practice to evolve, there must be a means of extending the reflection on material that is new or learnt from other situations. The practitioner might learn in a formal situation or use espoused theory.
- Extending this argument, some theorists consider that reflection-on-practice should take into account ethical, social and political issues in order that personal and professional development can occur.
- Schön's notion of reflection-on-action is encompassed in Kolb's experiential learning cycle as the processing of experience.
- The concept of a time frame for reflection is helpful. There are some arguments that reflection takes place as anticipation of an event, but the view taken here is that that anticipation can equate to a combination of reflection-on-action – that is, on previous actions – and imagination.
- Schön sees reflection-in-action as the response to unexpected events and it is knowing-in-action that controls action generally and many interpret reflection-in-action as guiding action. Van Manen's view that a distillation of reflection-on-action is what guides action seems to be helpful as a means of accounting for observations. Eraut (1994) would abandon the word 'reflection' in Schön's writing.
- Several consider that 'stop and think' periods represent reflection-on-action and, therefore, are reflection but are distinct and different from what Schön calls reflection-in-action.

There are many and diverse criticisms of Schön's work, but it covers what it covers and did not set out to describe reflection in detail, only to show that there were distinctive aspects of professional life that accord with some reflectivity in the processes of practice. Argyris and Schön (1974) and Schön's writings raise important debate about the nature of theory and practice in the professions.

Perhaps it is helpful to view the work on reflection as an adjunct to these other considerations rather than central to them. It is then appropriate to value the questions that Schön's work raises. Some questions prompted by Schön's work and the developments of it are the following.

On the assumption that reflection-on-action is in accord with the common views of reflection, are reflection-in-action and reflection-on-action the same or different mental activities?

- Is reflection or some other mental process enacted during action?
- Is espoused theory really as unrelated to theory-in-practice as Schön suggests? (As this section was written, a metaphorical speculation arose that relates to Schön's observations on theory and practice in the professions. It is included at the end of this chapter.)
- Following on from this, are there distinct qualities of reflective practice?
- Does the mental process of reflection alone operate in the anticipation and planning of events or might it be a combination, for example, of reflection-on-action and imagination?
- Are the activities that Schön characterizes as being distinctive to professional activity indeed the sole preserve of professionals or are they also found in everyday action?

Conclusion

Donald Schön's work has inspired a great deal of other research, writing and educational activity on the concept of the reflective practitioner. The task of this chapter has been to explore what he said about reflection. Precise identification of a role for reflection in practice was not the main task of Schön's work. This chapter suggests that Schön is, indeed, not very precise about the use of many of his terms, even though he tends to define them quite narrowly and, in particular, does not make a reliable case for the existence of reflection-in-action, which is the more contentious of the roles he gives reflection. The role of reflection-on-action accords with the role of reflection in experiential learning and the common-sense use of the term. Reflection has a role in learning and informing action and, we can add, in the building of theory to guide practice or action.

Speculation on the theory and practice of professions

This chapter closes with a metaphorical speculation about theory and practice in the professions and, in particular, where espoused theory 'fits' into practice and professional education. Argyris and Schön (1974) have, in a significant manner, drawn attention to the distinction between espoused theory and theory in use and have argued that, in real situations, practice is guided by theory – in use.

A more realistic concept of the mental activity that guides action could be that of a network of knowledge, a part of a cognitive structure (as with the constructivist view of learning – see Chapter 9). This network of knowledge is composed of espoused theory and the idiosyncratic processing of espoused theory that has occurred as a result of experience in practice and other sources of further learning. These components have been assimilated and, in response to the new learning, the cognitive structure has accommodated to a new understanding.

In metaphorical terms, perhaps we 'leave on the shelf' one pristine copy of the espoused theory (Volume A) that we have been taught because we are told of its importance. We draw a second copy into everyday use and, as we assimilate knowledge from experiences in practice, we accommodate the espoused theory into a usable network of knowledge that further guides practice (Volume B). Unless we are asked to describe it, the usable network of knowledge that guides practice remains tacit and untranslated into language. Knowledge that guides practice may not be organized in a manner that enables us to describe it or explain it easily. Such difficulties in describing practice are observed by Schön (1983) and others. If we are asked to explain how we guide our practice, we might struggle with the difficulties to start with and then may resort to talking about what we think guides our practice. At this point we reach for our fairly pristine copy (A) of the espoused theory. This is what we were told, while in training, would guide practice. This situation could give rise to the impression of a gap between theory and practice when one does not exist. The anomaly is in what the practitioner reports that they do, not in what they actually do.

In a parallel way, if we are asked to teach another person about a professional activity, we may reach for the copy of espoused theory (A) – and the gap between theory and practice appears again. This speculation is supported by a number of writers in the field of nursing who are concerned with the theory–practice 'divide' (Cox, Hickson and Taylor, 1991, and Gray and Forström, 1991, for example).

Pursuing the metaphor in the case of the process by which a novice become competent, as new practitioners we have learnt from espoused theory and usually some limited practical work experiences. Later, through assimilation of new knowledge from practice, from mentors, and other life experiences in the gaining of maturity, the espoused theory with which we started is relatively unrecognizable in a rich network that might be what Schön terms knowledge in use – our volume 'B'.

To Schön, or the outside observer, the experienced practitioner displays two areas of knowledge. There is the pristine copy of espoused theory (A) and theories-in-use that now bear no recognizable relationship to espoused theory, but may well have drawn on it to a greater or lesser degree in the novice stages of practice (B). To Schön or the observer, these appear to be different, while they actually started out the same, with one having evolved (B) and the other as it was originally (A).

Chapter 5

Reflective practice in the professions – a theoretical stance

Introduction

The work of Donald Schön was discussed in the previous chapter. As we have seen, it has been the inspiration of much work on reflective practice in the professions and, hence, provides a prelude for looking at reflective practice in broader terms. Two points are worth noting here about some of the work that emanated from that of Schön. First, there is a tendency for interpretations of reflection-on-action to be broader than Schön's own use of the term. Second, there has been a tendency to adopt Schön's model as 'fact' and theorize on this basis rather than treat the model as speculative.

This chapter reviews wider interpretations of the role of reflection in reflective practice and how much consensus there is on the identity of reflective practice.

Reflection and professional characteristics

Reference has been made to the somewhat evangelical attitude to experiential learning and the Kolb cycle. This enthusiasm is also characteristic of the way in which both the professions of teaching and nursing – and to a lesser extent social work – have taken up the ideas of reflective practice. In teaching and teacher education, reflective practice has been described as 'the emergence of . . . a conceptual thrust' (Smyth, 1989), 'an important rallying point in current efforts to reform teaching' (Wildman and Niles, 1987) and perhaps a potential focus of effort 'to unify the vast array of educational reform initiatives that will lead us into the twenty-first century' (Vaughn, 1990). It is acclaimed as 'a goal in many teacher preparation programs' (Hatton and Smith, 1995).

In a similar way, the enthusiasm for reflective practice is demonstrated in nursing. Kelly (1994) talks about how reflection has 'caught the imagination of nursing . . .'. Emden (1991) refers to reflective practice as being of great significance in nursing, and, revealing sarcasm, Lauder (1994) refers to 'the reflective doctrine' that 'has become the Holy Grail that will rescue nursing practice and education from ignorance and the performance of ritualitic behaviours'.

The reasons these professions, in particular, have taken up the banner of reflection and reflective practice with such enthusiasm makes inferences about the professions' perceptions of reflection and could suggest similar reasoning in both. Various general reasons have been mooted for the enthusiasm for reflective practice in these professions. One lies in the ethos of these particular professions. Nursing, teaching and social work, for example, represent hermeneutic knowledge consitutive interests (Habermas, 1971), with subject matter that is interpretive and not rooted in fact to the same extent that scientific disciplines are. The methods used in nursing and teaching, for example, involve review, interpretation and reconstruction of ideas and reflection is employed in these processes. Another reason is that practice in these professions is often based on rapid action and the proof of expertise in the subjects emerges from the actions taken, not the quality of thought that might have gone into the actions (Argyris and Schön, 1974; Schön, 1983). Thus, for the teacher managing a class of difficult children, the teacher's action at any point matters more than their knowledge of the dictates of theory or even their own prior theorizing about their action. A similar situation exists for the nurse encountering a crisis. Action is what counts.

Because it is action that counts, these professions display a characteristic difficulty in relating theory to practice. Practitioners in teaching and nursing are continuously dealing with uncertain or ill-structured problems that require rapid responses (Palmer, Burns and Bulmer, 1994), with no time for resorting to theoretical ideas (Smyth, 1989; Wildman and Niles, 1987; Kirby and Teddlie, 1989). Schön (1983) talks about professions where deliberation plays a large part in determining the manner of operating to achieve a particular end. The practitioner makes the choice between alternatives for action or recombines them as is appropriate. This form of uncertain knowledge, however, is not characteristic of other professions that have taken up notions of reflective practice, such as engineering.

Politics and empowerment in the professional context are further reasons for the interest in reflection, particularly in teaching. Calderhead and Gates (1993) cite increasing centralization and control in the teaching profession and consider that reflection-on-action can lead to reactionary empowerment. Some teachers welcome reflection as a means of extending themselves intellectually, examining their own ideologies and enhancing their professional role when the pressure on them is to behave more like technicians (Wildman and Niles, 1987; Calderhead and Gates, 1993). Perhaps cynically, Calderhead and Gates suspect that reflection was eagerly seized as a research topic, and in what might be a perceptive comment that could clearly relate to nursing as well, Richardson (1990) suggests that adherence to the notion of reflective practice raises the status of a profession.

A reason, in these last decades of the twentieth century, for these professions needing to build status is that they are largely female. In a circular argument, the gender characteristics of nursing and teaching have been used to account for the interest in reflection. Women predominate in nursing and in particular areas of teaching (Clarke, James and Kelly, 1996). Clarke, *et al.*, base this contention on Balkan (1966) for whom the characteristics of being open and willing to share ideas were associated with women. They suggest that these qualities are related to reflective practice.

A justification for the interest in reflective practice in nursing (but not teaching) concerns the rapid development of nursing theory to justify the new place of nursing in higher education. Those who have developed this theory are nurses, and not generally those who have moved into nursing from other disciplines, and they are nurses who have often recently been in practice. They are therefore keenly aware of the need to relate theory to practice. In this development there may also have been conscious or unconscious reasons for ensuring that nursing theory differs markedly from its partner, medicine, which has traditionally been male dominated and, until recently, has displayed a strong instrumental orientation. Perhaps some of the recent changes in medical education could, in turn, have been influenced by the developments in nursing.

The function of reflective practice

Interest in reflection and reflective practice in teaching, nursing and social work is not uniform throughout different roles in these professions and there are various relationships that provide contexts for professional learning and practice. All have different involvements with professional learning and different reasons for using reflective practice. The contexts are expressed in the following interactions:

- educators teach novice practitioners;
- novice practitioners are learners in the profession;
- practising professionals are in practice with learners, patients and clients;
- practising professionals are learners in continuing professional development;
- learners/patients/clients learn and are subject to the actions of practising professionals, which may engender a process of learning (knowledge, skills and behaviour).

In education, the main interest in reflective practice has come from teacher education more than those engaged in teaching or who are concerned about learning. One might speculate that the interest has something to do with the work role of teacher educators, perhaps more than about teaching as such. However, while teacher educators promote reflection among teachers, they seem to have less tendency to consider reflection as a method for their own practice than do nurse educators (see, for example, contributors to Palmer, *et al.*, 1994; Gray and Pratt, 1991; Mezirow, 1990).

In contrast, in nursing, the ideas about reflective practice have been applied more in the realm of the professionalism of the nurse and less in nurse education. The nursing literature seems also to have remained closer to Schön's work on reflection-on-action and reflection-in-practice than is the case in teaching. Generally, the stance taken in the nursing literature is more accepting of the value of reflection and more concerned with the 'real life' use of it. Some of the teaching literature seems to jar on efforts to identify reflection in order to discover if it is useful. For probably the same reason, there has been less concern in nursing with the definitions and models of reflective practice, but the general lack of clarity as to the nature of reflective practice is noted (Kelly, 1994; Fitzgerald, 1994).

A generalization that seems to apply to teaching, nursing and social work is the fact that there is relatively little concern for the effect of reflective practice on the subjects of the professional's action – the learners, patients or clients in the case of the professions under discussion. Since the improvement in learning or care of the patient or client is deemed central to the purposes of these professions, this seems to be a surprising omission. With this in mind and referring to teaching, Copeland, Birmingham and Lewin (1993) ask a critical question: 'Do students of highly reflective teachers learn more or better or even differently?' Similar questions could be asked of other professionals.

The fact that reflective practice seems to have become tied up with the essence of being a professional rather than the activity of facilitating learning or caring may have much to do with the manner in which the literature has built on Schön's original work on the reflective practitioner as it also concerns itself with the professional aspects. There is justification for focusing without concern for the impact on their clients if it enables the practitioner to feel more comfortable in what can be a difficult role. Feeling that they are doing a job thoughtfully can have beneficial effects on the manner in which the work is done. However, whatever the objective of promoting reflective practice in reported work is, there should be a clear statement of what that objective is – and at the moment that is not clear.

What is reflective practice?

The nature of reflective practice might seem evident until questions are asked such as that of Copeland, *et al.* (1993) – whether or not students of reflective teachers perform better. Similarly difficult questions for reflective practice include the following.

- How is a reflective professional or reflective practice to be recognized?
- What is it that the reflective practitioner is intended to accomplish (Vaughn, 1990)?
- Are there values or ideologies associated with reflective practice (Copeland, et al., 1993)?
- Can all professionals learn to be reflective – and would this be desirable?
- Can newly trained professionals be usefully reflective? (Perhaps the ability to reflect on practice is built up over a career.)
- What is the career trajectory of highly reflective professionals (Copeland, et al.)?
- Are reflective professionals always good or better than their less reflective colleagues?

The issue here is not a distinction between reflective and non-reflective professionals, but between more and less reflective professionals or more or less reflection. On the assumption that every adult reflects to some extent, a response to most of the questions above hinges on the meaning of 'more reflective practice' or 'more reflective professionals'.

Morrison's notion of reflection or reflective practice in teaching as 'a conceptual and methodological portmanteau catch-all term' (Morrison, 1996) has already been employed. This lack of consistent definition matters for if the notion of reflective practice is important in professional life, it is correspondingly important that students and practising professionals understand what it is that they are attempting to achieve (Morrison, 1996). If it was only the content of the definitions that differed, but they were broadly targeting the same areas of functioning, there could be resolution or acknowledgement of disagreement, but this is not the case as the definitions are so different in their nature and application. In the discussion that follows, some of the ways in which reflective practice has been applied in the professions are illustrated.

Reflective practice as a set of abilities and skills

Calderhead and Gates (1993) identify reflective teaching as being largely a list of abilities set in the context of appreciating the political context of teaching and gaining empowerment. They include teachers' abilities to discuss their own practice, appraise ethical and moral issues in teaching, take greater responsibility for their own development and develop personal theories of educational practice.

The use of the word 'abilities' tends to imply a combination of skilled activity and content. Few talk of reflection purely as skills, but Bright (1993) is an exception: 'Reflective practice is an active, dynamic, action-based and ethical set of skills, placed in real time and dealing with real, complex and difficult situations'.

The paper by Atkins and Murphy (1993) has been mentioned in the context of experiential learning and it is influential in the nursing literature. As was demonstrated in Chapter 3, it seeks to analyse the events of reflection. From the analysis, the skills that are required to reflect are derived. While this may seem to be a logical process, the query as to whether or not the events of reflection are teaching or learning events may throw some doubt on the value of the exercise. The definition of the first 'skill' as being that of self-awareness also seems somewhat strange. Other skills that they mention are those of describing the experience verbally or in writing, critically analysing the material and synthesizing new and previous knowledge. The last 'skill' mentioned by Atkins and Murphy is that of evaluation, which is 'the making of judgements about something' – this perhaps sounds more deliberative than reflective. A number of features of this list of skills seem to locate it firmly in situations in which reflection is guided in the classroom.

Reflective practice and criticality

Proctor (1993) emphasizes criticality in reflective practice. On this view, reflective practice is the process of looking back in a critical way at what has occurred and using the results of this process, together with professional knowledge (with technical and ethical aspects), to tackle new situations. Such a view accords, in a broader manner, with Schön's reflection-on-action (1983). Proctor suggests that widening the range of considerations and developing personal criteria for the evaluation of situations are also involved.

As the first chapter indicated, criticality has been widely associated with reflective practice and is sometimes taken to be the main purpose for reflection (Smyth, 1989), but it can mean different things – a critical view of the content of an action (as Proctor, above) or of the self or of the context of the professional or profession. Smyth (1989) provides an example of the third of these and provides a set of guiding questions as a basis for reflection to empower and politicize professionals in teaching (see Chapter 6).

The use of reflection to encourage emancipation by means of a broad and critical review of a situation seems to be represented in teaching more than nursing where it is often related to the Habermasian classification. The apparent status hierarchy that is sometimes promulgated in work that favours the politicizing or emancipatory forms of reflection over those that concern classroom events is evident in some of the literature – Smyth being an extreme example of this. He stresses the concern that while empowerment underlies the advocacy of reflective practice in teaching, in many instances, it actually tends to be presented in an unempowering manner, encouraging teachers to work in an unreflective manner 'prescribing what teachers ought to teach within tight guidelines, while co-opting one another into policing the implementation of predetermined goals'. Smyth generalizes that when one group thinks that another group should act in a particular manner (in this case, be more reflective), there is an imposition of the will and agenda, which itself can be the subject of critique.

Smyth argues that the activity of teaching requires that it be set in its historical, political, theoretical and moral context because, removed from this, it becomes a technical process. Reflection is the 'active and militant' tool that enables that contextualization. The aim is that teachers will take greater responsibility for exposing the tensions 'between particular teaching practices and the larger cultural and social contexts in which they are embedded . . . placing themselves in a critical confrontation with their problems' (Smyth, 1989). Van Manen (1977) deals with similar issues in his analysis of curriculum development processes.

The development of a critical stance by means of reflection suggests that particular issues in teaching will be tackled, but it also has the connotation of sharpness and precision, suggesting continuous evaluation in the process of reflection.

Reflective practice as a state of mind

Reflective practices may also be interpreted as a gentle process of noticing and being concerned. In earlier chapters, the reflective orientation of the person was discussed and the process termed 'being reflective'. There are some references to this quality in the literature of reflective practice. Vaughn's suggestion is that reflective practice is 'as much a state of mind as it is a set of activities' (1990), and this appears to match Van Manen's use of the term 'mindfulness' to describe reflective practice (1991). Similarly, Jaworski's definition of reflective teachers, for example, does not incorporate connotations of criticality, yet suggests useful and purposeful activity that has an element of concern for the subject of the action – the learner in this case. For her, reflective practice involves 'noticing aspects of [their] own practice, perhaps triggered by some form of surprise, or by some question from an external observer, they recognize and work on issues of concern. Their thinking, reinforced possibly by its articulation, puts them in a more knowledgeable position for future decision making and professional action' (Jaworski, 1993).

Jaworski, like Schön, but unlike Proctor, implies that the reflective process works on the material of the stimulating event or surprise and she does not indicate that other information and knowledge is brought to bear on the process. A particularly interesting feature of Jaworski's definition is the idea that the resolution is aided ('possibly') by the articulation of the issue.

Reflective practice as an orientation to problem solving

Several writers see reflective practice in teaching largely in terms of solving the problems in practice (Kirby and Teddlie, 1989). This can be the proactive seeking of 'problematic situations', 'a conscious process of identifying problematic issues in their practice and pursuing solutions that bring about valued effects on student learning' (Copeland, Birmingham and Lewin, 1993) or the seeking of understanding (Grimmett, 1988; Russell, 1993).

Reflective practice, intuition and emotion

The descriptions above attempt to define what reflective practice is. Valli (1993) notes that in the literature there is an absence of reference to emotion and the process of intuition. She relates her observation to Houston and Clift (1990) who consider that definitions of reflective practice are rooted in Western culture, which emphasizes analysis and problem solving, not negotiation nor contemplation. Houston and Clift comment on the domination of a view of the world that stresses detachment, objectification and non-involvement of the emotions. While the practice of reflection can overcome these tendencies, the process of reflection itself within the professional context may be subject to cultural pressures.

A number of other writers describe elements or forms of reflection that might be similar to intuition and seem to integrate emotional reactions and cognition. Korthagen (1993) describes 'non-rational' reflection, which he contrasts to 'rational reflection'. Non-rational reflection is the result of right-hemisphere processing, which is not logical and may account for situations in which 'certain cues from the environment activate a gestalt triggering an immediate interpretation and reaction' such that rational or logical analysis is circumvented.

While the descriptions above suggest that intuition is a form of reflection, Dewey's views were fairly similar. Dewey (1933) considered that intuition results from the summarizing of prior reflection and conscious thinking that becomes habitual and comes to characterize experts in their fields. This recalls the comments of Van Manen, that the actions of professionals are guided by the outcomes of reflection transformed into more tacit competence. This explanation might also account for Schön's notion of reflection-in-action. Korthagen argues that this form of reflection should be recognized and nurtured in teacher education. Using the term 'holistic reflection', Clarke, James and Kelly (1996) suggest that representations of reflection, such as poetry writing, dance, drama or graphic methods, can elicit materials that 'make possible unique forms of understanding that are not possible through rational means of knowing'. However, if intuitions are seen as a form of outcome of reflection, which is probably unconscious, LaBoskey (1993) suggests that they require to be subjected to the normal conscious reflective processes to check their appropriateness in given situations.

The patterns of reflective practice

While there is no evidence of a common definition emerging for reflective practice, another angle that has been used to approach the topic is an attempt to recognize patterns of reflective practice or of reflection in practice in the form of models. The models endeavour to capture the elusive qualities of reflective practice for practical application.

Van Manen (1991) proposes a categorization of reflection as follows:

- thinking and acting in a common-sense manner on an 'everyday' basis – Van Manen clearly separates reflection and action;
- reflection that is focused on events or incidents – this is a more specific form of reflection than the first and matches Schön's ideas of reflection-on-action;
- reflection on personal experience and that of others – this is more systematic reflection with the objective of reaching understanding, it is a higher order reflection, which may be on several events or on the results of reflection that has already occurred, and could be seen as reflection-on-action that goes well beyond the event, a category that is not obviously covered in Schön's work;
- reflection on the manner of reflection – this is self-reflection on the nature of knowing or meta-cognition on the way in which knowledge works.

In this manner of organizing views of practice, there is a hierarchical arrangement from reflection that is focused on 'everyday' problems towards a meta-cognitive view that is critical of the act of knowing itself. Van Manen distinguishes between reflection on experience and reflection on the conditions that shape our experience. His model is more comprehensive than most others, allowing for the views of some that reflective practice is essentially a critical and political stance. Other models that deal with reflective practice similarly are those of Grimmett, McKinnon, Erikson and Reichen (1990), Valli (1993), LaBoskey (1993), and Goodman (1984). James and Clarke (1994) use a higher order of analysis on which to base their conceptual organization of reflective practice. They use Van Manen's earlier classification (Van Manen, 1977), described in Chapter 2, relating it to the Habermasian model of knowledge constitutive interests, but they also have an additional category of reflection on the self and personal behaviour.

Reflective practice and other forms of practice

Given the confusion over the characteristics of reflective practice, one of the most helpful approaches is that taken by Jones and Joss (1995) in the literature of social work. These writers compare reflective practice with other forms of practice – such as practical professional, technical expert and managerial – on a range of factors involved in professional functioning, including self-image, theoretical orientation, knowledge base, practice theory, the relationships implied with the client, attitudes towards professional development and the nature of critique. In this manner, some of what might be defining characteristics of reflective practice begin to emerge. For example, the writers talk of the reflective practitioner with a self-image as a facilitator, for whom there is important recognition of the uncertainty of the professional situation, the knowledge base of the profession and, thereby, the problems that need to be resolved in practice. The reflective practitioner will cope with this uncertainty by putting the relationship with the client at the centre of practice with an attempt reflectively to develop negotiated and shared meanings and understandings as a joint process. It is interesting to apply this to the idea of reflective practice in other professions, such as nursing and teaching.

Is reflective practice associated with a stage of professional development?

Implicit in most of the literature on reflective practice is the notion that attaining this form of practice is a matter of education or training. However, it is possible that processes such as maturation and personal development may be involved. Gregorc (1973) identified stages in professional (teacher) growth and infers that there is stage of a teacher's development as a teacher at which she may become more reflective. Having passed through the 'becoming stage' and the 'growing stage', a teacher may or may not progress to 'the maturing stage', which is when they have ' made a strong commitment to education and functions beyond minimum expectations'. Gregorc continues, 'In this stage the individual tests concepts about education [themselves], others, subject matter and the environment. By opening the door to reality, faulty concepts are "exploded". The person is forced to restructure [their] view of reality'. This sounds like a period of transformation in the teacher's view of themselves in their role that might follow, as the quotation suggests, the testing of concepts and other reflective activity. This is reinforced by Gregorc's observation of teachers. He says that self acceptance, deep knowledge of subject matter and an openness and willingness to share ideas are characteristic of the teachers who successfully move through the stages, or moved more quickly. These characteristics are associated with reflectivity elsewhere, for example in the work on the development of reflective judgement (King and Kitchener, 1994).

In Gregorc's work, age had no direct relationship with the stages, but there is a suggestion that another factor in the development of reflective practice may be their stage of formal professional education. This would be relevant to any educational activity with practising teachers. While Gregorc's work is with teachers, it seems likely that its principles might be applicable to other professions.

The features of reflective practice

The main conclusion of this chapter is that, in theoretical terms, there appears to be no one form of practice that can be called reflective practice, but there are many different ways of regarding it. There is no consistency within or across professions. There is a general sense that reflective practice is good, but the identity of the main beneficiary is not clear – the professional or their clients?

In 'local' situations, the imprecision of the definition may not be a major issue, but it matters for the theoretician and in discussions about reflective practice between two or more agencies (say a teacher educator and teacher or writer to reader). It matters particularly in the education of novice professionals who are most likely to meet the inconsistencies of the definition. In these cases, honesty about the imprecision is better than a pretence that we are dealing with an exact science.

Some of the features that tend to be identified as characteristics of reflective practice are summarized below:

- reflective practice involves the mental process of reflecting, which may or may not be characterized by what we have called 'being reflective';
- the subject matter of reflection is likely to be one's own practice, paying more or less attention to the setting of the practice;
- reflective practice may refer to reflection on the everyday events of practice or the conditions that shape reflection, such as political influences;
- reflection may be ongoing or a reaction to a specific event or an unexpected occurrence or observation of a problem; it is characterized by states of uncertainty; it may have an ethical or moral content;
- it may be in response to an externally posed question or task or arise from personal considerations, but the material will be such (say, unstructured) that there is no immediate solution;
- reflective practice may have a strong critical element;
- the end point of reflection in reflective practice may not be resolution of an issue, but attainment of a better understanding of it;
- reflection will have involved the process of thinking, but it may be aided by the process of articulation of the thinking orally or in written form;
- review and reconstruction of the ideas surrounding reflection will be aimed at understanding or resolving the issue in the context of a general aim of improving practice, specifically or generally;
- still within the overall context of improving practice, the immediate aim may be self-development or professional development or self-empowerment or empowerment of the educationalist within the political sphere;
- there can be emotional involvement, either in the content of reflection or as a product of reflection, and this may or may not be acknowledged;
- reflective practice may bear some relationship to the process of intuition;
- reflective practice is usually enhanced when there is some sharing of the reflection with others;
- a useful approach to developing further understanding of the nature of reflective practice is exemplified by the comparison of reflective practice with alterative approaches to practice (as in Jones and Joss, 1995).

Conclusion

There is no one behaviour or one consistent set of behaviours that is reflective practice. What constitutes reflective practice behaviour has been characterized above by listing behaviours that have been associated with reflective practice.

The outcomes of reflection in reflective practice include learning and action, empowerment and emancipation. Reflective practice may also imply the general orientation of being reflective.

Chapter 6

Reflective practice in the professions – a practical stance

Introduction

The previous chapter reviewed theoretical approaches to reflective practice, seeking evidence of consistent approaches to reflective practice or a common meaning. The use of the term 'reflective practice' seems to be idiosyncratic within and across professions and the conclusion arrived at a the end of the chapter was that there is no useful common definition, only a number of common characteristics. The implication is that users of the term need to negotiate and agree the meaning of the term for themselves.

This chapter takes a more practical approach to reflective practice and describes some ways in which the concept has been applied in practical situations. Again, the literature this chapter draws on largely concerns teaching and nursing, but examples have been chosen for their potentially wider applications.

Reflective practice as a means of relating to learners/patients/clients

In discussions of reflection on professional situations, the focus on the practitioner and practice has been noted. The improvement in practice is usually specified as a desirable outcome, but there is another perhaps more significant outcome of the action on the client of the professional (such as the facilitation of learning) and this real end point features little in the literature of reflection. Moon (1996a) points out a similar issue in the conduct of training those with a role in promotion of health where the real focus might be on the improvement of the health of their clients, with improvement in their professional practice being instrumental in that process. However, health improvement is rarely mentioned.

In the discussion of reflective practice in the previous chapter, some issues are concerned wholly with the professionalism of the teacher, but Van Manen's levels of reflection (see Chapter 2) are posited in a manner that is also relevant to action at the professional–client interface. The content of his book (1991) takes this a great deal further and is written to inspire novice teachers to a reflective or mindful stance in their early work with pupils. The previous chapter briefly considered the notion of mindfulness as a theoretical interpretation of reflective practice, but here it is examined in its more practical implications. Previously, mindfulness has been equated with the behavioural orientation of 'being reflective' (as in Chapter 5). Van Manen suggests that mindfulness is a quality of the behaviour of a person that links thought and action in a relationship between the self and others. The quality of this relationship is maintained by means of reflection on or about actions and represents a concern in the relationship between teacher and learner. It aims to produce a positive educational experience for the learner (or the child – Van Manen considers this in the context of parenting as well). Daloz (1986), in a similar way, discusses the manner in which a reflective teacher or mentor can affect the quality of learning and experience of the learner or mentee.

Because of their reflective and wordy nature, the accounts of Van Manen and Daloz of the effect of reflective practice on the educational process are difficult to operationalize and impart to novice teachers in a formal education situation, but then this is clearly not the aim of their writings. Rather, the aim is to inspire the individual reader to reflect on the content at a deeper level and make a link between the accounts of reflection in teaching and the crucial outcome of learning.

While Van Manen and Daloz consider the nature of reflective teaching and how it relates to learning, Barnett (1992) is concerned with the qualities of teachers who will facilitate reflective learning. He considers that, among other actions to encourage reflection, higher education teachers must act as role models in order to encourage reflection in their students. They need to become reflective practitioners themselves. Unfortunately, as in higher education, sometimes the structure of educational programmes seems to work in opposition to this. Mass higher education is generally resulting in the reduction of small group work with students when small groups are where the qualities of reflectiveness on the part of a teacher can be evident. Similarly, the modularization of courses may mean that students do not have contact with one teacher over a sufficiently long period of time to allow them to reflect on or to observe or interact with the reflection processes in their teachers.

Developing reflective practice in experienced practitioners

The desirability of reflective practice in teaching is assumed in the literature – that it is good to be a reflective teacher. However, much of the literature is about reflection in student teachers. Sometimes it is difficult to dissociate the literature that concerns the development of reflective student teachers from that of reflective practising teachers, and as these two groups are substantially different in their likely uses of reflection, this might be a little surprising.

Wildman and Niles (1987) describe a scheme for developing reflective practice in experienced teachers. This was justified by the view that reflective practice could help teachers to feel more intellectually involved in their role and work in teaching, and enable them cope with the paucity of scientific fact and the uncertainty of knowledge in the discipline of teaching.

Wildman and Niles were particularly interested in investigating the conditions under which reflection might flourish – a subject on which there is little guidance in the literature (some of their work contributes to Chapter 13). They designed an experimental strategy for a group of teachers in Virginia and worked with 40 practising teachers over several years. They were concerned that many would ' be drawn to these new, refreshing conceptions of teaching only to find that the void between the abstractions and the realities of teacher reflection is too great to bridge. Reflection on a complex task such as teaching is not easy'. The teachers were taken through a programme of talking about teaching events, moving on to reflecting on specific issues in a supported, and later an independent, manner.

Wildman and Niles observed that systematic reflection on teaching required a sound ability to understand classroom events in an objective manner. They describe the understanding in the teachers with whom they were working, initially as being ' utilitarian . . . and not rich or detailed enough to drive systematic reflection'. They suggest that teachers rarely have the time or opportunities to view their own or the teaching of others in an objective manner. Further observation revealed the tendency of teachers to evaluate events rather than review the contributory factors in a considered manner – in effect, standing outside the situation or progressing to the higher levels of reflection in terms of Van Manen's model (1991).

Helping this group of teachers to revise their thinking about classroom events became central in the work with them. This process took time and patience and effective trainers. The researchers estimate that the initial training of the teachers to view events objectively took between 20 and 30 hours, with the same numbers of hours again being required to practice the skills of reflection.

Wildman and Niles identify three principles that facilitate reflective practice in a teaching situation. The first is support from the administrators in an education system, enabling them to understand the requirements of reflective practice and how it relates to teaching students. The second is the availability of sufficient time and space. The teachers on the programme described how they found it difficult to put aside the immediate demands of students in order to give themselves the time they needed to develop their reflective skills. The third is the development of a collaborative environment with support from other teachers. Support and understanding were also required to help teachers on the programme to cope with the products of their reflection. Becoming reflective meant, for example, that they became aware of aspects of their professional life with which they were not comfortable, and they required support to cope with the situations or change them. Wildman and Niles make a summary comment: 'Perhaps the most important thing we learned is that the idea of teacher-as-reflective practitioner will not happen simply because it is a good or even compelling idea'.

The work of Wildman and Niles suggests the importance of recognizing some of the difficulties of instituting reflective practice. Others have noted this, making a similar point about the cultural inhibitions in the teaching profession about reflective practice. Zeichner and Liston (1987) point out the inconsistency between the role of the teacher as a (reflective) professional decision maker and the more usual role of teacher as technician, putting into practice the ideas of others. More basic than the cultural issues is the matter of motivation. Becoming a reflective practitioner requires extra work (Jaworski, 1993) and has only vaguely defined goals with, perhaps, little initially perceivable reward and the threat of vulnerability. Few have directly questioned what might lead a teacher to want to become reflective. Apparently, the most obvious reason for teachers to undergo work towards reflective practice is because teacher educators think it is a good thing. There appear to be many unexplored matters about the motivation to reflect – for example, the value of externally motivated reflection as opposed to that of teachers who might reflect by habit. LaBoskey (1993) talks about the process of changing 'common-sense thinkers', who are externally motivated to reflect, into 'pedagogical thinkers', who reflect habitually.

Providing useful insight into this transition towards reflective habits in the field of nursing is the writing of Emden (1991) who describes how a nurse might become a reflective practitioner as a result of a relatively short exercise involving the process of observation and reflection. She contrasts this method with the usual pattern of written reflection over an indeterminate period of time. She acknowledges that the processes are not new, but their use to focus on development of a personal view of nursing is an application of value, but also a potential source of unease. The process involves a preparatory period of anticipation of a clinical situation in which the whole range of elements that make up the experience – the sensory aspects and behaviours, including the role of the observer – are considered. Emden also suggests that feelings and a relevant history of the setting are drawn into the process of anticipation and some reading is done. The experiential phase involves close observation of, and involvement in, the chosen clinical setting for around 18 hours. This will include the writing of field notes. The processing phase requires a review of the experience and the field notes in order that further meaning is derived from them. From her standpoint of critical theory, she sees action to be an important outcome. This will ensure that reflection is more than simply a mental exercise, although intellectual exercises can achieve significant new understanding that builds towards change over a longer period and so perhaps they should not be so decried.

Also from the profession of nursing, Johns (1994) developed a series of questions to guide the reflective process in practising professionals. The guided process consists of a core question and a series of further questions that is, he suggests, a model that provides 'a comprehensive and valid means of "knowing" the breadth and depth of reflection'. The questions have relevance to other professional situations and so have been adopted in a modified form in a teacher training situation.

Johns suggests that the process of using guided reflection needs to be supervised, preferably by the practitioner's line manager. He recommends that the reflection is written in a 'reflective diary', with one side of the page consisting of the descriptive material (with actual dialogue where possible) and the other side consisting of the reflection and exploration. The incidents recorded will probably be situations of doubt or difficulty and he suggests that they are worked through on the same day. He also asks nurses to challenge themselves each day on something that they normally do – 'Why do I do that?'

The guiding questions of Johns (see Figure 6.1) are limited to the lower levels of reflective activity on Van Manen's model and do not extend the trainees' thinking to a consideration of the conditions that shape the reflective activity itself – the meta-cognitive dimension. The addition of questions developed by Smyth to probe the higher order areas of reflection can complement those of Johns. Smyth suggests that the initial experience of events in practice are described in personal narrative, by means of which he anticipates that the material will be drawn into identified theories in use (Argyris and Schön, 1974). Then he proposes that the events be analysed critically by asking questions, such as 'What do my practices say about my assumptions and beliefs about teaching?', 'What views of power do they embody?', 'Whose interests seem to be served by my practices' and 'What is it that acts to constrain my views of what is possible in teaching?' (Smyth, 1987).

Reflection in developing theory of practice

Schön's work demonstrates in a general manner how theory of practice is built on the basis of reflection. As nurse educators, Gray and Forström (1991) considered that their colleagues were not paying sufficient attention to the importance of clinical practice, particularly with regard to its generation of theoretical knowledge. They demonstrate how, in returning to a clinical situation, they used reflection in a manner described by Boud, Keogh and Walker (1985) to develop practice theory of nursing.

Core question

What information do I need access to in order to learn through this experience?

1.0 Cue questions

Description of experience

1.1	Phenomenon	Describe the 'here and now' experience.
1.2	Causal	What essential factors contributed to this experience?
1.3	Context	What are the significant background factors to this experience?
1.4	Clarifying	What are the key processes (for reflection) in this experience?

2.0 Reflection

2.1 What was I trying to achieve?
2.2 Why did I intervene as I did?
2.3 What were the consequences of my action for myself, the patient/family, the people I work with?
2.4 How did I feel about the experience when it was happening?
2.5 How did the patient feel about it?
2.6 How do I know how the patient felt about it?

3.0 Influencing factors

3.1 What internal factors influenced my decision making?
3.2 What external factors influenced my decision making?
3.3 What sources of knowledge did/should have influenced my decision making?

4.0 Could I have dealt better with the situation?

4.1 What other choices did I have?
4.2 What could be the consequences of these choices?

5.0 Learning

5.1 How do I feel about this experience now?
5.2 How have I made sense of this experience in the light of past experiences and future practice?
5.3 Has this experience changed my way of knowing empirics, aesthetics, ethics, personal?

Figure 6.1 *Johns' model for structured reflection*

Gray and Forström chose to work in areas of practice in which they had some expertise and interest in order to ensure that they could make adequate observations on which to reflect. They emphasize the need for familiarity with the context and suggest that novice nurses or even experienced nurses in an unfamiliar context may not have the experience on which to conduct fruitful reflection. They report how they used journals to work through the recommended sequence of stages in reflection – recollection of salient events, attending to feelings, re-evaluating the experience and integration, validation and appropriation. There was a gradual realization of the difficulty of the task of reflecting in such a way as to build theory and they felt that a longer time period was required to enable them to use the reflective technique to greatest effect and thereby develop theory. They felt, too, that the support of a regular discussion group to facilitate the development of theory from the journal entries would have helped.

As a result of their investigation of reflection as a means of building theory of practice, Gray and Forström suggest that nurse academics should be encouraged to engage in the process and be given some relief from their other duties. Nurses at all levels should be involved, but practising nurses engaging in the process need time and the support of a regular meeting. The activity must be seen as one that is supported as a legitimate part of the job and accepted by administrators. Interestingly, these conditions are very much in accord with those specified by Wildman and Niles (1987) in their relatively similar work with teachers.

Cox, Hickson and Taylor (1991) are also concerned with the development of theory of practice in nursing and continuing nurse education, but they are concerned that the reflection should enable a shift from an awareness of personal realities to new understandings. They advocate the use of a journal as a means of recognition of the issues in practice, but they consider that there could be a stalling effect if reflection is always a lone process. They are concerned that there might be difficulties in overcoming distortions in their own understandings to enable them to face up to questions that challenge practice. They suggest that there is a need to focus on their self-imposed task of developing understanding.

Cox, et al., advocate that reflection is used in a more critical manner and is intended to lead to constructive action so that the constructed realities of the practising nurse are challenged and enabled to change and improve practice. Cox, et al., present a paper that has the encouraging rhetoric of many of those writing about critical reflection, but the examples of it are (probably realistically) down to earth. The sharing of personal reflections with others could be a critical factor in taking the reflective process beyond self-affirmation. It may be that the work of Gray and Forström lacked this dimension.

Some examples of reflection in initial professional education

Reflective practice in mentoring

As was commented on earlier, professional educators show an interest in creating reflective students, but do not report on their own needs for reflective practice. Reid (1994) is an exception and reports on how she uses a journal to facilitate her activity in providing support for her students in their ability to reflect. She uses Gibbs' reflective cycle (Gibbs, 1988), a form of the experiential learning cycle, to support her work. The cycle has the following stages:

- description – 'What happened?';
- feelings – 'What were you thinking and feeling?';
- evaluation – 'What was good and bad?';
- analysis – 'What sense can you make of the situation?';
- conclusion – 'What else could you have done?';
- action plan – 'If it occurs again, what would you do?'.

Developing reflective habits in students

The arguments in favour of teaching student professionals to reflect are reported as the early formation of the habit of reflecting on practice (Zeichner and Liston, 1987), the development of the ability of students to be critical of their experiences of training (Smyth, 1989) and the improvement of their use of reflection in action (Hatton and Smith, 1995). Schön's book (1987) on educating the reflective practitioner implies that the skills of reflective practice are to be initiated within the context of initial training. There are others who query the initiation of reflective practice for students, usually on the basis that students do not have access to the body of knowledge and experience in the day-to-day work of the professionals that is the real content of professional reflection. For example, McIntyre (1993), talking of teaching, queries the value of inducing a critical or political form of reflection on the basis that if things 'go wrong' in a student's teaching, the student's reaction will be to examine their own deficiencies rather than consider how the regime might in some way be culpable. It is not unlikely that some students will use their critical skills to turn on the training situation itself in a manner that is more impetuous than it is useful to them, even if there is some ground for their concerns.

There are other writers also who remark on the way in which the environment of professional education can be unsympathetic to the processes of reflection. Most initial professional education follows an apprenticeship model in which students are required to learn a body of knowledge to enable them to cope with their early days in the practice situation, and the ethos is not to criticize or question and be creative only within limits. Copeland, Birmingham and Lewin (1993) advise that 'A conservative approach is considered safest'.

This, too, is far from the 'active and militant' reflection advocated by Smyth (1989).

In the literature, there are several descriptions of programmes in which reflection is integrated into professional education, and there are reviews of a range of reflective practitioner programmes, such as that of Valli (1993). Sometimes the programmes operate on the conventional apprenticeship model, with reflection taught as a skill or performed as an element of the learning, but in some instances it has been given a more all-encompassing role and the whole programme is dedicated to the development of the reflective practitioner.

Whole programme approaches to instituting reflective practice

The most obvious example of a programme approach to developing reflective practice is that of Schön who advocates the use of a practicum as a setting in which the pressures of normal practice are removed and where there is a better opportunity to institute good practice using coaching techniques. Coaching requires very high staff to student ratios and, as a whole programme approach, would thus often be impractical. Several writers report use of a practicum as a part of a programme (Hatton and Smith, 1995, for example) and note that difficulties may be incurred in transferring the reflective practice from the stress-free environment to the real world.

Zeichner and Liston (1987) provide an example of a teacher education programme in which the total content is orientated towards development of the reflective practitioner. Reflective activity is integrated according to a number of principles. In terms of students, 'the programme seeks to prepare students of teaching who view knowledge and situations as problematic and socially constructed rather than as certain'. In terms of the curriculum, they say that it '. . . should reflect in its form and content a view of knowledge as socially constructed . . . .This requires a curriculum for student teaching that is reflective rather than received, one that is based on enquiry that challenges the traditional relationships which exist between student teachers and teacher educators. The teacher educators endeavour to act as models of the moral craftsperson teacher'.

These elements of the programme are expressed via four curriculum components. These are seminars that focus critically on the role of the teacher (such as on the relationship of conventional theory to practice), personal journal writing, students' processes of enquiry, and supervisory discussions on the students' classroom teaching practice. Evaluative studies suggested that many areas of the programme were successful, but collaborative interactions between students and the ideal of the teacher as a 'moral craftsperson' were less successful. This may be one part of the programme that suffers from the difficulty that students may have in talking about the teacher's role before they have lived in it.

Zeichner and Liston also considered impediments to the implementation of the programme. Among the factors mentioned are the dominance of the view of initial teacher education as an apprenticeship, the resistance or reluctance of some students to engage in reflective processes and the pressure on the relation-ships between students and staff and university and school staff. Significantly for the study of reflection, students found it difficult to function in the reflective 'teacher as decision maker' role engendered by the course when their personal experiences of teachers before their training and within the schools was of 'teacher as technician', a role 'our society and its institutions seek to maintain'. The use of reflection to enhance decision-making skills in professional education and practice is not an outcome of reflection that is commonly mentioned. Chapter 14 provides a case study on the use of reflection in enhancing effective decision making.

It is interesting to compare the all-encompassing nature of this teacher education programme, which is geared towards the production of reflective practitioners, with the sketchy descriptions of abilities required for reflective practice in the previous chapter. In addition to more concrete capacities to reflect, a programme of this type certainly accords with the notion of reflective practice described by Vaughn (1990) as a state of mind rather than a set of activities.

An approach based on an evaluative tool

Hatton and Smith (1995) approach the development of reflective practitioners in a completely different manner. Crucial for them was the development of a tool that demonstrated evidence of different qualities of reflection. The evaluative tool was then used in the gradual design and redesign of activities to foster reflection in a teacher education degree at the University of Sydney.

Initially, Hatton and Smith instituted a number of different strategies in the later years of the four-year course. These included special seminars, a practicum, action research and micro-teaching, with associated reflective tasks in written, video and audiotaped forms and interview. They found that the written reports provided the best evidence of reflection and subsequently these formed the source of data for the research. By analysing the written work, they classified four types of writing, three of which they identified as forms of reflection. These were as follows, listed in order of increasing sophistication:

- 'descriptive reflection' – a reflective description of events;
- 'dialogic reflection' – with some stepping back from the event and explora-tion with the self of reasons for the event;
- 'critical reflection' – exploring reasons for an event in the broader social, ethical, moral or historical contexts.

Hatton and Smith comment that they found few examples of critical reflection in the work of these pre-service students. This might support the contention that student teachers need to come to terms with more routine activities in teaching and learning before they can meaningfully put them into the context of politics and power in schools in order to write an effective critique.

The use of this research tool gave Hatton and Smith evidence that students were learning to be reflective over their period of training. It also demonstrated that reflection was particularly fostered in situations where students interacted verbally with 'trusted others'. Supervised peer group discussions of micro-teaching episodes were also valuable for the encouragement of reflective activities.

Approaches using journal-writing

There are many examples of the use of journals to support learning on professional courses. Morrison (1996) provides insight into the theoretical framework on which his journal exercises were based. Reference is made to Morrison's work in Chapter 15, which focuses on practical issues in the use of journals to enhance reflection. Morrison describes a teacher education programme in which reflection is engendered by means of a single but coherent and structured method – the use of a learning journal. Morrison acknowledges the complexity of the literature on reflective practice for the academic and questions how a student teacher can grasp it. To overcome this, he categorized reflective practice into two models. The first, which is related to Schön's work (Schön, 1983), deals with reflection-in-action and reflection-on-action, and the second with individual and social empowerment by means of critical reflection. These forms of reflective practice fit neatly into Van Manen's framework of levels (see Chapter 2).

The learning journal promoted in Morrison's programme is maintained by students throughout their courses and the contents are discussed with a named personal tutor. Among the purposes described for the journal are the charting of experiences and development, noting the interactions between personal and professional development and academic work, student empowerment and a development of meta-cognitive abilities. Morrison notes, as have others cited earlier, that for some students the idea of reflection is alien and they need extra tutorial support.

Effective learning from reflective journals usually implies the imposition of some form of structure in order that learners can make sense of the material and move towards learning from it. The structures, in this case, were a series of questions to prompt reflection. Morrison reports that, from the evaluation of the journals and the process of writing them, the questions seem to be helpful in prompting students to explore thinking that they might not otherwise have done.

The account, by Holm and Stephenson (1994), of learning to be reflective has been mentioned in the context of the stage approaches to reflection (see Chapter 1). It has an unusual place in the literature as an account of learning to reflect because it is written by the authors about their own experiences in learning to be nurses. One of the values of this piece of work is its description of the difficulties of learning to reflect.

In an informal manner, Holm and Stephenson describe the process of becoming able to reflect over the period of their education. They observe that early on the course, their writing tended to be descriptive and lacking in analysis. They mention that there was anxiety about how to reflect and that this led to a stage in which they wanted help and constructive criticism from tutors to show them where they were going wrong. They then began to grasp the idea that reflective processes were engendered by particular questions that they learned to identify. From the initial questions, they learned to question 'the given' and use reflection to bring clarity to unclear situations in their nursing practice.

Along with an assertion of the values of reflection to students, Holm and Stephenson mention that the process of reflection enabled their learning from events; their appreciation of different viewpoints on situations; the amalgamation of theory and practice and it enabled them, as student nurses, to have a sense of control over their own learning. They mention the value of the work for their professional development learning profiles, but, interestingly, they do not mention that reflection makes them better at nursing or caring for patients.

Conclusion

This chapter has considered the various more practical approaches to professional reflective practice. The examples given are diverse and bring us no nearer to a unified view of reflective practice. As with the last chapter, they provide a picture of a range of activities that apply reflection to achieve a variety of purposes within practice.

Taking an overview of the discussion of reflective practice in Chapters 4, 5 and 6, it seems that reflective practice has been interpreted in both a broader and richer manner than Schön's model, although it is largely his writings that have initiated the wide interest in reflection. Among the purposes for, or outcomes of, reflection illustrated in these chapters are:

- learning or material for further reflection;
- action or other representation of learning;
- understanding of the process of learning;
- the building of theory;
- self-development;
- decision making or resolution of uncertainty;
- empowerment and emancipation;
- other outcomes that are unexpected, such as images or ideas that might represent solutions to problems.

Added to this list, but different in character from the other purposes mentioned, is the state of 'being reflective' because it seems to summarize a number of references in the literature to reflection that are more related to a state of mind than an activity.

Chapter 7

The role of reflection in counselling, therapy and personal development

Introduction

There have been various references to reflection on the self in earlier chapters, often in the contexts of the achievement of emancipatory states or professional development. The different uses of the term 'reflection' overlap and separating them to describe them in a meaningful manner inevitably is a matter of making the best sense, rather than perfect sense, of the situation. In terms of making sense of reflection in personal development, some say that professional development is largely a matter of personal development (Harvey and Knight, 1996), while for others they are quite separate. The overlap varies according to the conceptions of both.

In this chapter, the focus is on reflection in personal or self-development where someone is intent on self-awareness and/or better personal functioning. The initial division used to organize this discussion is one between personal development in situations starting from deficit and those in which the start is from relative normality. In terms of deficit, personal development mainly takes the form of adopting the role of client in counselling or therapy, in which the guidance of the reflection is partly the responsibility of another. In counselling and therapy that really aims to promote mental health, the aim will be to enable the client to be able to take an increasing role in determining the nature of her own processes of reflection and learning towards mental wellbeing.

In a non–deficit situation, personal development encompasses any activity that might contribute towards growth or development of the person. This will not all be down to reflection. However, for example, growth may occur when a person puts themselves in a challenging position and faces up to difficulties, but the decision to put themselves into that position may have been determined by a reflective process, a coming to understand what is needed.

In practice, there is an overlap between the deficit and growth models because the notion of relative normality is imprecise and the same techniques or activities may be applied in either case. However, it is the intentions behind the activities that determine to which they belong. The division is largely one of convenience.

Reflection in counselling and therapy

If the use of the word 'reflection' in the literature on self-development, particularly counselling and therapy, was taken to be the criterion for inclusion in this chapter, there would be little content. It is not a term employed widely in this field, although the activity of thinking back on prior ideas in a purposeful manner in order to learn or to act differently is exactly the activity that leads to self development or the development of self-knowledge in either of the categories described above (in Egan, 1990, for example). Reflection, as a term in the literature of counselling, may be used in a different sense to that of this book. The word is used to describe a technique of the counsellor of repeating back or paraphrasing the words of the client or slightly changing them. The intended result of this is to facilitate more reflection in. the client or enable them to reflect again on their own words and perhaps find greater meaning (for example Brammer, Schostrom and Abrego, 1989; Dryden and Feltham, 1992 and 1994).

Most methods of counselling and therapy could be characterized as situations in which clients, either alone with a therapist or in groups, voluntarily reflect on their histories, views of the world, behaviour, human and material environments, and beliefs and values. The intention is to learn to feel or act differently with respect to an element or elements in their lives. Working with a counsellor or therapist, they will engage in this process of reflection within a framework of guidance that has been developed according to a particular philosophy or approach to counselling or therapy. The usual aim of the guidance is, initially, to draw out the nature of the problems or deficits in the client, then enable them to learn from them and, with the support of the counsellor, find a manner in which to resolve them through actions or change or reframing of their attitudes. The client is engaging in the acquisition of new information as well as reflecting on what they already know.

There are many different approaches to counselling and therapy and in real situations several different approaches might be combined. The nature of the relationship between the counsellor and the client is another variable in the situation. Some counselling (if this term can really be used here) even occurs in the use of specially developed interactive computer programmes, though it could be said that there is a virtual relationship with the person who wrote the program. However, in the more usual situation, a major dimension of the relationship between client and counsellor, and the manner in which the guidance of reflection is handled, can be described by a continuum with client-centred or non-directive counselling at one end and directive, 'therapist as expert' counselling at the other. This continuum has been emphasized mainly in the work on client-centred approaches by Carl Rogers (1961) and the directive approaches of Freudian psychoanalysis.

Client-centred approaches rely on the trust the counsellor has that the client has the capacity for healing and learning and, with support, will find their own route, by reflecting, towards a solution. There is trust that this capacity will emerge given the right attention, space and time. Directive therapies assume that the counsellor or therapist is expert in guiding reflection towards resolution. The problem with the extreme versions of this view is that the client does not learn to reflect in a way that will enable them to help themselves if the problem re-emerges. Most counselling and therapies lie between these two extremes.

The form the guidance by the counsellor of the reflective processes of the client takes characterizes the approach of the counsellor. Particular forms of counselling will usually emphasize some part of the process. The guidance may be relatively direct, in which the client is helped to talk of their experiences. Personal construct counselling emphasizes the effort made by the counsellor to understand the world as the client sees it by using particular techniques, such as the repertory grid (Fransella and Dalton, 1995). Other forms of counselling may use metaphorical forms within which both client and counsellor/therapist engage. Examples of the latter are gestalt therapy (Perls, Hefferline and Goodman, 1951) or Jungian and Freudian psychotherapies, which are couched in more elaborate symbolisms. The reflection may be represented non-verbally – for example, in terms of drama (drama therapy) or in graphic form, in music or dance or in other forms of physical activity. The reflection here relies on tacit knowing (Polyani, 1966) and the resolution may or may not be expressed orally. The assumption is that change can occur as a result of the form of expression, even if the client is unaware of the process of change. Reflection, in other words, can lead to unexpected results.

Reflection for personal development and growth

Reflection is a part of counselling and, similarly, it underpins self-development. In this case, the framework of guidance is more under the control of the individual and, in the same way, too, personal development may imply the need to acquire new information and assimilate that into the reflective process.

Personal development in the non-deficit mode covers a range of activities for which different words are used, not always consistently. There is an implication of improvement and thus of change from one state to another with the likely involvement of learning. The subtleties of meaning may matter relatively little until the personal development is viewed as a component of, for example, professional development and there are other stakeholders rather than simply the individual. What follows relies largely on the literature of personal development in professional development because the more analytical material concerns this field. There is a large amount of popular literature on reflection in self-development, but it tends to be too anecdotal in nature to include here.

Much that is written about professional development hints at an important role for personal development activities (whichever words are used), but relatively few writers have been explicit about the link. Winter (1995), followed by Harvey and Knight (1996), points out that professional development is dependent on the development of an individual's self-awareness, while Eraut (1992) puts more emphasis on the use of propositional knowledge in professional development.

In his references to personal development, Eraut implies a useful conceptual structure from awareness of self to the application of the awareness for personal improvement and improvement in terms of one's life position. The first part of what follows reviews the development of the structure as a means of grasping what personal development might mean.

Eraut uses the term 'personal knowledge' to describe the personal meanings that an individual constructs as a result of experiences (Eraut, 1994). This includes assumptions and impressions, many of which may not be accessible at a conscious level. He uses the term 'self-knowledge' to include self-awareness and 'knowledge of one's own knowledge and skills, when and how to use them and when to look beyond one's own resources' (Eraut, 1994). He therefore includes the capacity to use the awareness and knowledge of self to understand its limitations, its strengths and weaknesses. Self-management is the process of using self-knowledge in order to achieve a particular end. The 'end', in the case of Eraut's writing, is the growth of professional behaviour that enables the tasks of the professional to be executed in an appropriate manner.

Eraut conceives of the various forms of personal development described above as contributing to 'control knowledge', which is a usefully pragmatic term for ' knowledge that is important for controlling one's own behaviour'. A person needs 'understanding' in order to effect something as complicated and variable as control of personal behaviour, and Eraut (1994) describes control knowledge as encompassing:

> self-knowledge about one's strengths and weaknesses, the gap between what one says and one does and what one knows and does not know; self-management in such matters as the use of time, prioritization and delegation; self-development in its broadest sense including knowing how to learn and control one's own learning; the ability to reflect and self-evaluate, that is to provide oneself with feedback; and generalized intellectual skills like strategic thinking and policy analysis, which involve the organization of one's own knowledge and thinking.

While this list of ideas describes professional situations, it also seems to be a useful summary of what might be involved in, or the outcomes of, any successful personal development. In effect, Eraut talks about personal knowledge as the structure of understanding and it concerns our knowledge about ourselves and our functioning in relation to the demands of the environment. Control knowledge is broader still, including various life skills, and could be construed as the totality of the manner in which a person meets their world.

Generalizing the meaning in Eraut's schema and interpreting the elements in terms of tasks towards personal development suggests that they could be restated as follows:

- self-awareness is the development of an awareness of the self and one's view of the world;
- self-improvement is an intentional development towards improvement in some area of life;
- empowerment and emancipation are the attainment of the level of overview and control of the self that enables emancipation in thought or understanding at least – this might be expressed as the ability to behave in a different manner that is closely related to current needs.

If the three categories above, based on Eraut's work, are seen as describing the tasks that will enable eventual personal growth towards emancipation, the question arises as to the degree of dependence there is on each previous stage. Reflection that focuses on self-awareness only, for example, is unlikely to bring about substantial change and personal growth. Awareness does not imply actual change. Harvey and Knight (1996) imply this point when they consider the role of reflection in the professional development of teachers: 'Our claim is that reflection needs to be extensive, to involve examining lurking assumptions about what we do and why we do it'. It is significant that the aim for the professional development that is proposed by Harvey and Knight is transformative learning, which has similar connotations of meta-functioning as that expressed in the idea of control knowledge (Eraut, 1994). Transformative learning relates also to the meta-critical state necessary for emancipation and, in this second manner, also suggests the progression of self-development through the three elements of self-development sketched above.

While it is suggested here that work is needed in all three areas of self-development in order to achieve emancipatory states, writers on self-development have instead put emphasis on specific areas of the three elements, sometimes neglecting the others or simply not providing such detail.

Elements of self-development

Self-awareness

Reflection that leads to awareness of the self and awareness of one's personally constructed view of the world are explored below.

Eraut uses the constructivist view of learning (see Chapter 9) to describe the manner in which an individual constructs meaning and interprets their experiences in the terms of that meaning. This forms an important basis for the understanding of both professional and personal development. Eraut (1994) suggests that our understanding of the world is unquestioned 'unless a special problem arises and even then we are unlikely to probe very deeply'. The opportunity for personal awareness often comes in the moments of 'special problems' if a person is then encouraged to review their understanding. Mezirow (1990) talks in a similar manner and suggests that most of the time we 'trade off perception and cognition for relief from the anxiety when the experience does not comfortably fit these meaning structures'. Most of the time we work to maintain the integrity and credibility of these cognitive structures of under-standing. To gain awareness requires special effort. While reflection in the context of an educational process may gradually lead to change of meaning schemes, Mezirow suggests that rapid change may be triggered by an 'eye-opening discussion, book, poem, or painting or by one's efforts to understand a different culture that challenges one's presuppositions'.

This description of personal knowledge in the early stages of professional education is particularly difficult because of the undeveloped nature of some personal knowledge that is brought to a professional education situation and the manner in which that can form the basis of, and thus perhaps distort, the development of further knowledge. Taylor (1997) suggests that 'It is this form of knowledge which is likely to distinguish those professional education courses which are preparing students for interpersonal work with students from other kinds of professional course such as engineering where personal knowledge may have less direct bearing on practice'.

In teacher education, for example, student teachers will have built up personal meanings in their own school and learning experiences that may influence their subsequent learning. Novice social workers may have particular conceptions of personal adequacy or poverty that can affect the manner in which they construe their professional learning. Like the knowledge of a professional about how they makes decisions in the context of their practice, this personal know-ledge tends not to be immediately accessible (James, 1997). Personal or guided reflection is the process by means of which these pre-existing schemes of experience or cognitive constructs can be recognized.

The literature on professional education clearly acknowledges the importance of these preconceptions of professional action as potentially shaping the novice professional's learning and development. The task of the educational process is not just to promote awareness of prior conceptions, but to develop the understanding to form an appropriate basis for further learning.

Apart from some group work, perhaps the most usual reflective structure for developing self-awareness in formal situations is journal writing. The use of reflective journals is discussed by means of examples in professional development in Chapter 15. Here, though, it is worth noting that there are many examples in the literature of the use of journals in initial nurse or teacher training, specifically to increase self-awareness. For example, while James (1993) describes the use of such a tool in order to explore nurses' pre-professional experiences, this tool also draws into the area of professional development those experiences that are not directly related to nursing but will nevertheless contribute to nursing (such as family responsibilities). Knowles (1993) describes the use of a related technique that employs the taking of life histories to reveal and explore relevant personal constructs in prospective teachers. He describes these as containing the content of 'internal dialogues about teaching and schools that pre-service teachers use' and, within these dialogues, the content of practical arguments that underpin decisions about how to act in a learning situation in a classroom.

A more specific example of self-awareness development via journal writing in initial teacher training is provided by Korthagen (1988). In the context of various reflective writing, pre-service mathematics students were asked to hand in reports on their approach to particular mathematical problems. 'In this way, not only the mathematical product is stressed, but also the mathematical enquiry process' – and the students' interaction with that enquiry. The use of reflection to explore how it feels to be a learner in the relevant discipline (or how it feels to be the patient of a nurse) does not seem to be commonly reported, yet it could provide some useful learning for novice and trained professionals.

The encouragement of self-awareness is much broader than simply being aware of prior experiences and conceptions. Candy, Harri-Augstein and Thomas (1985), and later Harri-Augstein and Thomas (1991), emphasize the role of a person in construing their meaning using their current awareness of self and situation as a starting point for further development:

> If people are aware of what they are presently doing and can be encouraged to reflect on it and to consider alternatives, they are in an excellent position to change and try out new ways of behaving . . . . If people's awareness of what is happening to them can be heightened, and if they can internally examine life events, then they can make more of each experience. This is equally true of entering a new job, relating to a new marriage partner . . . [or] making contributions to a postgraduate seminar.
>
> (Candy, et al., 1985)

Candy, et al., describe specific ways in which people are enabled to reach this state of self-awareness – for example, by means of 'reflective learning devices' such as the reading recorder. Harri-Augstein and Thomas (1991) use these general principles as a basis for learning in academic, industrial and business training. Also, they propose the notion of 'learning conversations' as the process by which a person reflects on the state of their current understanding or awareness of a particular issue and the process by which they will attain further knowledge and understanding.

Self-improvement – building on awareness

A student teacher sits in front of a journal entry, aware of how negative she felt about teachers when she was at school and of the conflict that creates in her in now as she wants to be a teacher herself. Another student is aware that there are certain situations in his teaching practice in school that bring with them feelings of anger. Awareness alone does not necessarily imply improvement of the situation or change, though it might lead to additional confidence and a sense of personhood and pride (Boud, Keogh and Walker, 1985).

Some structures for guidance of reflection clearly build in tasks that can support development beyond simple awareness. Progoff's intensive journal workshops and the subsequent use of the journal enabled unemployed people to find confidence and value their lives (Progoff, 1975). Progoff's intensive journal was developed over ten years while Progoff worked with groups. He suggests that the development of active methods:

> enable an individual to draw upon his inherent resources for becoming a whole person . . . . [The journal] systematically evokes and strengthens the inner capacities of persons . . . . It establishes a person's sense of his own being by enriching his inner life with new experiences of a creative and spiritual quality. Since these experiences happen to him and are recorded by him in his Intensive Journal while they are actually taking place each person accumulates a tangible and factual validation of his personal growth as it is in process.

In other words, the process of using the journal is designed to be more active than simply writing reflectively and it is intended that reflection and growth should occur simultaneously. More information is given about techniques used with the intensive journal in Chapter 15.

The development of the sense of personal worth that can emerge from work on self-awareness such as that described by Progoff is linked by several writers to the work of Belenky, Clinchy, Goldberger and Tarule (1986). Cooper (1991), for example, notes that those women in Belenky's work who were in the group characterized by 'silence' have little sense of personal power, and that the use of reflective diaries, supported the process of empowerment via the establishment of identity, can begin to enable response to the question 'Who am I?'

Progoff's work led to a relatively elaborately structured journal. Others who have wanted to ensure that professional education students move on from the state of self-awareness in their self-development have provided particular questions to prompt growth. For example, Morrison (1996; see Chapter 6, earlier) provides his students with questions to support development by means of reflection, such as 'What have you decided to do next in your course? Why have you taken this decision?' or 'How are your studies frustrating your personal needs and personal fulfilment?' or 'What criteria are you using to decide what to do next in your studies?' In the context of questions to support reflection on academic development, reflection is guided by the following types of questions: 'In what ways has your scholarship developed (qualitatively and quantitatively?' and 'Have you seen your studies becoming easier, more difficult, much the same, and why is this?' Chapter 6 also mentioned the questions used by Johns (1994) for a similar purpose of drawing the reflection on particular experiences into learning.

Writing also contributes to self-improvement by focusing on deficits. Themselves reflecting on ways in which journal writing appears to help their students to progress in their professional development as teachers, Calderhead and James

(1992) say that writing seems to help students to focus on specific difficulties and allows help to be offered by tutors. Journals, they say, ' foster a sense of ownership and responsibility for one's own professional practice, possibly leading students to make more purposeful decisions about their own development and to feel more enthusiastic and involved in the betterment of their own teaching'. They also suggest that writing about anxiety-provoking incidents that students may have otherwise ignored appear to enable the situations to be tackled more effectively.

Also reflecting on writing, reflection and self-development, Walker (1985) talks of writing enabling experience to be separated from personal interpretations of the experience so that more realistic growth from the experience can occur. He says:

> The creative interaction between the person and the person's self-development helps incorporate new realities into that self-development. It can prevent the situation arising where new knowledge lies on top of old knowledge without integration taking place. Creative interaction with one's own development helps to ensure that new knowledge is incorporated in, and integrated with, existing knowledge.

The descriptions above have largely focused on reflection in the context of personal writing, although many who promote such methods advocate some sharing of the content (Progoff, 1975; Walker, 1985; Morrison, 1996, for example). Others emphasize the qualities of working with others to facilitate the process of growth or change. It is interesting to note that the techniques that promote emancipation are more likely to work in groups than they are with individuals alone.

Taylor (1997) describes the use of group work in the education of social workers. The overt purpose of the groups is to enable social work students to use their pre-course knowledge and conceptions as a basis for personal growth into professionals. In such situations, it is difficult to distinguish between personal knowledge and the generation of professional knowledge and self-development. For different students and at different stages of the course, the balance will vary. The maintenance of these distinctions in order to prevent the group process of learning from becoming like group therapy can be aided by deliberate reference to existing propositional knowledge and to preconstructured learning objectives. Taylor suggests that working with groups of these students enables them to explore the socially constructed nature of meaning, contribute personal experiences to the learning of others and provides a mutually supportive environment to facilitate growth. For some students, growth via this process of mutually shared reflection is harder than for others.

Empowerment and emancipation – the potential for change

Emancipation is linked in the literature with the thinking and writing of Paulo Friere (1970) and the process of 'conscientization'. This was a process of group liberalization that was engendered in learning circles and 'popular education' in Latin America. It is related to the third level of human interests described by Habermas (1971). Mezirow (1990) uses the term 'perspective transformation' in a more general manner to describe how people can become 'critically aware of how and why [their] presuppositions have come to restrain the way [they] perceive, understand and feel about [their] world, of reformulating these assumptions to permit a more inclusive, discriminating and integrative perspective and of making decisions or otherwise acting upon these new understandings'.

In Mezirow's use of the term, perspective transformation can be applied to groups or individuals and it has been applied, in particular, to adult education. For Mezirow, the significant element in the process of self-development towards perspective transformation is criticality. It is by means of critical reflection that the presuppositions on which learning is based are challenged, but, in terms of 'the most significant learning in adulthood', critical self-reflection is involved in the reassessment of 'the way we have posed problems and . . . our own orientation to perceiving, knowing, believing, feeling and acting'. Sometimes, however, support to maintain and act within the context of the new perspective, once it is achieved, is more difficult than working towards the changed orientation.

There are several examples of perspective transformation in Mezirow's book (1990) — for example, consciousness-raising. Consciousness-raising in groups defines its end point in emancipation and implies the provision of group support for the stage of action. In the broad review of consciousness-raising by Hart (1990) in Mezirow's book, it is clearly indicated that development occurs via awareness and growth towards emancipation. Hart (1990) describes it as a process of understanding:

> Understanding is both a process of completion and of opening up the view on the terrain of unexplored interpretations of experience and of possibilities for action. The woman who remembers the scene and understands its arrangement participates in it once more but on a higher and more mature level . . . . At the very moment at which a woman understands . . . she looks at her entire life in a new way.

Hart describes this process of 'collective theorizing' as 'a joyful event as it offers fresh interpretations that unfreeze numerous possibilities for individual and collective action within a better-understood social reality'.

Consciousness-raising is, in essence, not a personal process. Emancipation is of the group and not primarily of the individual. The focus is maintained on the group growth, by ensuring that meaningfulness of individual experience is always related to the meaning of the common group. Thus, in a woman's group, a personally reported issue such as wife beating is seen in the context of oppression of women in general.

A different form of collaborative work towards emancipation is human collaborative enquiry, where a group reflects in order to raise consciousness about a particular issue. An example of the use of this work in a professional context is that given in Miller (1990). Miller describes the reflective processes undergone among a group of teachers who met over a three-year period. The objective of the teachers was to understand how to work in a liberating manner in a busy and difficult environment. To support the group meetings, they used dialogue journals (see also Chapter 16) and personal writing as a further means of supporting and extending the value of their activities. The title of the book – *Creating Spaces, Finding Voices* – seems to describe the outcomes of the work well.

The level of emancipation in self-development is not an obvious aspiration in most initial professional development. One view is that novice teachers might need to become acquainted with their full professional situations before they are in a position to be critical, though the development of an aware and critical stance is a useful orientation. Smyth (1989), working with novice teachers, appears to be using this principle. The material of personal narrative writing is analysed critically in a political context. This is done by asking, for example, 'What do my practices say about my assumptions and beliefs about teaching?', 'Whose interests seem to be served by my practices?' and 'What is it that acts to constrain my view of what is possible in teaching?' (quoted from Smyth, 1987).

Barnett (1997) does not see the novice status as making the initial development of this emancipatory stance premature, but sees the role of higher education as being to support the development of the state of critical being:

> what the modern world requires of higher education [is] to provide the basis of an emancipatory process in which students, by means of their own powers of self-reflection through their lifespan, come increasingly into themselves, maintaining their critical distance from the world around them while acting purposively in it . . . . Reflection, then, is on the agenda of higher education in expanded form.

Conclusion

While reflection as a term is not much used to describe processes of self-development, that reflection facilitates development and growth of a person is assumed. In this chapter, self-development has been organized on the basis of deficit – in counselling, therapy and self-development from a state of normality for the purposes of exploring the role of reflection. Reflection could be seen as a tool that facilitates personal learning towards the outcome of personal development – which ultimately leads towards empowerment and emancipation. Some self-development work is non-rational (Korthagen, 1993) and may bring about unexpected outcomes within the context of self-development.

Part II

Reflection and learning

Chapter 8

Taking stock of reflection

Introduction

Up to this point, a variety of different interpretations of the idea of reflection have been considered:

- the everyday use of the word;
- its use in the theoretical approaches of Dewey and Habermas;
- its use in experiential learning;
- the manner of its use by Schön;
- its application in the notion of 'the reflective practitioner';
- its involvement in professional activities, such as decision making and theory building;
- its application in counselling and self-development activities.

Apart from reflection in higher level learning itself, these cover most of the major areas of work and writing on the term in the literature as it stands. They yield a complicated and confusing mass of different interpretations of the term, though, as has already been suggested, perhaps the picture is simpler than it first might have seemed. This chapter takes stock, gathers some loose ends and considers where this discussion of reflection has taken us. What are the common denominators of reflection that should be taken into consideration as we move into a review of the role of reflection in higher level learning?

Taking stock

Reflection seems to be a useful concept. It is applied in many fields and as a concept it helps those in learning and professional situations to make sense of an area of human functioning. As the idea of reflection is commonly understood, it seems likely that it is a concept that is useful in everyday functioning as well.

While the activity of reflecting seems to be understood in common-sense terms, it is when the concept needs to be communicated in formal or academic terms that there are problems of definition. Earlier chapters have demonstrated that some major divisions in the interpretation of reflection exist between those who relate their work to Dewey or to Habermas, Schön or Kolb. It could be said that these theorists have different disciplinary origins, but the application of their thinking in papers on reflection does not follow the disciplinary division. The tendency of literature to draw from one or another of these writers to accord with the proposed line of an argument in any writing tends to maintain the division in the literature, even if some complementarity of the approaches is evident.

The existence of different accounts of reflection without a common definition at their root means that particular features associated with the term have been accentuated or diminished in the definition of the word in order to apply it to the topic in hand. The development of this situation may have been caused by the fact that most writing about reflection relates to a task – such as professional development or the process of learning from experience. For example, the idea of reflection on practice puts emphasis on the manner in which reflection facilitates a reviewing of past action in order to perform better the next time. In contrast, it is the critical purpose that is emphasized when the term is used in relation to social and personal awareness and emancipatory outcomes in consciousness-raising.

Instead of different emphases on the features associated with reflection, some definitions are narrow, in effect separating parts of the commonly understood activity of reflection by denoting particular purposes for it or conditions under which it takes place. Examples are Schön's reflection-in-action and reflection-on-action where reflection and action are conceptually linked (1983) and the concept of reflective judgement (King and Kitchener, 1994). Narrowing a definition of reflection makes research more manageable, but then confuses the situation if the narrowed definition is not set, at some stage, into the broader, more generally understood, notion of reflection. For example, it is not apparent from the literature whether Schön sees his pair of definitions of reflection-in-action and reflection-on-action as encompassing all of reflective activity or describing only one corner of it.

Despite the range of interpretations of reflection, properly, the concern of many writers has not been simply to struggle with definitions of the word, but to focus on what can be done with reflection – how best to use it in the presenting circumstances to improve the learning or practice or other required outcome. Other writers, such as King and Kitchener have been concerned with the research implications of the construct. In a pragmatic manner, writers on task-related aspects of reflection or constructs for research have followed academic practice by presenting a brief review of the literature, which includes examples selected to favour the case that they wish to make. This process tends to further diversify the understandings of reflection rather than bring ideas together.

Associated with this is another phenomenon that has strengthened the growth of the literature on reflection. Models such as those of Schön are founded largely on non-empirical work. There are relatively few empirical studies of reflection and these do not tend to be aimed at defining the word itself. Indeed, one of the problems associated with the research that has taken place is the difficulty in creating operational definitions for reflection and reflective practice. This may even have discouraged experimental work. Without theory being tested, there has tended to be what could be called a 'solidification' of ideas, by which is meant that, as a result of the absence of empirical studies, there is too great an acceptance of particular models in the literature. Examples are those of Schön and Kolb. Models such as these were originally presented in print once or twice with the due tentativeness because they are founded on speculation, but began to be interpreted in later papers as if they were facts (Usher, 1993). For example, while some of the earlier literature speculated on the accuracy of 'the reflective practitioner' or Schön's contention that there is a difference between reflection-in-action and reflection-on-action (Boud, Keogh and Walker, 1985), more recently writers have fitted their observations to these constructs as if they are empirically established (Atkins and Murphy, 1993; Morrison, 1996, for example). Care is needed to maintain the appropriate critical view.

In metaphorical terms, the growth of thought (knowledge and speculation) on reflection is bush-like. It started from a single shoot – reflection as a simple mental activity. Two or three more grew from that one shoot – Dewey and Habermas, and then Schön and Kolb – and more branches have grown in many directions from those. Once a branch has started growth in one direction of thinking about reflection, others have grown out from there, following the processes described above – sometimes with a mass of uncritical theorizing on the basis of speculative models.

There is nothing wrong with this bush-like growth if it can result in purposeful and useful applications of the process of reflection. The difficulty of interpretation does, however, create a problem for those who wish to investigate reflection in a more theoretical manner, or to apply it to a new area of activity. As this book attempts to do both of these, we are brought directly into confrontation with the confused state of the literature.

Before looking at the role of reflection in higher level learning, therefore, it is necessary to strip back the idea of reflection to its basis, both in everyday understanding and its applications. What is reflection, what is the common denominator behind the elaborated models of reflection in the literature? Chapter 1 suggested that reflection may be a simple mental process that is apparently complicated by the different frameworks of meaning that have been imposed on it in its different applications in practice and in the academic and professional literature.

Some loose ends

Taking stock also means reviewing what is missing. Throughout the previous chapters there have been numerous situations in which the word 'thinking' could have been used with the same understanding as reflection. There have also been several instances where reflection has been mentioned alongside emotion, affect or feelings. These loose ends now need to be attended to, even if resolution proves to be impossible.

Cognition and reflection

General research on cognition has been relatively sparse in psychology – research tends to have been applied to specific problems (Erdos, 1990; Eysenck and Keane, 1995). Alongside the vague definitions of reflection, the fact that reflection, as such, has not often been a topic for research and is generally not a recognized construct in psychology, makes it difficult to reach useful conclusions about the relationship between cognition and reflection. Sometimes it is a matter of noticing how the words have been used in the literature. In many cases, reflection as word is used in the context of discussion about thinking, but, as in the general definition arrived at in Chapter 2, it has connotations of purpose and application to complicated or uncertain situations (Dewey, 1933). Alternatively, it tends to be used to describe thinking that is meta-cognitive, relating to its own process – thinking about the process of thinking (Swartz, 1989) – or in discussions of critical thinking (for example, Brookfield, 1993) or all of these (Lipman, 1991).

There is often not much help available to disentangle cognition and reflection beyond that of noticing the connotations implied within any given text. Perhaps the only generalization that it is useful to make here is that reflection is narrower than cognition or thinking, though it is probably justifiable to say that reflection is a form of cognition or thinking. Where there is use of the word reflection in the psychology literature, it seems to be used in the same way that it is in the education and professional development literature.

Emotion and reflection

The psychology literature on the role of emotion or affect and cognitive processing is in its relative infancy. The links between the processes are acknowledged and are being explored, but any conclusions are largely related to specific examples at the present (Gilhooly, Keane, Logie and Erdos, 1990; Eysenck and Keane, 1995). The psychology literature thus helps little in determining the relationship between reflection and emotion.

Most of the accounts of reflection in the literature describe or account for reflection in cognitive terms, not mentioning affective functions and, in context, these descriptions might seem to make sense. There are exceptions (such as Boud, *et al.*, 1985; Mezirow, 1990; Korthagen, 1993), but as soon as personal experience of reflection is involved – such as the writing of journals (Walker, 1985; Holm and Stephenson, 1994) or the use of reflection in personal development or counselling – the inextricable link between emotion and reflection becomes obvious even when the subject matter is relatively intellectual (Boud, Cohen and Walker, 1993). Where, in the literature, emotion has been associated with reflection, the influence from the writing of Boud, Keogh and Walker (1985) is often obvious (as in Atkins and Murphy, 1993).

Yet, the nature of the role of emotion in reflection is rarely addressed directly. There seem to be three possibilities that are not mutually exclusive. Reflection could be a part of the process of reflection. Alternatively, it could be the content of reflective processes in the same way as cognitive material. The third possibility is that it has a role that impinges on the process of reflection.

If affect is part of the process of reflection, the suggestion is that it is actively contributing to the way in which a person is reflecting and to the outcome of that reflection. In this context, it is interesting to note Bruner's observation that, in search of a memory of something, it is often a feeling about the content of the memory that reaches consciousness in advance of the content itself (Bruner, 1990). This indicates at least that a close link exists between emotion and cognition. This is, perhaps, the most problematical of the three possibilities.

There seems to be little problem in recognizing that an emotional state can instigate reflection. The material of counselling is usually emotional, though the question might be whether it is the feeling that we reflect on or the cognitive understanding of the feeling – is it the actual feeling of sadness that is the subject matter of reflection or the knowledge that we are feeling sad? It would seem from this that an actual feeling can be the outcome of reflection. This is evidenced in the actual expression of tears or laughter and so on when we are reflecting. Mortimer (1998) describes both the development of understanding of personal emotions and the experience of catharsis for some of the students who kept journals during part of a degree course.

The third possibility is the one to which Boud, Keogh and Walker make main reference – that emotion influences or steers the process of reflection so that it is not under immediate voluntary control (see above). Mezirow describes this as 'psychic distortion' and talks about the sources of these influences in childhood experiences (Mezirow, 1990).

A conclusion to this discussion is an acknowledgement of the relevance of emotion to reflective processes, particularly in practical situations, but an acknowledgement, too, of uncertainty about the nature of that relationship.

Taking stock – the literature and the common sense

Chapter 1 suggested that, in common-sense terms, reflection seems to imply a process of thought that is performed for a purpose or at least has an outcome.

We reflect on possible solutions to a difficult situation, but may sometimes find that a solution just 'pops up' when we have not been consciously reflecting on it. The sudden solution may be akin to the 'eureka' experience, when an important idea emerges unexpectedly in what may seem to be an act of creativity. The reflection that occurs in undirected meditative states may seem to be anything but purposeful in terms of subject matter, but the fact that people find meditation useful suggests that it does have some form of rewarding outcome. Dewey's view that reflection occurs when a person experiences cognitive discomfort – a problem needing to be solved – appears somewhat narrow in view of this experience. Once again, what seems important in a general definition of reflection is that it is driven either by purpose or by the expectation of some form of desired outcome.

While there is value in the assumption that everyone reflects, descriptions of the application of reflection in experiential learning, professional work or self-development appears to confirm its value in its more formal role. The upsurge of interest in it is evidence that the concept 'makes sense' or 'feels good', both to those who engage in it and those who propel others towards engaging in it, for example as professional educators. The enthusiastic literature of experiential learning and reflective practice supports this assertion, too. A problem may be that some do not feel comfortable with reflective activity and the possibility of them learning to reflect could be difficult. There may also be some professionals who are not reflective and yet manage well.

That solutions to difficult problems or creative ideas can suddenly appear or that the habit of 'sleeping on a problem' is believed to work suggests that reflection might not need to be a process we are conscious of. In professional practice, for example, much of the material of reflection appears to be tacit. People act effectively without being able to verbalize the mental process that has led to their action and it seems likely, therefore that, in some situations, we are more conscious of the outcome of reflection than we are of the process itself. Many sources suggest that reflection seems to be applied in situations where the subject matter is not straightforward. Thus, they say, while a person might reflect on the possible solutions to a difficult situation, they would not reflect on the answer to a mental arithmetic sum nor on the route of a known journey or someone's address. This is in accord with the empirically based work of King and Kitchener (1994) on reflective judgement described in Chapter 2. The idea that reflection is a mental activity applied in situations where there is an unpredictable or uncertain response or with material that tends to be complicated is confirmed throughout the literature.

Some of the professional literature seems to imply that a person will only reflect when another tells them so to do. This would not fit the common-sense view of reflection. Sometimes people reflect because they are given a purpose for reflection, sometimes because they happen to decide to reflect on something for their own reasons. Reflection does not seem to necessitate external motivation, nor can external motivation coerce engagement in general reflective activity or on any particular topic.

While no one can force another to reflect, it is possible to create conditions in which another is induced to reflect. The privacy of reflective activity and the usual inability to detect reflection, makes it a difficult topic to research. Unless it is managed carefully, the privacy of reflection creates difficulty in its use in educational situations. Asking a student to reflect on an academic topic and giving them time in which to reflect might mean that they do indeed reflect, but perhaps on a topic that is of importance to them, such as sorting out a problem with a friend. There is no guarantee that they will reflect on the subject matter presented. If, however, the student is asked to reflect on the role of emotion in a Jane Austen novel and told that they will have to talk about it to the class, then they are more likely to reflect on that topic. In other words, in a situation where one person requires another to reflect as in educational settings, the process of reflection may be encouraged by the specification of the outcomes that the other expects. If the student is willing to be encouraged to reflect towards a given end, they may be willing to follow guidelines provided by the other. It is therefore the quality and nature of the guidance of reflection and outcomes that are required that are highly significant in the improvement of the use of reflection in learning and teaching situations.

As was noted above, a person cannot determine the course of reflection in another, but, equally, we may not be able to determine the course of our own reflection because our processes of reflection steer themselves round emotional barriers or avoid areas of blockage (Boud, Keogh and Walker, 1985). Boud and Walker describe the experience of trying to reflect on particular experiences in order to learn from them, and yet finding that their attempts to do so were frustrated (Boud and Walker, 1993).

An area of controversy in the literature occurs regarding the time frame in which reflection takes place. There is no difficulty in applying the term reflection to retrospection, but some writers have applied the term to thinking about events in the future – in effect, to anticipation and planning (Van Manen, 1991, for example). It has been suggested earlier that such planning and anticipation is a mixture of reflection on past experience, knowledge (the product of learning and reflection) and imagination of the event anticipated (see Chapter 2). Reflection could be said to be involved in anticipation and planning, but it needs to be combined with imagination to bring extend its application into the future. The word 'reflection' has the connotation of a link to the past – going back over ideas and experiences or gathering current ideas so that thinking or learning may be progressed.

In terms of a time frame, there have been many references earlier to reflection-in-action, which, according to Schön (1983), occurs at the same time as the event. Reflection-in-action – or the ability to respond to the unexpected in practice situations – is apparently a cornerstone of his work (1983) and of his proposition about the distinctiveness of professionals. On the basis of its occurrence, he argues for a special type of training. However, there is no empirical evidence that distinguishes between reflection-in and on-action and their separate existence and, in particular, the existence of a form of reflection that occurs within action.

In a sense, the cycle of experiential learning puts reflection into a type of time frame in allocating it to a role in learning and clearly relating to reflection-on-action. As Chapter 3 demonstrated, however, even using Kolb's cycle, it is possible to interpret the nature of reflection in different ways. It is these differences that are critical in any study of reflection itself, and its relationship to learning, though they are not important when the whole cycle is being considered. It can be difficult, for example, to determine where reflection stops and abstract conceptualization starts. It was also suggested that if the material of reflection is material that has already been learnt, then the activity of assimilating the initial raw experiences, as would happen in the first revolution of the cycle, would not be reflection. Once some learning is generated, reflection has material to work on. Again, these distinctions may not be detectable in the messy, real-world situations whereas they are important in theoretical treatments of subject matter.

The widespread uptake of the ideas of experiential learning suggest that they make 'good common sense'. However, a suggestion that emerges from the study of the interpretations of the cycle of experiential learning is that it may not describe learning so much as sequence of guidance activities that will facilitate learning. The cycle might better be seen as a teaching rather than a learning model. This was evident particularly in relation to the manner in which reflection is described. That it guides practical activity is perhaps the main reason for its popularity and so it might be better to openly acknowledge that it is more about teaching than learning.

There are many examples of attempts to pin reflection down to skills or specific activities in the chapters on reflective practice. The concept of the reflective practitioner seems truly to be a 'portmanteau' term, as Morrison (1996) wrote. The ideas included do not seem to deviate greatly from the general range of conceptions of reflection, perhaps with one addition. In some writing, there is reference to the notion of 'being reflective', which seems to describe a general orientation to work and possibly to life in general rather than specifying a range of skills or activities, but this, too, is encompassed within the common-sense view of reflection.

The idea of a common denominator holds. There is little in the literature, it seems, to indicate that reflection is other than a relatively simple mental activity, the many diverse descriptions of reflection being characterized by the frame-works of inputs and purposes within which they operate. To reiterate Chapter 1, reflection seems to be a form of mental processing with a purpose and/or an anticipated outcome that is applied to relatively complicated or unstructured ideas for which there is not an obvious solution. Essentially, it is an input–process–outcome model. As the output accords with a purpose, in accordance with a purpose, it can be redrawn as input–reflective process–outcome or purpose. The purpose will relate, in general terms, to the framework within which the reflection is applied, so, for example, it will relate to the purposes of experiential learning or reflective practice or the improvement of learning.

Bringing the ideas together – an input–outcome model of reflection

What is the input material of reflection – what do we reflect on? Dewey suggested that reflection occurs when there is a problem or an uncomfortable situation, which seems a somewhat narrow view. From the literature and from common-sense reasoning, the input to the reflective process seems to include knowledge or material that has been learnt. This can be factual or theoretical, verbal or non-verbal and emotional components generated in the past or present.

These categories of inputs are not intended to be mutually exclusive. The Kolb cycle would suggest that raw experience should be present in the list, but the definition of reflection here implies that it is on material already learnt. This topic will be returned to after the further consideration of reflection and learning.

From the review of the literature and common sense reasoning, the outcomes or purposes of reflection are mostly those included in the list of outputs or purposes implied by the term reflective practice in Chapters 3, 4 and 5. From the brief discussion of emotion and reflection earlier in this chapter, tentatively added is emotion. Emotion can certainly be a result of reflection – whether or not it is an outcome in the manner of the other elements in the list, though, is somewhat uncertain. It may be more of an accompanying effect of reflection. Thus, reflection is:

- learning and the material for further reflection;
- action or other representation of learning;
- reflection on the process of learning;
- critical review
- the building of theory;
- self-development;
- decisions or resolutions of uncertainty;
- empowerment and emancipation;
- other outcomes that are unexpected – images or ideas that might be solutions;
- emotion.

Included as a different form of reflection is the personal orientation implied by 'being reflective'. This might be considered to cover input and outcome or purpose. The outcomes are not considered to be mutually exclusive and the result of any period of reflection is likely to be a combination of the outcomes. It is notable that some of the outcomes appear to be sequentially arranged, for example, and, on the basis of Habermas' views, emancipation is a consequence of forms of self-development and critical review.

The inputs to reflection and the outcomes or purposes of reflection identified above are summarized in Table 8.1. The model in Table 8.1 is not a model of

Table 8.1 *An input–outcome model of reflection*

Inputs to reflection	Outcomes of/purposes for reflection
⇒　⇒　**reflection**　⇒　⇒	
Theories, constructed knowledge or feelings	learning/material for further reflection; action or other representation of learning; critical review; reflection on the process of learning; the building of theory; self-development; decisions/resolutions of uncertainty; empowerment and emancipation; other outcomes that are unexpected – eg images　　　or ideas that might be solutions; ??emotion

There is also the capacity to 'be reflective', which seems to be an orientation to the activities of life rather than a mental process as such.

learning or practice, but a description of what we seem to understand about the process of reflection.

Despite the complicated literature on reflection, the broad interpretations of it can be incorporated into a relatively simple mental function model. Inputs that could generally be described as 'what we know' are processed by means of reflection to create a series of outcomes that then represent the purposes for which we would reflect. Most literature incorporates the idea of outcomes or purposes into the interpretation of reflection itself, so it seems very complicated. As elsewhere in this book, it is maintained that reflection is a mental process in itself and that the purposes for it or the outcomes of it are additional details that do not themselves characterize the process.

Moving on – reflection and learning

The literature on reflection, as it has been presented in different areas of study or practical application, has been reviewed in previous chapters. In all these situations, it has been seen that reflection is intimately linked with the process of learning – learning from, learning that, learning to do, learning to be. With the addition of raw experience, the inputs for reflection are the same as those for learning, and the list of outcomes or purposes of reflection could also be drawn to coincide with a list of outcomes from the process of learning. An exception might be seen to be reflection when making a decision, but making a decision is ultimately the same as writing a report where knowledge is manipulated in reach of an appropriate decision. Even the notion of being reflective suggests an alertness in relating to new ideas, together with a willingness to apply the learning to the situation. On this basis, it seems reasonable to consider that reflection is a part of learning.

Reflection seems, therefore, to be intimately linked with the learning process, but, despite this, and with the exception of experiential learning, reflection is not a common topic in the literature of learning. Boundaries of expertise and disciplines may be responsible for this anomaly, as those who study learning are not those who have studied, or needed to study, reflection, and vice versa. Reflection has been studied more by those who have wanted to apply it to real-world issues.

The association of reflection with learning provides another avenue for the exploration of the nature of reflection by focusing on what is known about learning and considering where it fits into learning. This also takes us further towards one of the aims of this book, which is to consider how a better use of reflection can be used to improve learning.

The stage approaches to reflection described in Chapter 1 suggest that there is a relationship between age and the developing ability to reflect, and this means that reflection may have a greater role in more sophisticated learning or higher level learning. The reflective content of such learning is evidenced by the frequent reference to reflection in descriptors of learning in higher education (Moon, 1995, 1996b, for example). Higher level learning is the focus of the next few chapters because the association between reflection and this type of learning seems to be significant.

The enthusiasts for experiential learning might argue that the exploration of reflection in learning has already been done and that the Kolb cycle demonstrates how reflection fits into learning. As has been suggested, however, the Kolb cycle of experiential learning and the elaborations of this described in Chapter 3 are like teaching models, suggesting what guidance might be given to learners in their learning from experience. The experiential learning cycle only hints at the psychological processes that might underlie what is observed. In this way, the writings on experiential learning only hint at the role of reflection. They do not take into account some particularly important developments in the in the literature on higher level learning that are particularly helpful in the further exploration of reflection in learning – the constructs of deep and surface learning.

There are few studies on reflection in the actual learning process of higher education, but some deal with its broader contexts. It is discussed in relation to particular issues, such as the development of critical thinking (Meyers, 1986) or in relation to adult education (for example, Mezirow, 1990) or problem solving (Boud and Feletti, 1991) or, as we have seen already, the development criticality (Barnett, 1997) and professional higher education (Morrison, 1996). In many cases, reflective processes are implied in higher education without being explicit and, as the following chapters will demonstrate, reflection could be said to have a central role in the deepening of learning, yet there is relatively little explicit discussion of this relationship.

It is by means of an analysis of the processes of higher level learning that the activity of reflection will be explored. Thus, Part II makes a deviation from the direct concern with reflection to explore the nature of higher level learning in order to locate the role of reflection in it.

Chapter 9

Reflection in learning – some fundamentals of learning, part I

Introduction

The next three chapters build a map of elements of higher level learning in order to locate the process of reflection within in, ultimately as a means of attaining better understanding of reflection and its role in learning. The first two of these chapters discuss issues of learning that are related to the construction of the map – in a sense, building the elements of the map as they go. This chapter begins with a brief overview of the difficulties of studying learning before it goes into further detail about the development of the map of learning and the representation of learning.

Unlike previous chapters, there is no conclusion to this chapter as it is composed of separate elements that are continued in Chapter 10.

Problems in the study of learning

Learning is a complex of cognitive and affective activities and there are reasons that mean that the study of learning is a complicated matter. First, descriptions of learning encompass different mental activities depending on the context. For example, student learning may refer to the whole process of learning and assessment of that learning, learning solely as the acquisition of knowledge or, in experimental terms, the learning of a simple isolated task. A second problem is that sometimes there is confusion between the processes of teaching and learning. A reason for this confusion can be the lack of vocabulary of teaching and learning. There is not, for example, a word that describes what a teacher teaches, nor what a learner learns. This is probably what has given rise to the misused phrase 'I'll learn you to (for example) ride a bike'. Here, however, the corresponding phrases have been adopted – the material of teaching and the material of learning. There is also not a regularly used word for the expression of learning and so the phrase 'representation of learning' is adopted here.

A third problem is that of conceptualizing learning. This is because the processes of observing learning are normally those of representation of that learning, which take either written expression or oral form. Representation might not be considered to be a part of the process of learning, yet it is clear that, at times, the process of representing learning is actually part of learning (Eisner, 1982, 1991). For example, the writing of this book is a process of clarification of – or learning about – the concept of reflection for the writer. On a smaller scale, the writing of an essay is a means of exploration of an idea and journal writing (see Chapter 15) is quite deliberate learning about the self or the self in relation to a particular experience. Most of the research on learning is research on learning with the associated representation of that learning, and it is possible to be an effective learner but poor at representing that learning in the manner required.

Similarly, because of the privacy of mental processes, it is difficult to separate learning from thinking (Marton and Ramsden, 1988). There is an assumption that they are different processes because they feel different, but this may only be because we have developed different words for them. The same reasoning might apply to reflection in learning. Some writers see reflection as part of learning (experiential learning theorists, for example), but for others it is distinct. In the act of writing a journal or meditation, reflection is seen as the main activity with the learning being secondary. It was commented earlier in the book that there is difficulty in distinguishing between thinking and reflection.

Developing a map of learning and the representation of learning

The role of reflection in learning is explored here by building a map of learning and the representation of learning. The term 'map' is used rather than 'model' because the latter word implies a static, established image, which seems inappropriate at present. The map is simply a means of making sense of what might be some of the processes of higher level learning. The map is based on the literature on reflection and student learning, supplemented by observation and personal reflection. As it attempts to make sense of observed phenomena in this way, this could be called a 'folk psychology' approach to learning (Bruner, 1990).

Research on learning in cognitive psychology is well advanced, but it does little to provide a picture of learning that is coherent or systematically applicable in the classroom. As Harvey and Knight suggest (1996), teachers need to have an organized understanding of the learning that they are endeavouring to promote – an understanding that enables them to work with and evaluate their day-to-day observations of learning and notice where these may become distorted. Teachers need an understanding that helps them to facilitate learning. To elucidate the role of reflection in learning, the same systematic view of learning and representation of learning is required. It is useful, too, if it is a mentally portable view of learning that can be carried into the classroom and applied to teaching or learning and the improvement of the reflective processes involved in situations as they occur.

There are two major sources of research and reasoning that provide the principle underpinnings for the map of learning. One source is that on cognitive structure, which was based on Piaget's work on accommodation and assimilation. It was further developed in the 1960s and 1970s in the writings of Ausubel and others (Ausubel and Robinson, 1969, for example) on cognitive structure and the constructivist view of learning. The other source is the line of research and reasoning on student learning that emanated from the Gothenburg School in the late 1970s and early 1980s and continued in several places, in particular the University of Lancaster in the 1980s (Marton, Hounsell and Entwistle, 1984) and continues currently (see, for example, Ramsden, 1992; Marton, Hounsell and Entwistle, 1997). The research is based on considerations of what learners do when they learn, how they conceptualize learning and how they approach learning tasks. Other helpful literature that contributes to the understanding of learning is based on closely informed reflections and observations on the processes of learning that take account of research data where they exist (Harvey and Knight, 1996, for example). As learners, we are all experts on learning even if what we know cannot be immediately articulated in an organized manner.

One of the reasons some accounts or models of learning are not mentally portable is that the flow of information about the events of learning is inter-rupted with detailed descriptions of the ideas that support the model. This makes it difficult to obtain a picture of the whole process. For this reason, the supporting ideas for the map are developed before the presentation of the map itself in Chapter 11.

The supporting ideas are the:

- constructivist view of learning;
- notion of cognitive structure;
- materials of learning and the learner;
- stages of learning
- environment of learning;
- deep and surface approaches to learning and the representation of learning.

The supporting ideas are presented in a sequence that enables a progressive introduction of the material that underpins the map. It starts with the more general material (the constructivist view and cognitive structure), then moves on to consider the material of learning, the stages of learning and the way in which the approach to learning relates to the representation of learning. The environment of learning affects all the elements in the map. In order to make the map more comprehensible, relevant sections of it are presented as the information is built up in the material that follows.

The constructivist view of learning

The recent developments in student learning have been based a constructivist philosophy. Previous emphases in studies of teaching and learning had focused on the activity of the teacher, suggesting that the structure of teaching – or of instruction – is the key to learning. This view implies that knowledge is transmitted from the teacher to the learner. It stresses the content and organization of the curriculum as being the basis of learning and implies that knowledge is built from ideas that the learner gradually assembles. When the learner finds incorrect ideas, they replace them like bricks in a wall. On this empiricist model of teaching and learning, the learner's prior academic ability and knowledge is seen as a guide to the teacher's strategy (Prosser, 1987) and its role in new learning for the learner is as a foundation on which the new learning is built or sometimes the foundation may be replaced.

Under the influence of such thinkers as Kelly (1955) and Rogers (1961), there was movement towards a view of learners as the determinants of what is learnt. On this learner-centred constructivist view, the teacher's role is that of a facilitator of the learning, and the prior ability and knowledge of the learner determines the learner's approach to a learning task. This view conceives of a more active role for learners, particularly for those who choose to be engaged in meaningful learning (see below) where their intentions become more significant than those of the teacher.

On the constructivist view of learning, the learner constructs their own knowledge and the knowledge is conceived to be organized more as a network (cognitive structure – see later) than as a brick wall (Novak, 1985; Strike and Postner, 1985). What is already known is employed in guiding the new learning in organizing the process of assimilation (taking in the material of learning). In meaningful learning, where the learner intends to understand the material of learning instead of just memorizing it, the learner accommodates or adapts an area of the network in response to the new learning (Pines, Fensham and Garrard, 1985). Whether learning is meaningful or not can only be judged by the learner because meaningfulness is an expression of the relationship between the material of learning and the learner's existing understandings. Teachers may seek to influence the learning by, for example, careful construction of the material of teaching to make it likely that it will be understood by the learner, by interaction to check understanding or by choosing specific forms of assessment that, in turn, influence the learner's approach to the learning or their intentions (Ramsden, 1992).

In these terms, rote learning or learning by memorizing occurs when the learner does not, or cannot, relate the material of learning to prior knowledge and will not wish to recall in the context of other knowledge. It results in isolated 'bits' of knowledge and, for this reason, a more descriptive term might be 'unconnected learning'. This is contrasted with meaningful learning, which is when the learner intends to understand the material of learning. Nichol (1997) describes the distinction between meaningful and unconnected learning as:

> Learning through memorization and . . . reproduction does not result in knowledge that can be used to reason and to solve problems in new contexts. For this [reasoning/ problem solving] to happen, students must learn by interacting with and transforming received information so as to own it and make it personally meaningful. They do this by actively constructing or reconstructing information input – i.e., modifying, revising, transforming, connecting, extending it, relating it to what they already know – in an effort to make sense of it.

(Note that the term 'transform' here is not used in quite the same manner in this book   see the discussion of transformative learning later in this chapter.)

Marton and Ramsden (1988) distinguish the constructivist view by means of its implication of a qualitative change in the learner – 'rather than a quantitative change in the amount of knowledge someone possesses'. The qualitative change is in the understanding that the learner constructs. While learners construct personal understanding and knowledge, this can occur within a set of guidelines that might be the form of thought embodied by the discipline (Bruner, 1966). The implication of this is that the thinking of disciplines does not exist separately from learners (Biggs, 1993). Similarly, Eisner (1991) says, 'I . . . believe that humans do not simply have experience; they have a hand in its creation and the quality of their creation depends upon the ways they employ their minds'. On this view, the meaning that a learner constructs is an element that has been selected out of larger possibilities and, in this sense, education can be regarded as 'a mind-making experience' (Eisner, 1991) – or perhaps more accurately, a 'mind-making' opportunity. The notion that the mind is constructed by the learner and that the ability to employ the mind appropriately is significant in the outcome of learning begins to hint at some of the roles that reflection might play in the learning process.

Evidence that supports the constructivist view of learning comes from studies of the application of study skills to help students improve their ability to learn. Both from research (Ramsden, 1992) and from observation in the classroom, it is evident that teaching students a bank of study skills does not usually have a long-lasting effect on their ability to learn (Gibbs, 1981). While some gain a certain level of confidence from study skills courses and may learn a few techniques, they gain more from a learner-centred approach in which they are helped to explore their own learning abilities, confront their deficits and experiment with change in their own time and on the basis of their own understanding. This is more effectively done within the context of the discipline studied. In other words, other than a few techniques, the most effective study skills are constructed by the learner within the context of their own learning. Raising awareness of personal study skills enables appropriate modification and reconstruction in response to different learning demands, and students who study well do appear to be more aware of their study processes than those who are less effective (Gibbs, 1981). Harri-Augstein and Thomas (1991) use the term 'self-organized learner' to describe someone who is able to deploy their learning and study skills effectively.

The cognitive structure

The function of the cognitive structure

The concept of the cognitive structure is central to the constructivist view of learning. The term 'cognitive structure' was introduced above as meaning 'what is already known' by the learner. It has been described as an ill-defined concept (White, 1985), which implies a network of 'facts, concepts, propositions, theories and raw perceptual data that the learner has available to him at any point in time' (Ausubel and Robinson, 1969), and some would add emotions to the list (Mezirow, 1990, for example). Learning is defined as being meaningful because it is linked into the cognitive structure and, more than the development of a linkage, there is a process of mutual accommodation of the cognitive structure and the new material of learning. In other words, an idea may be modified in order to 'fit' pre-existing ideas or the cognitive structure modifies to fit the incoming information. Reference is made to this process in terms of personal development (see Chapter 7).

To clarify this, the older view, described above, was of learning as an accumulation of the material of learning. The difference between the older and current view of the cognitive structure is demonstrated in the notion of 'meaningfulness' (Ausubel and Robinson, 1969). If the cognitive structure is an accumulation of learning that provides a link for new learning but does not modify (accommodate), then the quality of meaningfulness is attributable to the material of learning – how well it relates to the existing knowledge in the cognitive structure. In these terms, if it is meaningful and if the learner has adequate prior knowledge, it can be learnt. If it is a nonsense symbol and, in their terms, meaningless, it can only be memorized.

Let us now pursue the case for 'meaningfulness' being a quality of the learner's learning process, rather than an inherent quality of the material of learning, by using Ausubel and Robinson's evidence because they subvert their case for the cognitive structure as being an accumulation of knowledge. They say, in their example, that 'lud' is a nonsense syllable that 'makes no sense'. In fact, 'lud' has connotations of comic depictions of judges ('my lud') to most British people and is, therefore, meaningful and has a place in the cognitive structure. Any set of letters can be nonsense and meaningless to one person, but meaningful to another as a name, an acronym, the initials of a company and so on. Its meaning-fulness will be determined by the guidance of the prior knowledge in the cognitive structure of the individual. It is suggested here, therefore, that the cognitive structure does more than simply accumulate the material of learning and accommodate in response – it is active in guiding the learning of new material (Pines, Fensham and Garrard, 1985).

This guidance function of the cognitive structure is very significant in meaningful learning. Mezirow's definition of meaningful learning (1990) stresses this function of the cognitive structure:

> Learning may be defined as the process of making a new or revised interpretation of the meaning of an experience, which guides subsequent understanding, appreciation and action. What we perceive and fail to perceive, and what we think and fail to think are powerfully influenced by habits of expectation that constitute our frame of reference, that is, a set of assumptions that structure the way we interpret our experiences.

Mezirow applies the term 'meaning perspective' to the organizing role of the cognitive structure. The active and informed guidance of new learning may be less important in for younger and less sophisticated learners (interestingly, it is to these kinds of learners that Ausbel and Robinson's work largely applies) than is the case for serious adult and higher education learning. Indeed, for this latter group, its role is vital in enabling learning that has qualities of meaning-fulness and understanding (see later).

Habits or styles of learning may either be influential or influenced by the 'guidance' activity of the cognitive structure. Mezirow considers that some learners are open and receptive to new learning, even if it is unfamiliar, while there are others who have a narrow orientation and tend to accept new learning only if it is directly in accord with their cognitive structure. Taking this to its logical conclusion, what we already know, in its guiding and organizing role, can act as a gate-keeper to learning or a means of selection. As Eisner (1982) says, humans do not passively receive images of the world, but, by means of selection and organization, they are active in making them. If learners are able to select how they inform themselves, they can ensure that they are not confronted by new ideas. Mezirow talks of people being trapped in their meaning perspective and unable to develop as people. He sees some of the mission of adult education as being to emancipate people from a self-imposed restrictive view of the world to one that is open to new ideas and the changes in their lives that these may imply. The possibility of a change in a person's life view is encompassed in the notion of transformation (see Chapter 11).

Related to the process of the learner selecting what they learn is the setting up of predictions or anticipations of learning. For example, in terms of the specific processes of learning, fluent reading appears to be like a process of predicting ahead of time the meaning of the text so that the visual activity becomes one of checking or confirming the form of the words from minimal

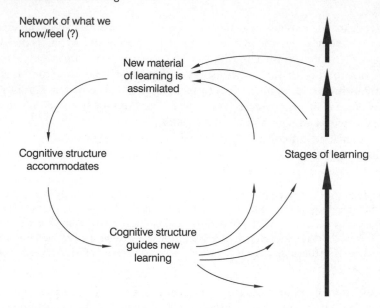

Network of what we
know/feel (?)

New material
of learning is
assimilated

Cognitive structure
accommodates

Stages of learning

Cognitive structure
guides new
learning

Figure 9.1 *The cognitive structure as it is depicted in the map of learning and the representation of learning shown in Figure 11.1 (see page 138)*

cues (Moon, 1975; Smith, 1988). Interpreting the anticipatory role of cognitive structure in broader terms, Eraut (1994) talks about the way in which ideas that have been learnt, in determining new learning, 'order the future as well as the past'.

The cognitive structure is depicted diagrammatically in Figure 9.1 as it is shown in the map of learning and the representation of learning in Figure 11.1. The diagram incorporates the ideas of assimilation and accommodation and the guidance function of the cognitive structure.

The cognitive structure and subject matter

The subject matter of learning also interacts with the cognitive structure and this interaction characterizes the nature of learning at any given time. We do not simply learn, we learn something. The new material of learning does or does relate to areas of the existing cognitive structure – it does or does not conflict with existing ideas. In this way, the process of learning at any time is contextualized. Marton and Ramsden (1988) say, 'The thesis we want to advocate is that learning and thinking skills are not separate entities that have a life of their own. They are ways of dealing with and reasoning about various aspects of subject matter and their character should be defined by the imperatives of that subject matter'.

The nature of the organization of the cognitive structure may also interrelate with the sequence of teaching the subject matter, both in small-scale terms and on a larger scale. In small-scale terms, the way in which a text is organized on a page was found by Ausubel (1962) to interact with the verbal ability of a learner. Ausubel gave learners an unfamiliar text and gave some of them an advance organizer – a short introductory passage to help them mentally organize the information in the text. Learners who had lower than average verbal ability appeared to be helped in their learning by the advance organizer, while students who were of average or above average verbal ability were able to learn without the organizer. He suggests that learners of higher verbal ability are capable of better organization of new material of learning around relevant, more inclusive concepts and so they do not need as much external organization of the meaning as do those with less ability in this area. This research suggests that 'higher verbal ability' may equate to greater ability in organizing incoming verbal information.

Regarding the larger scale of learning subject matter, it has been observed there is a tendency to learn specific details about a subject and generalize across the specifics (Marton and Ramsden, 1988). Throughout education, subjects are not learnt in terms of generalities to begin with. Children in primary school learn details about topics, learning the rules that enable a generalization of knowledge during subsequent education. As they progress, they are increasingly required to make generalizations themselves by reflecting on how multiple details can be developed into an integrated understanding.

The pattern of learning specific details and developing them towards generalizations accords with the notion of a cognitive structure that initially comprises networks of assimilated specifics about a topic that, with more input and inducement to generalize, accommodates to a more generalized network within which the specifics are located. 'Inducement' here might include teaching and explanation, but probably also maturity and developing skills in learning and representation. The progress might also be aided by personality traits, such as interest, curiosity and open-mindedness.

In the context of professional continuing development, Eraut (1994) suggests that, over someone's life history, there may be a pattern of periods of assimilation of detailed information and periods of accommodation and reorganization of the cognitive structure towards new outlooks. On the basis of the difficulty of 'teaching an old dog new tricks', older people may tend more towards assimilation of information into unchanging cognitive structures.

These organizing processes could be said to call on the cognitive housekeeping activities of reflection, ordering and reordering the patterns to make a sense of the cognitive structure that accords with incoming information and a sense of the incoming information that accords with the cognitive structure. In the map of learning and the representation of learning, the cognitive structure is therefore central to the operation of learning and thence reflection.

The materials of learning and the learner

The issue here is whether or not different forms of the materials of learning involve different learning processes. An apparent difference in learning that is emphasized in some of the experiential learning literature is that between learning from experience and formal (classroom) learning. However, the discussion in Chapter 3 demonstrated that there is often no explanation of what is meant by 'experience'.

For many, particularly those who use Kolb's experiential learning cycle, experience implies a physical event in which the learner has been involved and much learning is of this nature, even in formal education settings. Most higher education includes some form of experiential learning, but some of the examples below illustrate how difficult it is to distinguish what may be learning from experience from what is learning from the language and the concepts used in the classroom:

- the English student attends the theatre;
- the English student reads the play for herself;
- the English student acts in the play;

- the biology student examines a drawing of the structure of a leaf;
- the biology student examines a series of slides of the same leaf;
- the biology student pulls the leaf off a tree and looks at it;

- the theology student examines an ancient text;
- the theology student examines a new edition of the ancient text;
- the theology student listens to a teacher talk about and quote from an ancient text.

These learning situations illustrate how difficult it might be to distinguish between learning from experience and learning in the formal education setting. The last example of the theology student listening to a teacher does, however, bring out a possible distinction – that between mediated and direct learning.

'Mediated learning' is a term employed by Laurillard (1993) to describe the situation in which a student learns about something from or via a teacher and does not experience the matter of the learning directly. Thus, the student is taught about the geology of a volcano and does not see it, feel it or hear it. Laurillard says that much formal learning is mediated by others in order that one of the purposes of such education can be fulfilled – namely, that more can 'be learned than that which is already available from experiencing the world'. She argues that mediated learning, which might be called second-order learning, is different from learning from experience because it is developed by means of 'artificial structuring', using such processes as argument, exposition, interpretation and reflection. In other words, as information, it has already been processed and restructured in terms of the discipline.

In contrast to mediated learning, Laurillard suggests that we must learn such 'everyday' activities as table manners by means of mechanisms designed for learning from the natural environment. She says that 'knowledge derived from experiencing the world at one remove must logically be accessed differently from that known through a first order experience' because of the different ways in which the knowledge has been acquired.

Much of the continuing argument below follows from the earlier consideration of 'experience' as an ill-defined term. Laurillard's argument that knowledge learned via a textbook is accessed differently from that learned from experience is very significant when it comes to the development of a model of learning that will have explanatory power in both 'real world' situations and in educational environments – and a model that will demonstrate the role of reflection in either.

Laurillard is saying that what goes on in the 'natural environment' of learning table manners is fundamentally different from that which occurs in the classroom where the student reads or listens to a lecture on an abstract topic. Is it really different, though or is it a matter of the degree of difference? Clearly some of the learning of table manners will occur as a result of the experience of reinforcement and punishment, but some learning is likely to be from verbal instruction or feedback. On direct comparison, a verbal explanation of table etiquette from a thoughtful parent is unlikely to be as complicated as the explanation to the student of an abstract concept of physics, but, in terms that take the relative powers of comprehension into account, both explanations could be equally taxing. A geology student will link the learning about volcanoes to a cognitive structure that accords with the disciplinary subject matter, but there are likely to be linkages to some real-life experience, such as of rock and mountains, heat, light, fire and so on. A child will link the table manners learning to their cognitive structure areas of family rules, what happens at the table or other experiences of punishment, according to their own experiences. On this basis, it seems hard to maintain the argument that mediated and non-mediated learning represent completely different forms of learning. Even on the basis of later access to the knowledge, we cannot predict how any individual will have experienced learning and reconstructed it in their cognitive structure, and how this will influence later representation.

Laurillard justifies the differentiation of the types of learning again when she refers to representation. She says that 'symbolic representation is the means by which the academic knowledge is accessed' and asserts that 'It makes little sense to access one's knowledge of the [real] world through words and symbols, but it makes sense to assess one's knowledge of descriptions of the world in this manner'. Because we tend to represent knowledge in particular ways does not mean that we can never act differently and does not necessarily mean that we learn differently. It is certainly possible to describe knowledge of the world in words and symbols, just as new forms of assessment are requiring students to represent their second order learning in different actions or competences. In saying this, the difficulties of describing practice (recall Chapter 4) are noted.

Laurillard's arguments about characteristic forms of representation can be regarded from a different angle. As mentioned earlier, Eisner (1982) argues that we learn from the process of representing our learning. Under circumstances unconstrained by the formalities of education, we choose how we represent our learning according to our skills and the requirements and purposes of the situation. We then gain further meaning – or learn from the act of representing the learning and that meaning becomes part of the material of further learning. An Ordinance Survey map, for example, might clarify meaning in a different way from a set of written instructions about a route.

Eisner goes on to argue that the constraint on the forms of representation of learning (that is, assessment) set by many educationists can be interpreted as an influence that unnecessarily shapes learning. Extrapolating from this argument, it would seem that learning that is subject to assessment becomes characterized by the nature of that assessment. Eisner is suggesting that the type of learning that is derived from processes of representation (such as essays or project work) is itself shaped by the form of representation used. This is an influence in addition to the more usual observation that the learner's expectations of the form of the assessment modify the manner in which they go about learning – that assessment drives the learning that precedes it (Ramsden, 1992).

Laurillard's analysis of learning and teaching in her book (1993) lays a foundation against which the contributions to learning of a wide range of media can be analysed. The notion that information that reaches the student via a teacher is a description of the world and that this is different from the direct experience of the world is important. Laurillard is suggesting that the teacher's interpretation of the material of learning will influence the nature of the material of learning that reaches the learner. Clearly, it will have considerable influence, but, as has been indicated above, the learner's cognitive structure will also have an influence. The guiding role of the cognitive structure might determine how much attention the learner gives to new learning and how they perceive it (Eisner, 1991). In other words, there are many influences on, and modifications that occur to, the material of learning as it is learned. Whether it is or is not in mediated form seems to be only one of a range of other factors that modify the material of learning in the process of its transmission in the learning process.

Thus, what has been argued here so far is that Laurillard's assertion that there is a significant difference in the learning process between second order learning and learning from experience is not well supported by the evidence that she provides or by the constructivist view of learning in which the learner is an active learning agent. The material of learning derived from raw experience may be different in nature from mediated or second order learning and direct learning, but many learning situations will involve both forms of learning and there is probably no useful distinction to be made when it is the learning process that is being considered.

Ausubel and Robinson (1969) support the view that there is no clear distinction between mediated and non-mediated learning. Respectively, they use the terms 'reception' and 'discovery' learning as equivalents for mediated and non-mediated learning. They also suggest that these are a 'dimension' of learning in the sense that they are opposites on a continuum. Ausubel and Robinson consider that most learning is a mixture of degrees of discovery learning and reception learning and therefore they do not distinguish qualitatively between mediated and non-mediated learning.

While the material of teaching may be an important source of influence on the learning process, the cognitive structure of the learner is important in its influence on the learning that is achieved. It might be reasonable to assume that differences between mediated and non-mediated types of the material of learning are dissipated by the interactions of the cognitive structure with the new knowledge and the outcome of the learning is further knowledge, albeit with different qualities. For example, an industrial site that has been visited will have generated many more associated ideas – networked connections – with sounds, smells, stray observations and so on that are more firmly linked into the cognitive structure as a result than would be the case if it were merely described. The learning from a description of the site might be linked into the cognitive structure in different ways, according to the emphases of the description, and there would be fewer links and connections related to sounds, smells, stray observations and more to other theoretical ideas. Presentation of a video might come somewhere in between. Again there do not seem to be useful 'real world' distinctions to be made between mediated and non-mediated learning or classroom and experiential learning. The role of the cognitive structure of the individual learner in this relationship with the material of learning seems to be a variable to which few accounts pay sufficient attention.

Here the focus has been on the material of learning. The suggestion that the learning process is different according to the form the material of learning takes has been questioned. In fact, most learning situations are likely to involve a range of different materials of learning. The work experience situation – a typical experiential learning site for students – includes activities that the student will observe, but also people speaking about what is happening. In their cognitive structure, the student may have theoretical knowledge that they will apply in order to facilitate further learning from their experiences while they are on site. The student's learning task is to integrate these inputs and form a coherent, valid and appropriately critical picture of the events. Their cognitive structure may contain a theoretical framework to which the new learning will be related or else the theory may follow, to be associated with and later restructure what was learned from the event. The fact that some of the material of learning is more 'real world' – direct experience of events, 'non-mediated' – and some is 'descriptions of the world' and therefore 'mediated' is not taken to be a useful distinction.

The stages of learning – an introduction

Here, the stages of learning to be used in the map of learning and the representation of learning are briefly introduced. While the stages are properly discussed in Chapter 11, for the sake of clarity, they are named here. Five stages are identified and they are arranged hierarchically – that is, to have reached the stage of making meaning from learning, means that the person will already have passed through the stage of making sense of it. The stages of learning are:

- noticing;
- making sense;
- making meaning;
- working with meaning;
- transformative learning.

The sources that have informed the identification of these stages are the general literature on learning (such as that on perception), the theory of the cognitive structure, the literature on deep and surface approaches to learning (see below) and on student learning, and (for the stage of transformative learning) the theory of human interests (Habermas, 1971) and perspective transformation (Mezirow. 1990). The names of the stages have been assigned according to convention (for example, transformative learning) or according to the processing that, it is hypothesized, occurs at that stage. Despite the fact that the word 'processes' appears more apt than 'stages', the former word does not suggest the potential for progression from one stage to another that the latter does and this is also important.

The concept of different stages in the progression from simpler forms of learning to more complicated ones and that the stages might depend on a progressive sequence is supported by a series of experiments on 'wait time' reported in Tobin (1987). 'Wait time' is the 'duration of pauses separating utterances during verbal interaction' – for example, pauses in speech or silence after a question has been asked. Tobin reviews a number of studies and concludes that, within limits, lengthening wait time during teaching facilitates learning at a higher cognitive level (that is, deeper learning or that which has been processed at several stages) than would otherwise occur as this allows learners more time to think about or process the material of learning.

The environment of learning

It is relevant to introduce discussion on the environment of learning at this point because there are general ideas and particular concepts (limiting factors) that need to be introduced and others reinforced (such as the interpretation of environment on the constructivist view of learning). These will inform the discussion of approaches to learning and the representation of learning.

Biggs (1993) suggests that a useful basis for the analysis of learning environments is a systems approach. The more immediate factors in the environment are seen by Biggs as the 'micro-systems', contrasting with factors of an institutional and societal nature that Biggs terms macro-systems, such as those identified by Oates and Watson (1996) as factors at an institutional level that can directly determine teaching and learning effectiveness. Some of the factors affecting modern learning environments are learner numbers, a decreased unit of funding, organizational culture, fear of change or the sense of tradition in an institution and so on. Macro-systems often impinge on the learner via micro-systems. Examples of micro-systems are the student and their study, the teacher and the teaching. De Corte (1996) describes a 'powerful learning environment' as being exemplified in those 'situations and contexts that can elicit and keep going in higher education students the appropriate acquisition processes and activities for maintaining the intended disposition toward productive learning , thinking and problem solving'.

This discussion of learning environments and the manner in which they affect learners will focus on two important issues that underpin the current view of learning and the representation of learning. These are the importance of the perception of the learner and the interactive behaviour of variables in any environment.

Looking first at the importance of the perception of the learner, the constructivist view of learning suggests that the learner constructs their own meaning by using their uniquely developed cognitive structure to guide their noticing and perception of the material of learning. The learner actively constructs their view of the world and, correspondingly, reacts to the environment as they perceive it to be. While it is possible to make reasonable predictions about the manner in which a person will learn under a particular set of conditions, in the end this is guesswork. The literature on student learning is demonstrating that ideas held by teachers about the nature of learning, perceptions of what is expected at university or, more specifically, what an essay is, are not necessarily the same as those held by students (Marton and Saljö, 1997; Beaty, Gibbs and Morgan, 1997). A student's conception of learning may determine the approach they take, which may or may not be appropriate to the course requirements. That the student's view of their environment may differ from that of the institution or of their teacher is a fundamental issue in research on approaches to learning (see below).

Another fundamental issue in the consideration of the environments of learning is the ways in which factors interact in the environment. Biggs' use of the terms micro- and macro-systems were described above. The notion of 'system' emphasizes the interactive nature of the factors in the learning environment and encourages it to be viewed in a holistic manner, much as would any ecological system in the natural environment. It also enables the application of the concept of equilibrium, where an ecosystem acts to maintain a state of balance. Using Biggs' example, the attempt to change the quality of teaching in a department is not best achieved by providing intensive training for a few of the lecturing staff, but, rather, by working with all the staff (Biggs, 1993). In a similar way, as discussed in Chapter 6, Wildman and Niles found that administrators need to be involved in the process of enabling teachers to become more reflective.

If the teaching/learning environment can be equated with the functioning of an ecosystem, concepts that underlie the functioning of an ecosystem can be applied here, too. The concept to be introduced and applied in the development of the map of learning and the representation of learning is that of limiting factors. I have (1975) applied the principle of limiting factors (Odum, 1968) to the interaction of factors that influence the adoption of reading strategies. The definition of limiting factors includes the idea that they have a particular manner in which they interact in an environment. Originally the idea of a limiting factor arose in the ecological context of nutrients, and there it was a substance that affected the survival of plants in an ecosystem. The idea was expanded to apply to any environmental condition. The presence and success of organisms depends on a number of different conditions in the environment. A limiting factor is a condition that approaches or succeeds the limits of tolerance of the organisms because it is the factor that is limiting their existence at that time.

In terms of the learning environment, the concept of a limiting factor has very general application. For example, the ability of a good student to represent their learning effectively in an examination might be limited by constant symptoms of hay fever (the limiting factor) on the day of the examination. Alternatively, a limiting factor may, influence the student's ability to learn a particular topic. For example, despite normal ability, a student may have emotional blocks concerning reflection on a particular area of learning. This is a limiting factor to the normal learning.

In terms of learning, then, a definition of a limiting factor might read:

> the success of learning depends on a complex of conditions, so any condition that approaches or succeeds a particular tolerance so as to limit the quality of learning is the limiting factor in that situation.

The definition of a limiting factor in ecology has been expanded to include the notion of 'factor interaction'. The implication of this is that the effect of a variable that is acting as a limiting factor can be mollified by the effect of another. Thus, in the second example above, a conversation with a tutor that generates extreme interest in the subject matter could mollify the effect of a student's emotional resistance to studying it. In terms of strategies for reading from texts (see next chapter), I have found that the ability to learn from reading a text is improved by the use of particular reading strategies (patterns of movement through the text, back and forth and at different speeds) only if the general verbal ability is below a particular level. Above that level of verbal ability, a reader could learn from a text regardless of the strategy used (Moon, 1975).

As a result of these different forms of influence on learning, it can be said that a learning environment shapes learning. On this basis, it is possible to design a learning environment to encourage a desired form of learning (Eizenberg,

1988; Entwistle, 1992; Biggs 1993). Here is a summary of the issues and factors that may be important to learners in a learning environment.

- A learning environment is a complex of factors that affect learning in an individual or a group. The factors may act directly on the learner or, on a constructivist view, may be mediated by their perception. In that sense, we can guess at some influential elements in the environment but not others without working with the learner and their perceptions.
- In a learning environment, factors interact in a variety of ways. The ecological notion of 'limiting factors' is a useful concept with much relevance to the interaction of factors so as to facilitate or discourage good-quality learning.
- A learning environment shapes learning and it is possible to design it so as to favour a particular type of learning.

Chapter 10

Reflection in learning – some fundamentals of learning, part 2

Introduction

The previous chapter began to review the information that underpins the development of the map of learning and the representation of learning. The topics covered there were the constructivist view of learning, the notion of cognitive structure and the materials of learning and the learner. The stages of learning were introduced and the environment of learning was considered.

This chapter continues to review underpinning ideas in the same way. It concerns the approaches to learning. Probably a more helpful construct than any other in the realm of student learning has been the identification of deep and surface approaches to learning. Sometimes a third approach – that of the strategic learner – is added. As a field of interest, it has been, as Biggs (1993) has said, 'a broth stirred by many' over the last 17 years, but it remains the background of much study of student or higher level learning, even though it is not sufficiently known by teachers or learners themselves.

This chapter describes the background and characteristics of deep and surface approaches to learning and how they relate to some of the concepts introduced in the previous chapter. The identification of deep and surface approaches to learning has strong implications for the development of the map of learning, but also accords comfortably with the observations of teachers in classrooms and learners about their own learning patterns. While the first half of this chapter is a theoretical consideration of approaches to learning, the second half views approaches to learning in the context of the 'real world' of higher level learning.

Deep and surface approaches to learning and the representation of learning

Background

The idea that approaches to learning might influence the outcome of learning had its principal origins among researchers in Gothenburg, Sweden. There, instead of the more usual work on learning – monitoring of the effects of changed conditions on learning – students were asked how they conceived of various learning tasks that they were set in experimental situations (Marton and Saljö, 1984). Initially, the tasks consisted of the reading of texts. These 'phenomenographical' studies showed that students either approached a task in order to elicit the meaning that the writer intended to covey, typifying a deep approach to learning, or so as to learn for simple recall purposes the elements in the texts without the sense that they needed to understand the whole text. This latter pattern typifies a surface approach to learning. It relates also to the discussions of the constructivist approach to learning in which the importance of the student's perception of the task is recognized.

Entwistle (1988) describes these approaches in the context of the reading of an article by a group of students. The intention of students adopting a surface approach 'was to memorize those parts of the article that they considered important in view of the types of questions they anticipated afterwards. Their focus of attention was thus limited to the specific facts or pieces of disconnected information which was rote learned'. Students who took a deep approach to learning '. . . started with the intention of understanding the meaning of the article, questioned the author's arguments, and related them both to previous knowledge and to personal experience, and tried to determine the extent to which the author's conclusions seemed to be justified by the evidence presented'.

The students' focus of concern for the 'whole' or for elements of the whole was the subject of earlier work by Pask (1976), who distinguished learning strategies or styles as 'holist' and 'serialist'. Later, Svensson (1984) used the concepts of 'holist' and 'atomistic' strategies. The greater efficiency of approaching a task as whole and relating the specific elements of which it is composed to a generalized conception of the whole accords with the manner in which the cognitive structure appears to operate once some understanding has been established. Ausubel's advocacy of advance organizers (see Chapter 9) to provide a helpful initial structure for ideas also fits this conception when the material of learning is new or when there is no prior understanding of the learning.

More work on approaches to learning was carried out at Lancaster University and in Australia (Biggs, 1993). For convenience and to enable its wider application, some of this later work relied on inventories of approaches to study instead of learner self-reports of approach to learning (Entwistle, 1988, for example). The inventories were shown to be a reliable means of discerning how students approach different types of study. In the Lancaster studies, a third approach to learning was defined – the strategic approach. Learners who adopt a strategic approach to learning are concerned to achieve the highest grades possible, and their approach to learning is tailored to this aim (see below). In the Lancaster studies, too, there was a focus on learner 'intention' as well as the approach adopted. Learner intention has a sharper sense of purpose.

Below are reproduced the descriptions of deep, surface and strategic approaches to learning (Entwistle, 1996), which are based on more research and deliberation than earlier descriptions.

Deep approach
Intention – to understand ideas for yourself by:

- relating ideas to previous knowledge and experience;
- looking for patterns and underlying principles;
- checking evidence and relating it to conclusions;
- examining logic and argument cautiously and critically;
- becoming actively interested in course content.

Surface approach
Intention – to cope with course requirements – by:

- studying without reflecting on either purpose or strategy;
- treating the course as unrelated bits of knowledge;
- memorizing facts and procedures routinely;
- finding difficulty in making sense of new ideas presented;
- feeling undue pressure and worry about work.

Strategic approach
Intention – to achieve the highest grades possible – by:

- putting consistent effort into studying;
- finding the right conditions and materials for studying;
- managing time and effort effectively;
- being alert to assessment requirements and criteria;
- gearing work to the perceived preferences of lecturers.

The identification of the strategic approach to learning as a distinct category seems to be somewhat disputed. For one thing, the strategic approach is only evident when the learning is to be assessed (Entwistle, 1997). An alternative view is that strategic learners are skilled at deploying deep and surface approaches in accordance with an accurate understanding of what is required to obtain high marks in assessed work (Ramsden, 1992). They are not only motivated by deep interest and wishes to be effective, but also the need to be efficient regarding their workload. They will do this particularly by taking note of assessment requirements. From the description above, the most effective approach to academic learning is that where the learner takes a deep approach, does not identify with statements that describe surface learning, but is aware of strategies for obtaining high marks.

The deep approach to learning demonstrates the learner's intention to assimilate the new material and, in so doing, allow the current knowledge and understanding to be modified so as to accommodate to the new. This accords with the operation of the cognitive structure as an adaptable network of what is already known, which in turn can guide and organize the assimilation of further ideas. The term 'transformative learning' has been used to describe this openness to changed understanding, and is the most advanced stage named on the map of learning.

The deep approach is of particular significance to a study of the role of reflection in learning. In its use of words and phrases such as 'relating ideas', 'looking for patterns', 'checking' and 'examining cautiously and critically', it implies the involvement of reflective activity in the process of learning. It is noticeable, too, that one of the defining characteristics of surface learning is that it does not involve reflection.

In terms of surface learning, there might be some accommodation of the cognitive structure, but there is no general aim on the learner's part to understand in a manner that might change their view of this area of learning as a result of the new knowledge. There is a sense of the learning being disconnected. Harvey and Knight (1996) describe it metaphorically as being 'lodged in a separate file, hardly linked with related sets of concepts and meanings'.

The approach to learning and its outcome in representation

The approach to learning would not matter if it did not have implications for the retention and representation of that learning. The idea that the material of learning is 'lodged in separate files' implies that the way in which learning is represented (for example, in an essay or examination) might be influenced by the manner of its learning. The manner of learning in the map of learning is represented by the stage of learning reached.

There is a problem in measuring competence in representation of learning in a sufficiently broad manner to yield generalizable results and, yet, in a sufficiently sensitive manner as to determine the effect of deep and surfaces approaches for the representation of learning. The 'SOLO taxonomy' (Biggs and Collis, 1982; Biggs, 1988) is one means of making a measurement. 'SOLO' stands for 'structure of learning outcomes' and, while the taxonomy initially appears to be simplistic, it has been applied widely in education and underpins the classification of at least one higher education degree. It is easiest to consider it initially in relation to written or oral accounts, though it could have application in the solving of problems and other forms of representation. Its focus is on the level of abstraction of the contents of the representation of learning and the degree to which ideas are sensibly and coherently related.

The SOLO taxonomy consists of five levels that describe the structures of the represented learning. They are:

- pre-structural – there is no appropriate structure to the task;
- unistructural – only one general element is represented;
- multistructural – more than one general element is present in the representation, but they are poorly integrated in a serial or unrelated manner;
- relational – here there are relevant elements present and they are integrated in a coherent and interdependent manner; development of any appropriate new structure is competent but not generalized to new situations;
- extended abstract – the coherent structure is developed into an effective and coherent new structure in a competent manner, from which there are generalizations to new situations.

A criticism of the SOLO taxonomy is that, while its wide applicability is valuable, it does not take sufficient account of differences in representation caused by the actual content of the material. The structure of a response may be determined, for example, by the nature of the task set, such as an examination question, rather than the competence of the learner (Dahlgren, 1997).

The SOLO taxonomy was used in research to determine whether or not the approach to learning bears a relationship to the quality of the representation of that learning (Van Rossum and Schenk, 1984). Van Rossum and Schenk worked with first-year psychology students who were required to read a substantial piece of text and then respond to questions on it. They were also asked to describe their approach to the learning in relation to the kinds of questions that they anticipated being given. The responses to the questions on the text were allocated by trained judges to the levels on the SOLO taxonomy. There was a strong correlation between the outcomes of the learning in terms of SOLO levels and both the manner in which the students had viewed the task of learning and the way in which they reported actually tackling the task. Learners who had adopted a surface approach to learning could not represent their work at more than a multistructural level on the SOLO taxonomy. In other words, it seems that once the material of learning is 'lodged in separate files' as surface learning, the best possible manner in which it could be represented will be as disparate and relatively unrelated ideas (multistructural). Van Rossum and Schenk demonstrated that, if there was a deep learning approach, the representation could be in the relational or extended abstract form, although other factors could interfere with the outcome. In other words, other factors could act as limiting factors to the learning.

The Van Rossum and Schenk research is particularly valuable in the manner in which it links the phenomenographical method of researching approaches to learning to the outcomes-based typology (SOLO) of Biggs and Collis and a quantitative measure of learning. The approach of the students to their learning enables some predictions to be made about the quality of the outcome – the representation of the learning – in effectiveness of style and, to a lesser extent, the learning performance. As evidence of the learning process, the observer only has the learner's account of their approach and the representation of the learning. While it is only the form of the representation of learning that is available to the observer, the degree of abstraction and organization of the material that is presented by the learner is a guide to the form of the mental processes that give rise to it (Biggs, 1988).

Another study of the representation of higher level learning is that of Hounsell (1997) who focused on essay writing. He looked at the conceptions of the task of writing an essay and the approaches that students took. The most sophisticated approach was described as argument, where the essay is a manner of constructing meaning, involving study as 'an object of reflection'. It is an approach in which the ideas are worked towards the presentation of a coherent whole. Less sophisticated is the approach to essay writing in which it is the presentation of a viewpoint – an 'ordered presentation of a distinctive viewpoint on a problem or an issue'. This differs from the essay as argument, particularly in the poorer handling of data. The third approach is as arrangement. Here, an ordered presentation of 'facts and ideas' is given rather than work towards a coherent whole. The importance of the arrangement of the meaning in an essay relates to the basis of the SOLO taxonomy (see above).

In consideration of the representation of learning on the map of learning and the representation of learning, the concept of 'best possible representation' (BPR) is used to suggest the kind of representation that can occur in ideal learning conditions. The descriptions of the best possible representation are simply an indication of the qualities of learning that might be predicted to result from the qualities of processing. The structure and the wording is suggested by the SOLO taxonomy and Hounsell's work on essay writing, the implications of the work on deep and surface learning, and on the quality of learning that might be represented by the different stages of learning.

Following Van Rossum and Schenk, it is suggested that, under ideal conditions, the best possible representation is directly related to the stage of learning (and, thereby, the approach to learning) that ultimately determines, but also limits, the real quality of the representation of learning. So, a learner who has taken a surface approach and reached the stage of 'making sense' will be limited to a relatively low quality of representation of learning as their 'best possible representation'. In reality, however, the BPR may not occur. A learner may have effectively adopted a deep approach to learning, but is required to represent their learning as an essay and leaves it to the last moment, writing in an anxious state. While this learner's best possible representation could be at least well structured, they are likely to produce an essay in which the ideas are present but not well structured. In this situation, they under-perform in terms of their potential and do not reach their BPR.

Table 10.1 lists the five descriptions of best possible representations of learning that are used in the map that is depicted in Figure 11.1.

To summarize, this part of the map of learning and the representation of learning is suggesting that the quality of the representation of learning is limited by the approach to learning (deep or surface), which is expressed via the stage of learning that has been reached. In other words, a fundamental idea in the map of learning and the representation of learning is that, other environmental

Table 10.1 *Descriptions of the representation of learning used in the map of learning and the representation of learning shown in Figure 11.1 (see page 138)*

Stage	⇒⇒⇒	Best possible representation (BPR) of learning
		Meaningful, reflective, restructured by learner, idiosyncratic or creative
Stage	*(deep*	Meaningful, reflective, well structured
of	*surface)*	Meaningful, well integrated, ideas linked
learning	*approach*	Reproduction of ideas, ideas not well linked; memorized representation

factors being favourable, the approach to learning adopted by a learner is likely to act as a limiting factor to the representation of their learning so that the learner who has only processed the learning of a topic to the 'making sense' stage will not be able to produce a coherent account of how the topic relates to other areas of knowledge. The processing has simply been too limited and, in terms of Table 10.1, the BPR will be reproduced ideas that are not linked effectively. If, however, the representation is in the form of a set task and the demands of the task are well within the capacity of the learner's learning, the representation will not be limited in its quality and so the limitations of their processing will not be tested.

On the other hand, for a learner who has adopted a deep approach to learning a topic, the BPR will be less limited by the approach and if the representation is in the form of a task, they will probably have the capacity to demonstrate their learning effectively when given an easy task or a more difficult task. They could be said to have more room for manoeuvre. However, this may be where strategic approaches come in. It is possible that some who habitually take a deep approach to learning do not have the flexibility in response style or the examination/assessment skills to adapt their meaningful understanding to styles of question that require more superficial responses.

The approach to learning in the context of higher level learning

Ramsden (1992) summarizes the role of deep and surface approaches to learning: 'There is little room for doubt that they describe a primary difference in how our students learn'.

Attainment and the approach to learning

So far here the outcome to the approaches to learning has been dealt with in somewhat theoretical terms. In 'real world' terms, a number of studies indicate that the students who tend to use deep approaches to learning as their predominant pattern are those who tend achieve first or upper second degrees (Ramsden, 1992). It is not surprising that a student who tends to use a surface approach cannot attain the level of cognitive functioning that should be demanded by a good degree when their processing of the material of learning is limited.

While there is evidence that those with deep approaches to learning are more likely to produce qualitatively high-quality learning outcomes (Marton and Saljö, 1984; Prosser and Miller, 1989) than surface learners, it has also been found that they recall the content of their learning more effectively after a period of time than those with shallow approaches. In terms of the cognitive structure, the assumption is that deep approaches to learning involve greater accommodation of the cognitive structure to the new material of learning, and, in effect, it is therefore 'filed' more efficiently with relevant and associated ideas. It is not 'mislaid' as a relatively unclassified item.

Despite their better ability to recall, deep learners are not as consistent at reaching good grades as the surface learners are at failing to reach the good grades (Ramsden, 1992). As was suggested above, learners who achieve the highest grades in formal courses tend to be those who have strategic skills of study and the motivation to get good grades as well as taking a deep approach to learning. Some who take a deep approach to learning can become too interested in the ideas and not the representation of the ideas in the format required for assessment (Svensson, 1997). Also, not all kinds of assessment test deep learning – some test the breadth of superficial knowledge.

Consistency of approach

This treats learners as if they are consistent in their approach to learning. Ramsden (1992) introduces his chapter on approaches to learning with six quotations from students. He asks the reader to discern whether the students are talking of deep or surface learning and how many students are represented. There are, in fact, only three students, each describing two of their own approaches – one surface and one deep – in response to different tasks. Ramsden concludes, 'We can see that one cannot be a deep or surface learner; one can only learn the content in a deep or surface way'. A few pages later, however, he provides a less dogmatic, but very significant, comment that learners do have tendencies to approach different tasks in one way or the other, all be it with variation on occasions. This seems to accord with the general observations of teachers and learners themselves and some consistency of approach appears to be the assumption on which the validity and reliability of the questionnaires on study habits are based.

The approach to learning and discipline

As has been said earlier, learning cannot be dissociated from its content. There are some differences in the interpretation of the approach to learning in different disciplines and the demands of their assessment tasks (Ramsden, 1992). Ramsden (1988) provides examples of the interpretations of deep and surface learning in different disciplines and, in general terms, the teachers of the discipline will be able to describe the typical deep and surface learner in their own terminologies and forms of knowledge. This was evidenced in the development of the level descriptors and the degree to which teachers from different disciplines were able to agree common terminology (Moon, 1996b).

Influences on the approach to learning – maturity

It is unclear in the literature whether or not all learners at higher education levels are able to choose which way to approach learning, but there are certain factors that will influence the approach. Some of the literature that contributes to the understanding of reflection suggests that maturation may be relevant to the approach to learning that is adopted. The work on stages of reflective judgement (King and Kitchener, 1994) and that of others who have looked at the stages of 'coming to know' (for instance, Belenky, *et al.*, 1986; Perry, 1970) suggests that there is a process of maturation and development in the viewing of knowledge. It implies that relatively few reach the full ability to manage unstructured knowledge, integrate ideas and transform their understandings into a new view of the world. These qualities, which seem to characterize the full and mature development of deep learning, may not be fully developed in many who have not yet reached their twenties (King and Kitchener, 1994). The youngest students in higher education might just reach their twenties while doing an undergraduate degree and, on the basis of this, relatively few may have reached their full capacity for deep learning as undergraduates. The stages identified by Perry were seen as reaching a lower level than those of King and Kitchener, but some of the functioning implied may be more characteristic of those at postgraduate levels or who have reached sophistication in professional situations.

It is interesting to note that the level descriptors for higher education learning mentioned earlier (Moon, 1996a) intimate the expectation that all students at the end of an undergraduate degree will reach the understandings that are suggested in descriptions of deep learning. For example, regarding the cognitive descriptor for synthesis/creativity (level 3):

> The learner with minimum guidance can transform abstract data and concepts towards a given purpose and can design novel solutions.

It would seem doubtful that the learning of all students at level 3 can be described in this way, and, indeed, it is doubtful that all level 3 students are consistently deep learners – strategic learning appears to be playing a stronger role in higher education (Moon, 1997; Kneale, 1997).

Influences on the approach to learning – the teaching environment

The influence of a teacher in encouraging a learner to engage in material is a matter of how the learner perceives the teacher and their teaching as well as more objective qualities of the teaching, such as organization of the material, clarity and enthusiasm. Good teaching can facilitate a deep approach but will still not guarantee it. Poor teaching can discourage a deep approach – Paul Ramsden actually uses the term 'surface teaching' (Ramsden, 1992). Equally, poor teaching may create the incentive for the learner to find out about the material of learning for themselves learn at greater depth as a result. In this case, the learner needs access to information on what they are expected to learn, such as learning outcomes that relate to any tasks of assessment.

Trigwell and Prosser's studies of nursing students (1991) illustrate some of the factors in teaching ('the academic environment') that encourage deep learning approaches and good-quality outcomes of that learning. Features that were found to facilitate good-quality (deep) learning are:

> '[where] the lecturer gives adequate and helpful feedback, makes clear the objectives, the assessment criteria and generally what is expected of students, demonstrates the relevance of the course and attempts to make it interesting, creates opportunities for questions and time for consultations, is good at explaining things, makes an effort to understand students' difficulties and gives students the opportunity to decide what and how they learn.

These findings result from two studies – one of first-year students and one of third-year students. The ways in which a teacher could best promote deep approaches to learning might be expected to differ between the first and third years of a course according to the qualities of learning required at the different levels. For example, while clear explanations might be helpful to first-year students, they may discourage third-year students from seeking the information for themselves and deepening their learning as a result of being required to work at understanding. Again, this is an example of factor interaction (see Chapter 9).

Trigwell and Prosser make a further observation that also indicates that simplistic descriptions of 'good' learning environments may be misleading because of factor interaction. They observe that in an environment in which assessment is perceived to encourage a surface approach to learning, the opportunity to ask questions and the provision of clear assessment criteria can enhance the use of a surface approach rather than deepen learning. In other words, the nature of teaching can interact with students' expectations of assessment tasks to produce a resultant influence on the learning that could differ from what might be predicted.

Working with adult learners, Usher (1985) interprets the role of teacher as one of manager of the learning situation for students. Managing learning in order to facilitate a deep approach is a matter of managing the relationship of the learner to the subject matter (Marton and Ramsden, 1988). While the use of personal experience to make learning meaningful and thereby deep is a tenet of adult education, Usher observes problems in this approach, and some of the problems could apply to undergraduate learning, too. He found that those in the group he was working with were unable to use personal experience as a means of deepening their learning in other than a superficial and isolated surface approach. The students seemed unable to make the appropriate sense of their experiences and they had learned not to value their experiences in comparison with what they perceived to be scientific or academic knowledge. Usher found that the 'worst cases' were essays (in psychology) that were 'depersonalized, abstract and "out there" rather than "in here" [and were] representative of surface learning. In essence, real knowledge is seen by these students as reproductive, with the task of the learner to gain access to and acquire from the body of knowledge, with knowing as "right or wrong"' (Usher, 1985).

Usher illustrates his point by describing tutorial sessions on such topics as 'motivation', where the personal experiences of students might reasonably play a part. The students come to the session having done some required preparatory reading. They discuss the texts, but never at the depth or level of criticism of the texts and quickly they assume that there are few links between the theoretical stance and their own experiences or that making these links is inappropriate. The result is that the new learning does not relate to their cognitive structures and is isolated from personal understandings. It remains unconnected.

Usher suggests that compromise between the two approaches is required. Both the scientific, 'objectified' learning and a meaningful personal framework within which the learning can be located are required. Students need to appreciate that experience and theories are simply different ways of looking at something and that neither is right or wrong. Usher suggests that it is possible to incorporate both forms of knowing by starting with personal experience and using that to create a personal link to the academic material. There is a need for the students to start from a meaningful point in their understanding of the topic and develop their knowledge from there. The 'meaningful point in their understanding' might be seen as their current state of cognitive structure brought to awareness by means of reflective review. The new material of learning effects a secondary accommodation and deeper learning.

Influences on the approach to learning – the assessment environment

At the end of the discussion on the environment of learning, it was suggested that an environment could be designed to encourage a particular form of learning. The most influential element in that environment is likely to be the assessment regime. As has been said earlier, learning tends to be driven by assessment.

Students may adapt their approach to learning to the assessment task, but it is the student's perception of that task that influences their approach, not the reality of it. The learner can misconstrue the demands of the assessment task and it is important that students understand the kind of learning that they need undertake for success. Initially, this will be a matter of guesswork. Something that compounds this first point is that there are many stereotypes of assessment tasks, both among staff and students. Multiple choice tasks can more easily assess unconnected knowledge that has not been learned at depth, but they can be designed to assess learning at depth. Similarly, there is a tendency to consider that examinations only assess the disconnected knowledge of a surface learner. This need not be the case, and the period of revision that precedes an examination can be a valuable opportunity to integrate ('deepen') what has been surface learning.

Influences on the approach to learning – changing the learning environment

Eizenberg (1988) describes the way in which a whole anatomy department focused on attaining deeper and better-quality learning by means of a process of action research. This study involved shifts in the teaching, curriculum and institution in order to reach the goals set. The system moved from teaching an atomistic and sequential pattern of learning to a pattern that is organized holistically and hierarchically. The factors that appeared to be important in deepening the learning of students were the clarity of the curriculum goals to teachers and learners, appropriateness of the match between the curriculum, teaching and assessment, the identification of 'essential learning' and the use of thought-provoking textbooks. In the teaching, there was encouragement towards thought rather than memorization and an active engagement of students in the work of their course. The design of assessment tasks required understanding in the learners and the quality of their understanding was central in the marking criteria. Students were given good feedback.

Eizenberg's report describes how the whole orientation of the department to its students and their conceptions of their field of study were taken into account and, where necessary, measures were taken to modify the environment, always with the aim of deepening the approach that the students took to learning. For example, there was consideration of the perception that students might have of the subject of anatomy and the work with bodies, in relation to their preconceptions and the knowledge and forms of understanding that they were required to adopt.

The learner's conception of the learning task

Throughout the literature on student learning is the suggestion that learners' assumptions about learning tasks or their programmes of learning do not necessarily match those of their teachers. The point is made in relation to tasks (Marton and Saljö, 1997), in Hounsell's work on essay writing (Hounsell, 1997) and to whole programmes of learning (Beaty, Gibbs and Morgan, 1997). The same point has been made above in relation to student assessment tasks. If learners' conceptions of learning or the nature of the work they are required to do differ from the conceptions of the teachers, then apparently poor learning can be the result. For many learners, learning is conceived as a broad range of superficial knowing, not the higher education conception of knowledge as deep and applicable understanding.

Learners' interest, satisfaction, emotion and the approach to learning

Being interested in a topic seems likely to encourage a deep approach to learning. In the literature, interest in the material of learning is dealt with somewhat peripherally. The question might be posed as to whether or not a student who is interested in a topic will do other than learn at depth (Marton and Saljö, 1997) – unless, perhaps they are under pressure from an assessment regime. If interest is an element in the encouraging of deep learning, then it is appropriate to investigate what might inspire interest. One source is contact with other interested people. It might be significant that students constantly rank highly those staff who display enthusiasm for their subjects, and from this it follows that the degradation of the tutorial system in an era of mass education may influence student learning by reducing direct contact with the staff who might have inspired them. It has been suggested that the main losers might be the middle ability students who can 'take off' with a some personal inspiration, but will otherwise regard higher education as simply a stage towards the world of work (Moon, 1998).

Interest in a topic is related to the satisfaction gained from study of the topic. Interest is an incentive to learn at depth, and the satisfaction gained will be a positive reinforcer for more learning behaviour of that type. A corresponding relationship seems to exist between lack of interest and disengagement, resulting in a surface approach, which reduces interest.

Entwistle and Entwistle (1997) interviewed students who had completed their revision for finals. The quotations from the students indicate the role of satisfaction in their learning. Those students who took a deep approach to learning say that 'the experience of understanding generally had a feeling tone associated with it – there was necessarily an emotional response'. The insepara- bility of cognitive and emotional components of understanding was very clear in the comments made by the students. The Entwistles continue, 'understanding was experienced as a feeling of satisfaction, although that feeling varied in its expression from the sudden "aha", as confusion on a particular topic was replaced by insight, to a less dramatic feeling associated either with being able to follow a lecture or with an emerging appreciation of the nature of the discipline itself'.

The students who reached this deep understanding are described as having a sense of 'things clicking into place or locking into a pattern'. The Entwistles go on to suggest that they appeared to be gaining a state in which they acknowledged a 'provisional wholeness' in their learning – a notion that the current state of understanding was sufficient, but that they could envisage the possibility that it could develop further. This comment on learning seems to support the descriptions in this book about the cognitive structure and the manner in which it might operate. It hints at a description of learning that functions in two ways. First, it assimilates the new information and modifies the cognitive structure to accommodate it. Second, there might be a reflective process in which more accommodation might occur. This pattern is reflected in the hierarchy of the stages of learning used in the map of learning and representation of learning. The description of these students suggests that they were at least at the stage of working with meaning, but could see that more processing was possible (transformative learning).

The Entwistles report further how the sense of 'coherence and connectedness' described by the group of students enabled them to feel confident about explaining the content of what they had learned and applying it elsewhere. It might be reasonable to suggest that tasks that require 'explanation' are tasks that make demands on the students' capacity for deep learning because, in order to explain adequately, there is a need for initial understanding.

Another group of students in the Entwistles' study did not feel sufficiently confident to explain the content of their learning and described experiences of panic and anxiety. Such emotional reactions probably perpetuate a vicious circle. Students who fear situations in which work is assessed and may also fear failure tend to adopt a surface approach to their learning (Usher, 1985). In addition, students who perceive their workload to be excessive (for them) also tend to adopt surface learning approaches (Trigwell and Prosser, 1991). A cycle of anxiety generates a surface approach to learning, which, in turn, generates the sense of dissatisfaction in learning and it is hard to see how students can change such patterns. They might rely on assessment tasks that suit their surface learning. Counselling or good tutorial support, which enables a reorientation of learning approach, would be an alternative (Main, 1985). Another form of relief to the anxious and non-surviving surface learner might be the end of the module. A modular system can sometimes allow struggling surface learners to just survive, while an integrated system might allow them to fail and correspondingly allow the problems to be recognized and tackled.

The close relationship between the cognitive and emotional elements in understanding is an important observation in the Entwistles' work that has, and will again, be related to the processes of reflection.

Student ability and the approach to learning

In the discussions about the determinants of the learning approach in the literature, there is emphasis on the learner's perception of the task. An earlier study of reading for learning from textual materials suggests that quite different mechanisms may also be playing a part in determining either the approach to learning or the quality of the representation of learning. The research employed a 'reading recorder' (Harri-Augstein and Thomas, 1991) that maps a learner's track through a text against time. Thus a reader might read the text once quickly and then once more slowly or haltingly, with pauses for reflection, or may return through the text, matching ideas at various points in the text (Moon, 1975, 1976). I have demonstrated that these differences in patterns of reading are evident in a group of older school children. I showed that those who read the text in an uneven manner, who did not necessarily read smoothly from beginning to end, usually performed better on tests of their understanding of it than those who read it straight through once or twice in the same time total length of time. As well as their test on the subject matter of the text, the readers underwent a verbal reasoning test. The results of this test showed that while those who scored well on the verbal reasoning test normally used the uneven strategy, some of them could learn efficiently by using the smooth reads straight through the text. Those who performed less well on the verbal reasoning test could only learn effectively if they used the uneven strategies.

While this work with the reading recorder preceded most of the work on deep and surface learning, it is likely to have been testing similar constructs of the approach to learning. The use of the reading recorder graphically demonstrates the sequencing of the intake of information from the text that the learner chooses to adopt in order to learn. In my own work, the learners knew that they were to be tested. For most of them, the most successful strategies consisted of a quick read through the text and then an uneven, back-and-forth reading. This method presumably demonstrates that they are actively working through the structure of the text to pick out the main features in order to relate them to a view of the whole. However, some of those who scored highly on the verbal test appeared to be able to learn adequately from the text regardless of the pattern of their reading. A hypothesis formed on the basis of this might be that the learners' superior ability to organize the text or verbal meaning within their cognitive structure might have alleviated their need to physically move through the text in particular ways. However, it is also possible that the superior ability to learn from the text caused the student to adopt a particular strategy. One reason for a reading the text in a manner that resulted in deeper learning is that it interested them.

From my own work, described above (Moon, 1975, 1976), it appears that two more variables may need to be added to the list of factors that influence the approach to learning. These are the ability in verbal reasoning and the strategy (or, perhaps, habits) adopted for reading a text, but these factors appear to interact.

Deep and surface approaches to learning, and the map of learning

Any model or map of learning must account for the construct of deep and surface learning. The construct meshes with the ideas that have been proposed about the structure and function of the cognitive structure. The learning of the deep learner is actively integrated into the cognitive structure and, as a consequence, the cognitive structure accommodates to the new learning, possibly changing as a result of the learning. While the learning of the surface learner is guided and selected by the action of the cognitive structure, the learner does not actively relate it to knowledge already in the mind. The evidence for the existence of the strategic learner – who chooses their approach to learning according to perceived demands of the learning in relation to their ability – suggests that there is the possibility of movement between deep and surface approaches to learning, even though learners tend to develop patterns of behaviour in one or other direction.

It seems implausible that the approach to learning is a matter of one thing or another – either deep or surface processing. Entwistle (1997) suggests that much learning in education is intermediate between memorization and meaningful interaction with the material of learning in a deep approach, and this suggests that a continuum on the basis of orientation to meaning could be envisaged. Most learners' experiences, particularly of revision, suggest that we can range widely on the continuum on even one piece of work as enthusiasm drifts towards tiredness or boredom with different consequences for the quality of learning. This would mean that there is not really a distinct jump from surface to deeper learning, nor distinct shifts between the stages. For clarity and ease of depiction, however, the map of learning and the representation of learning is drawn with lines and, therefore, there is an apparent distinction between the stages and between deep and surface approaches to learning. Broadly speaking, on the map the stages of 'noticing' and 'making sense' relate to surface approaches to learning. 'Making meaning' relates to elements of surface and deep learning, and 'working with meaning' and 'transformative learning' relate to deep learning.

The representation of surface learning, without further processing, draws on the isolated 'files' – at the time of learning, links have not been made with other ideas and areas of knowing. The representation of surface learning is of bits of information that may be recalled, but do not demonstrate a coherent form, nor substantially relate to previous knowledge. Deep learning, on the other hand, can be represented in a coherent form because the ideas themselves are meaningfully related and the material is meaningfully related to a network of relevant ideas in the cognitive structure. As Marton and Saljö (1997) point out, however, the nature of the task set can determine the nature of the response rather than the quality of the learning. In such a situation, the task demand is the limiting factor rather than the quality of learning.

Up to this point, the description of the map of learning and the representation of learning has been based on the assumption that a learner taking a surface approach will be limited to representing that learning in a manner that reflects the nature of their learning. In other words, they will not demonstrate integration or deep structure – but this may not be the case. There have been several hints in the text above that it might be possible to 'upgrade' the quality of surface learning at a later time. This is a hypothesis that feels right from observation of learning and one that has important implications for the structure of teaching and learning. The mechanisms by which this process might occur are discussed at the end of the next chapter.

Chapter 11

Reflection in learning – mapping learning

Introduction

The previous two chapters have developed a range of ideas and constructs that underlie the process of learning as it is described on the map of learning and the representation of learning. In this chapter, the map is laid out – initially in the form of an overview and then in more detail. While the process of reflection is not mentioned yet, the purpose of the map is ultimately to demonstrate the role that reflection might have in learning.

A map of learning and the representation of learning

The map is speculative. It is based on theory, empirical work and observation, the work on deep and surface learning and the relationship between the two and the outcomes of that learning. It is also based on the ideas of the cognitive structure and its function in learning, and the processes of assimilation and accommodation. The map is presented as an attempt to make sense of a broad range of ideas that must logically relate to each other in some manner or other. It is a 'best fit' model and stands to promote thinking about the processes of learning and reflection on learning. It is also there to be questioned and modified in the trust that such reflection on the model will facilitate progress towards greater understanding of a complicated area of human functioning – an area of which educators and learners need to make better sense.

The idea of a map of learning and the representation of learning has been used to imply the progress through events in the processing of learning that may have one or another consequence for the outcome of learning. There is meant to be a notion of fluidity, suggesting that the learner chooses, or the learning environment determines, a route through the learning process with the major junctions distinguished, for current convenience, by the stages of learning that are identified below. The stages represent different levels of complexity of processing and suggest, thereby, that relatively unprocessed material of learning is limited, at best, to a corresponding form of representation. There is always a possibility of failure occurring because of the technical demands of the representation task. There has already been some suggestion that there might be ways in which learning that is initially is processed in a relatively low-level manner might be upgraded and carry on to be represented in a more sophisticated manner (see later in this chapter).

An overview of the map of learning and the representation of learning

The map of learning and the representation of learning is depicted in Figure 11.1.

The intention of this overview is to show how the map of learning might work as a whole. The map consists of two main parts – the stages of learning and the representation of learning. The learning is mediated by the cognitive structure. The quality of the representation of the learning is indicated as a number of descriptions of the best possible representation (BPR) that can be achieved at each of these stages. The BPRs are, in reality, a continuum from integrated, well-informed and well-structured outcomes to outcomes that are a simple representation of the original learning with no apparent mediation of understanding. An assumption is that, at any one session in which learning and the representation of that learning both occur – such as reading a script and subsequently answering a question on it – the stage of learning reached will act as a limiting factor for the quality of the representation of that learning. In other words, if students have learned from a lecture to the stage of 'making sense', they will not be able, without further processing, to represent that learning any better than by simply reproducing the material. The ideas will not be integrated in any new way. Because the first two stages of learning in the model involve assimilation of the new material of learning, it is assumed that they can only occur in the presence of the material of learning. The other stages can occur at a later time, when the learner reprocesses their knowledge.

The cognitive structure, as previously defined, is what is already known by the learner and a guidance/organization mechanism for the new material of learning. It guides the assimilation of new learning and at the stage of 'making meaning', the cognitive structure and new material of learning are assumed to undergo the mutual process of accommodation. The subsequent two stages represent, in effect, the further accommodation the cognitive structure undergoes. At the least, emotion is involved as an influence on the guidance of assimilation.

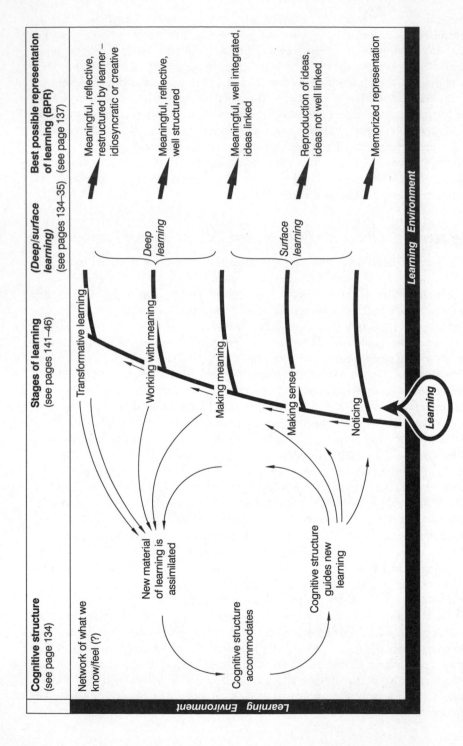

Figure 11.1 *A map of learning and the representation of learning*

'Noticing' is the stage of the acquisition of the sensory data. It is the initial sensory encoding of the material of the learning and it is a selective process, guided as much as any other stage by what we know already. The 'making sense' stage is one in which a coherency is sought in the material that is perceived. The stage of 'making meaning' is where the new material of learning is related to that which is already known in the cognitive structure. There could be some accommodation of the cognitive structure at this stage.

Up to the stage of 'making meaning' in learning, the learner is processing the new material of learning and is in direct contact with the material. At this stage they will have learnt the material reasonably adequately and be able to explain elements of it because the material is linked into the cognitive structure and that has accommodated appropriately. There is some sense of understanding at this level. Because the material of learning is now registered in the cognitive structure, any further parts of the learning process may be pursued away from the source of the original learning.

The next stage, 'working with meaning', occurs when the learner reflects on, or reasons with, the new learning in the context of the cognitive structure and not necessarily in the physical presence of the new learning (for example, the book or the teaching). This is a stage of greater accommodation – or re-accommodation – of the cognitive structure. This stage could be a process of 'cognitive housekeeping', thinking over things until they make better meaning, or exploring or organizing the understanding towards a particular purpose or in order that it can be represented in a particular manner.

It is not anticipated in this account that all learners will reach the stage of transformative learning as it is defined here. The operation of transformative learning appears to be the result of persistent work towards understanding, but there also seem to be times when sudden transformation of understanding can occur. These situations can be the result of a single piece of new learning or a new idea. The learning may be accompanied by strong emotional reactions, such as in spiritual transformation. Although the emotional reaction may be less dramatic, there are moments in normal learning situations when things fall into place, a substantial new view emerges and there is a sense of intellectual excitement.

To summarize the previous chapters, the stage in the learning of the material that a learner will reach will be determined, among many unpredictable factors, by their perception or the direct action of factors in the following list. The effect on learning of many of these factors may occur as a result of their influence on the approach to learning:

- teachers' explicit aims or expressed learning outcomes;
- a guess at what the learning situation requires them to do or understand;
- a guess at what they will be required to demonstrate in a representation of their learning, for example in an assessment task;
- what the learner supposes is the nature of the task from previous experience of similar situations;

- the complexity of the material of learning in relation to their cognitive structure;
- the complexity of the material of learning in relation to their ability;
- time constraints;
- their threshold of boredom or concentration or interest in the material;
- their strategies of learning;
- their intentions for the learning;
- their habits of approach to learning (deep or surface).

The learning environment is shown on the map as influencing all stages of learning. It might be more appropriate to describe it as interacting with stages of learning in the sense that a learner might choose to modify their learning environment if, for example, they feel that they are not reaching the stage of learning that they want or need to reach. For example, most people know that they learn better in one place rather than another and may vary their environment in response to this.

The metaphor of a jigsaw is useful in elucidating the path of learning in its initial stages on the map. The metaphor seems to represent some of the important processes that may be involved in the earlier stages of learning. However, beyond the stage of 'making meaning', the metaphor becomes strained. If the idea of the map is made clearer by the use of the metaphor, this might make the map more mentally portable and so more useful in practical situations.

The making of the jigsaw represents the learner developing their cognitive structure with respect to some area of learning – perhaps a topic of academic learning. At the start of the jigsaw building process the assumption is that the learner has some of the jigsaw pieced together, such as some of the outside edges and the corners but not the centre. They do not have a picture of the completed jigsaw, though they may have been given some idea of what it is – for example, a landscape. Initially, there may be some stray pieces of other jigsaws in among those that the learner wants. At the stage of 'noticing', the learner observes that some of the pieces have colours or shapes that match the pieces already on the board, some seem to match each other and will almost certainly fit into this picture. 'Making sense' is the stage of gathering together all the bits of the jigsaw that seem to be of a particular type and fitting those together. Following the metaphor further, there is a choice as to whether to find loose bits that match and fit them together to form coherent parts that are isolated or to work from the elements of jigsaw that are actually in place, such as the corners and outside pieces. This is –'making meaning'.

The metaphor of making a jigsaw illustrates the way in which assimilation and accommodation work in the first few stages of learning. The jigsaw maker is using the cues in the outline that is in situ to guide the placing of loose pieces or groups of pieces. Before this stage, they have on the board vague features of objects, colours and lines and what are obviously parts of things. They also have promising loose pieces or pieces that fit together but do not yet link into the whole. At the stage of 'making meaning', they can start to link the loose pieces and groupings of pieces into what is there already and, in so doing, see increasingly clearly what the vague features, colours and lines are depicting. The jigsaw is then completed to the satisfaction of its maker and, at this point, the jigsaw metaphor has served its purpose.

This overview has sketched out how the map works as a whole and now it is time to consider the elements and processes in more detail. Each stage is described below in terms of the relevant functions, processes and events. In addition to the metaphor of the jigsaw and to give more meaning to the stages of learning, each stage is illustrated by a series of comments from the learner about relevant issues in their learning.

The stages of learning

Noticing

Noticing accords with perception. It is the stage of acquisition of the sensory data from the material of learning (Eysenck and Keane, 1995; Eisner, 1991). It is a first filter and a point at which the cognitive structure guides and organizes the input of the material of learning on the basis of expectations and previous experiences, frames of reference and preferred modalities. It is a 'gate-keeping' phase where attitudes towards the material of learning, motivation and the emotional state have initial effects, although they appear to go on to affect the further stages of processing. The learner will only learn something if they notice it, but may be more likely to notice it if they are expecting to perceive it (Boud and Walker, 1993).

What is noticed is determined by at least four factors. The first is what the learner knows already – in other words, the content of their cognitive structure. Mostly, the current state of learning is not consciously brought to awareness when new learning is contemplated, though there is some evidence that greater personal awareness of this state is helpful to learners (Boud and Walker, 1992; Moon, 1996a). Such awareness helps with decisions about focusing new learning. On the basis of Ausubel and Robinson's work (1969), it can help to link the new material of learning with what is already known.

The second factor that determines what is noticed in learning is the perceived and given purposes of learning. Purposes may be those of the learner (such as interest) or those set for the learning by another. These may be described in terms of assessment criteria, the nature of an assessment task, statements of learning outcomes or the teacher's aims or, not infrequently, guesswork. Modifying these purposes may be other factors, such as any reinforcement system attached to the purposes that makes it more or less important to the learner.

Third, constitutive factors will affect the stage of noticing. Examples are self-esteem as a learner of this material or emotions associated with the material or situation, such as fear, excitement or boredom.

The last factor is that the learner will not learn what does not reach their attention. One of the roles of a teacher is to bring the material of learning to the attention of learners.

Issues in learning

Those issues that are relevant to this stage are illustrated in the following comments:

- 'I will just hold this in mind for the test tomorrow';
- 'I've just noticed the bit of information that I need . . .';
- 'I'm anxious: I can't take in these notes at all so near the exam';
- 'I've seen this before. I got really bored with it and I'm not going to bother with it'.

If representation of the learning can occur directly from the noticing stage, the best possible representation will be memorized representation and the form will be modified from the original only in terms of inaccuracies and loss of recall.

Making sense

Making sense is seen as a process of becoming aware of coherency in the material of learning, organizing and ordering the material of learning and slotting ideas together. It might be the limit of processing in elementary problem solving where there is no requirement for substantial previous knowledge, but the presented ideas need to be rearranged. The identity of the stage is suggested by the characteristics of surface approaches to learning.

Teaching that is directed at facilitating this kind of learning calls on the learner to gain a coherent view of the material in relation to itself, not in relation to previous knowledge. It is teaching that 'talks conclusions' (Riddle, 1997) without engaging the learner's own reasoning. It could be called 'surface teaching' (Ramsden, 1992).

Issues in learning

The issues that are relevant to this stage are illustrated in the following comments:

- 'Does this stuff make sense?';
- 'I just need to cram into my head as many facts as possible to do this test';
- 'Does this chemical compound go in this group or the other?';
- 'I think that we have enough facts to work out the solution to this problem';
- 'Sorting out what this seems to say is like doing a crossword'.

The best possible at this stage might have some coherence in itself, but will not be connected to deeper or broader meanings and forms of integration. In terms of the SOLO taxonomy, it will be at the multistructural level at most. On the map, the best possible representation is described as 'Reproduction of ideas, ideas not well linked'.

Making meaning

This is the stage at which the new material of learning is assimilated into the cognitive structure and, simultaneously, the cognitive structure accommodates it to make sense of the new learning and what is known. Accommodation results in meaningful learning and understanding that may be accompanied by a sense of emotional 'rightness' (Head and Sutton, 1985; Entwistle, 1996). Entwistle and Entwistle's subjects (1997) talked of learning 'locking into a pattern', but felt that there could be further understanding (see Chapter 10). In terms of academic learning, this form of learning is the basis of the productive accumulation and deepening of learning over a period of time. It allows the building of an understanding of the discipline.

Most good teaching will be supporting learners in reaching this stage of understanding, enabling learners to relate the new material of learning to what they know, which in itself, will bear a close relationship to established knowledge and understanding in the discipline. One difficulty in mass teaching situations is of ensuring that what the student knows does relate to the knowledge and understanding within the discipline. Working with the disciplinary knowledge in, for example, discussions in tutorials or the provision of good feedback on students' writing can help them to make the appropriate links in understanding.

Issues in learning

The ones relevant to this stage are illustrated in the following comments:

- 'How does this idea match those that we considered in last year's course?';
- 'Ah, now you have told me that, I can understand it!'
- 'So, for these reasons, I can see why I must do it in this way';
- 'This ties in with what I have been thinking';
- 'I understand the reasoning behind this sequence now';
- 'I am trying to get my head around this'.

The representation of learning that has been processed to the stage of 'making meaning' will mainly, at its best possible representation, demonstrate deep learning with the ideas being linked together and evidence of a holistic view of the subject matter. In terms of the SOLO taxonomy, it will demonstrate qualities of the relational structure. It is described on the map as 'Meaningful, well integrated, ideas linked'.

Working with meaning

In the stages of 'working with meaning' and 'transformative learning', the assumption is made that the learner does not need contact with the original material of learning. Indeed, the original material of learning may have been modified in the process of accommodation and is now part of the cognitive structure itself, with the potential to guide more learning. The learner may dip back into external resources for more information or to check on details, but in 'working with meaning' this process will be guided by the accumulating ideas resulting from the ongoing learning. This type of processing implies a major role for reflection, but the term is avoided here in order to develop the broadest possible overview of learning before examining specifically the part that reflection plays.

'Working with meaning' implies the ongoing accommodation of the cognitive structure and, where representation of learning is required, the manipulation of meaningful knowledge towards a specified end, such as a clarification of thoughts on some issue. This stage is a means of developing further understanding that cannot occur unless there is some understanding in the first place. Reorganization of material that is not understood is identified in the map as 'making sense'.

Teaching has an interesting position with regard to 'working with meaning'. It is essentially a private process because it is assumed that it can occur independently of further input, although the learner may seek new input or guidance in their organization of ideas. The teacher's opportunity to encourage learning at this stage is to coach from the 'front end' – by generating ideas, setting work, giving guidance or asking questions that provoke 'working with meaning'. Alternatively, a teacher can work from the 'back end' by making it clear that their marking of assignments will be on the basis of the learner's demonstration of a reprocessing or reformulation of the given information. Feedback would be on the success of attainment of this criterion.

The Entwistles (1997) described how students talked about their revision process and felt that they had not reached as great an understanding as was possible for their subject matter. The process of 'working with meaning' will consolidate the understanding by seating it more firmly in the network of meanings that make up cognitive structure, thereby perhaps leading to more accommodation of the cognitive structure. In using the term 'working with meaning', there is an implication that this is a form of processing that is involved in the representation of learning or occurs within the process of the representation of learning. It may be difficult to separate the initial mental process from the feedback obtained from trying out ideas on paper and 'seeing how they feel', whether they convey the appropriate meaning.

Below is a list of commonly experienced and cognitive activities that would seem to be involved in the stage 'working with meaning', but the categories are not mutually exclusive:

- organizing thought about something;
- the processing that enables planning;
- summarizing;
- thinking over something after the event in order to come to a conclusion;
- working with ideas in a discipline;
- critical analysis;
- integration of meanings and synthesis;

- deduction and problem solving that requires understanding of the elements involved;
- thoughtful reasoning;
- making a judgement;
- marshalling facts and ideas as evidence in argument;
- reflection-on-action.

In the process of 'working with meaning' a learner might simply review what they know without changing their understanding but increase their knowledge by being more aware of the content of that knowledge. This may be a matter of bringing the tacit knowledge to consciousness. However, when 'working with meaning' yields new conceptions, then new material of learning has been generated and the cognitive structure may need to accommodate it. This process could account for the manner in which much self-development and counselling works. The ability to work with meaning and generate new meaning is funda-mental to a deep learning approach and the generally accepted functions of a higher education system.

Issues in learning
The issues that are relevant to this stage are illustrated in the following comments:

- 'Putting these ideas together, I think I can work out how to present this argument';
- 'I will need to analyse what this is really saying in order to criticize it fairly';
- 'Let me sort out my thoughts on this matter and then I will give you an answer';
- 'Taking everything into account suggests that I do this as my next move';
- 'I am working out how to present my ideas so that they can understand'.

The representation of learning that has been processed in this stage at its best is likely to be a meaningful exposition that takes into account other personal and disciplinary knowledge in a manner that suggests reflection and anticipation. The ability to give appropriate explanations seems to be a good indicator of functioning at this stage (Entwistle, 1996). In terms of the SOLO taxonomy, such representation would demonstrate most of the qualities of the extended abstract level. On the map, the best possible representation is described as 'Meaningful, reflective, well structured'.

At this stage, it may not be very helpful to suggest that there is a limitation to the quality of the representation of learning (BPR) because 'transformative learning' is probably best seen as a further development of 'working with meaning' that has no clear boundaries. On the basis of work like that of Perry (1970) and Belenky, et al., (1986), it seems likely that not all people are capable of functioning at either of these stages, particularly the full meta-functioning of 'transformative learning'. Whether or not the capacity to function in this manner can be coached is an interesting issue.

Transformative learning

It was suggested above that this stage may not be very different from that of 'working with meaning' in a qualitative sense. 'Transformative learning' is identified separately, however, because references in the literature, such as those that derive from the Habermasian categorization of human interests (Habermas, 1971), identify a form of representation of learning that would require learning of a more sophisticated nature than 'working with meaning'. This learning involves a more extensive accommodation of the cognitive structure and the learner demonstrates that they are capable of evaluating their frames of references, the nature of their own and others' knowledge and the process of knowing itself. The process demands greater control over the workings of the cognitive structure and greater clarity in the processes of learning and representing that learning than does the previous stage.

A learner at this stage will be self-motivating and self-motivated, but may derive support from discussion and an environment in which their ideas can be tested by others. A mentor who can facilitate the process of learning to this stage may be effective in supporting a learner in developing their capacities to this stage with regard to a particular element of learning. In formal education terms, 'transformative learning' is the place of intellectual excitement and of the deeply satisfying discourse that can occur in good-quality tutorial work.

Issues in learning

Those relevant to this stage are illustrated in the following comments:

- 'I can see that my view was biased in the past. Now I am reconsidering the situation';
- 'What my tutor said has helped me to look at it in a completely new light';
- 'My outlook has changed and I am critical of the whole of our approach. Let me explain how';
- 'In those days I studied detail, now I defend my position on the basis of principles'.

The representation of learning at this stage of processing will demonstrate the learner's capacity to take a critical overview of knowledge and their own knowledge and functioning in relation to it. On the map, it is described as 'meaningful, reflective, restructured by learner – idiosyncratic or creative'.

Learning and the representation of learning – some further implications

If the fairly straightforward learning described above is deemed to be one form of learning, then there are two other forms that are built on this form. The first is learning from the representation of learning. The second, the possibility of upgrading learning, is more speculative, but it has important implications for the process of facilitating learning. Figure 11.2 shows a map of learning and the representation of learning with the processes of learning from the representation of learning and the upgrading of learning added.

Learning from the representation of learning

Learning occurs in the process of representing the learning (Eisner, 1991). Representation of learning in the form of an essay or report or oral expression gives the learner an opportunity to reflect on the ways in which the bits of knowledge, now expressed, relate together and to previous learning or how they work in towards the aim of the representation. In effect, by means of the representation that has occurred at any stage of learning, it is suggested that the learner can deepen and progress their learning. Learning from the representation of learning is, in itself, a means of upgrading learning (see below).

Upgrading learning

It has been suggested that stage of learning reached at a given time determines the maximum (best possible) quality of representation of that learning. Here it is suggested that learning might be upgraded to another stage after the original time of learning. On the basis of the map of learning, there might be several ways in which this can happen.

The first example of upgrading learning might seem to be where learning that has been processed to the 'making meaning' stage is later processed via 'working with meaning' towards 'transformative learning'. This upgrading implies a secondary and more fundamental accommodation of the cognitive structure and only differs from the normal process of learning in that it occurs later than the initial learning and can occur without it being necessary to have contact with the original material of learning.

From the point of view of teaching and learning, a more significant example of the upgrading of learning might occur when the material of learning is upgraded from the stage of 'making sense'. If a student has only made sense of some material of learning, they will not be able to represent concepts meaningfully related to each other in a new structure or relate them to previously held knowledge because they will not have integrated the new material meaningfully into their cognitive structure. From reasoned observation of learning, it seems possible for the material of learning at the stage of 'making sense' to be upgraded to stages of meaningful learning. This might occur if the learner deliberately recalls the material processed to the stage of 'making sense' and then consciously relates these somewhat isolated ideas to what they know already. In other words, they integrate them into her cognitive structure in the process of 'making meaning'.

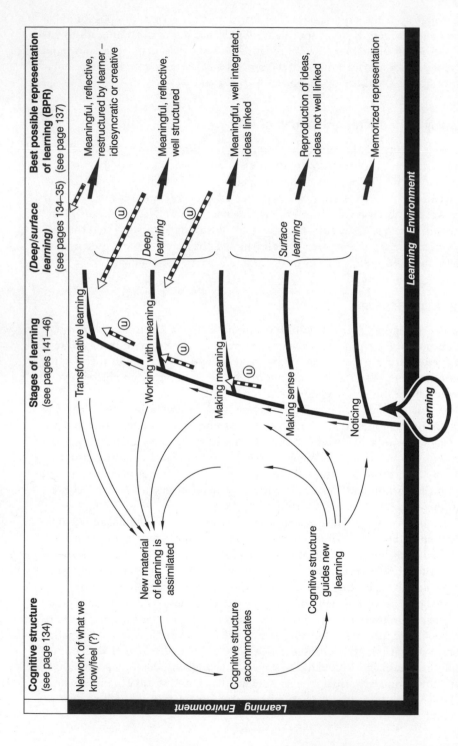

Figure 11.2 *A map of learning and the representation of learning from the representation of learning and the upgrading of learning*

This form of upgrading of learning may be the basis of much learning that occurs in higher education. When students make notes in lectures, it might well be unlikely that all of them are also continuously processing all of the material of learning to the stage of 'making meaning' (deep learning). Their opportunities, then, for deeper processing of the learning rest in later processes, such as re-reading or discussing the notes or doing revision for examinations or, perhaps most traditionally, in discussion in tutorials. It is notable that in mass higher education, tutorials or small group experiences in numbers that can allow interaction are diminishing. This may represent the loss of an important means for students to upgrade their learning to the quality required at higher education levels.

The discussion above suggests ways in which learning might be upgraded, but, if this can occur, it is unlikely to be an automatic process. The terms 'deliberately' and 'consciously' have been used. This is because it is likely that to upgrade learning will require the intention of the learner to develop a deeper understanding of what has been a lower stage of learning. It could be seen as an intention to 'deepen' learning.

The means of upgrading learning described above are closely related to parts of the Kolb cycle of experiential learning (see Chapter 3 and Kolb, 1984) and suggest reasons for the effectiveness of learning that is expressed in action. The cycle of experiential learning is reconsidered in the next chapter.

Developmental processes, complexity of material of learning and the stages of learning – observations and speculation

The map of learning and the representation of learning is an attempt to describe the possibilities for depth of learning for a mature and able learner. Indeed, the stages represent for such a learner a range of options in a learning task. The map may additionally relate to human developmental processes.

From the studies of Piaget, it can be assumed that adult forms of learning mainly occur from the early teens onwards. The literature suggests that the stage described here as 'transformative learning' may not be reached by all university students, and attaining this stage may be related, in some degree, to maturational as well as educational processes (King and Kitchener, 1994). It seems reasonable to suggest, therefore, that the maturity of the learner can act as a limiting factor to the stage of learning attained where learning demands are high.

Another variable in relating the stages of learning on the map to age or educational progress is the perception of the complexity of the material of learning, which interacts with the level of anxiety. If anxiety or academic pressure tend to influence learners to shift from deep to more surface approaches to learning (Entwistle, 1996), then the perceived complexity of the material of learning can also act as a limiting factor to the stage of learning and, therefore, the quality of the representation of the learning. If the material is difficult at any age or level of learning, and there is a requirement to learn it, learners may initially try to understand it by relating it to their cognitive structure in the 'making meaning' stage, but if they fail, they may resort to learning it by memorizing, representing their learning in the stages of 'noticing' or 'making sense'.

In the case of 'working with meaning' and 'transformative learning', however, when, it is suggested, the material of learning is already processed and integrated into the cognitive structure, a limiting factor may then be the complexity of the requirement regarding the representation of the learning – an assessed task or a problem that needs to be solved, for example.

There are other disruptive processes that can be envisaged. If a student who is capable of sophisticated stages of learning is given straightforward material of learning to learn, then it might be assumed that their cognitive structure will slot it into their networks of understanding and accommodate it easily. However, the material of learning might be adjudged by one person to be 'simple' because it slots easily into their cognitive structure, but the same material might be difficult for another, either because they have a cognitive structure with which it is not immediately compatible or it might potentially radically disrupt the current state of their cognitive structure with regard to a particular matter. For example, ethical issues might be simple to some and complicated to others. In a similar way, emotional factors may disrupt the learning in one person, whereas the same material of learning for another will be processed at a deeper stage. In other words, developing the complexity of the material of learning is not a variable that is independent of the learners, and it does not relate to the stages of learning in a simple manner. Returning to the ecological model of limiting factors, this might be a case of factor interaction.

It would seem that, for an individual, therefore, the stage of learning reached or the representation of learning is not directly predictable from the major variables of age or educational progress or the complexity of the material of learning. However, all of these can act as limiting factors on a learner's ability to learn and their understanding and they are relevant to the process of learning and representing that learning – alongside the influence of more ephemeral factors in the learning environment, such as teaching, assessment tasks and so on.

A further slant on the relationship between mental development, maturation and learning and its representation is contributed by Biggs and Collis (1982) in reference to the SOLO taxonomy. They suggest that at any level of learning ability, for a given task, the learner goes through the sequence of levels in the taxonomy. Thus, for a new and unfamiliar task, the learner's learning will progress from representation in terms of pre-, then uni-, then multistructural levels and so on. However, the speed at which a sophisticated learner might progress through the levels is likely to mean that their learning is never actually represented in the earlier levels.

In a corresponding manner, it would appear likely that when a learner tackles a new area of learning, the initial quality of that learning is likely to be relatively superficial and unconnected to their cognitive structure because it has not developed sufficiently to facilitate the new learning. In other words, the stage of processing is limited here by the lack of availability of guidance from the underdeveloped cognitive structure. This speculation relates to the previous observation that in learning new material, we tend to dwell initially on details without an overall view of the subject.

Conclusion

This chapter has systematically demonstrated the building of the map of learning and the representation of learning to provide a picture of learning that will enable the exploration of the role of reflection in the next chapter. In the latter part of the chapter the possibility of other forms of learning has been considered – from the representation of learning and the upgrading of learning. The roles of age and education in relation to the map and the operation of factors on the individual state of the learner have been considered too as they can influence the depth of learning.

Chapter 12

The place of reflection in learning

Introduction

The map of learning and the representation of learning has been developed because reflection appears to be intimately related to learning, yet the literature that links reflection and learning is sparse or lacking in detail. The map represents an effort to find a meaningful way of analysing the events of learning in order to locate reflection and speculate more clearly on its nature. A definition of the term that has been developed in the discussion thus far is: 'a mental process with purpose and/or outcome that is applied to relatively complicated or unstructured ideas for which there is not an obvious solution'. This remains to be tested in the view of learning that has been presented in the previous chapters.

The place of reflection in the map of learning and the representation of learning

The map of learning and the representation of learning is an hypothesis – a model that fits observations and limited empirical work – and therefore what can be said about reflection on the basis of its analysis is also hypothetical. Reflection seems to be heavily implicated in the processes of the more sophisticated stages of learning where there is manipulation of meaning that has already been developed in the cognitive structure. In this way, reflection is integral to a deep approach to learning. It is suggested that there are three main areas, in terms of the map, in which reflection is involved in learning.

- It is involved in straightforward learning. If the restructuring of the cognitive structure as it accommodates new learning is a form of manipulation of meaning, then the stages of 'making meaning', 'working with meaning' and 'transformative learning' involve reflection, though this is more the case in the latter two stages.
- Reflection is involved in learning that results from the representation of learning in that this feedback and reconsideration process also involves the manipulation of meaning.
- If learning can be upgraded in the manner suggested in the previous chapter, this process would also seem to imply reflection.

The suggested points at which reflection operates in the learning process as depicted by the map are plotted in Figure 12.1. The operation of reflection is described in more detail below.

Reflection in initial learning (in 'making meaning', 'working with meaning' and 'transformative learning')

'Making meaning' is a stage that involves relatively minor accommodation of the cognitive structure. 'Working with meaning' involves more reorganization of meaning in a process by means of which new learning or understanding is achieved from the restructuring of meaning in the cognitive structure. This may or may not lead to representation of the learning. In either of these cases, reflection could be said, metaphorically, to be acting in its 'cognitive housekeeper' role. In terms of the literature of reflection, this can be equated with reflection-on-action – the mental review or 'reliving' of an event or series of events, and the making of more or different meaning as a result. It is also suggested that, in conjunction with imagination, reflection might acquire an anticipatory role where it brings together past experiences and their meanings with imagination of the future situation (see Chapter 2).

Reflection in the 'transformative learning' stage enables the learner to take a critical overview and amass further understanding of a professional or social situation or the self or their knowledge, which can lead to emancipation. In other words, it can operate in a meta-cognitive manner, enabling a view to be taken of the cognitive structure and its functioning or of the whole self. Reflection in this stage is in accord with the emancipatory level of human interests (Habermas, 1971). Mezirow (1990) provides examples of ways in which reflection of this type can enable transformative learning, such as consciousness-raising groups and the use of critical incident analysis (Brookfield, 1990) and particular forms of journal writing, such as that of Progoff (1975).

Reflection in the representation of learning

Reflection in the representation of learning is also a means of upgrading learning (see below). The task in which learning is represented may be a deliberately

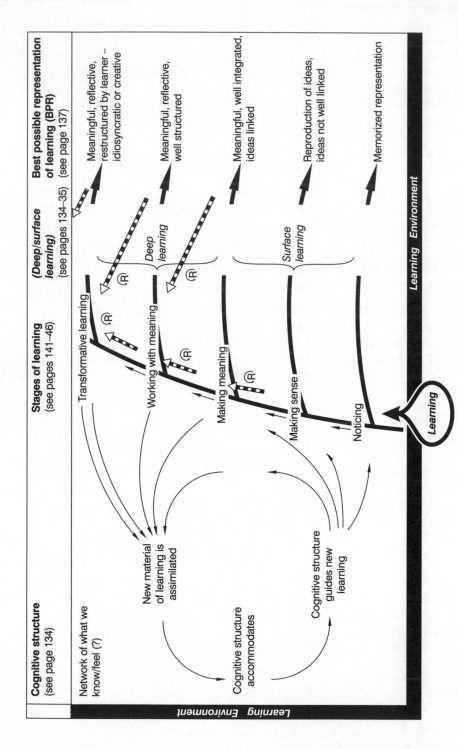

Figure 12.1 *A map of learning and the representation of learning and the role of reflection*

designed tool to facilitate reflection. Examples of this would be a learning journal where reflection is both the process and purpose of the work, the representation is a written piece, such as an essay or report where reflection is the process used to create the deeper and better-quality meaning. Alternatively, the representation may take spoken form.

Reflection in the upgrading of learning

The discussion on the upgrading of learning suggested that it may not be uncommon for learning initially to be surface learning that is relatively unconnected to previous knowledge. Reflection on these relatively isolated bits of learning is suggested to be the means of integrating the learning into the cognitive structure and relating it to previous knowledge. It was suggested earlier that there needs to be the intention to develop understanding or to deepen learning. Discussion of a topic in a small group could facilitate this form of reflection. Critical to its success may be the form of questioning that is used and the degree to which this stimulates learners to relate the new material of learning to previous knowledge and, thereby, learn meaningfully (Morgan and Saxon, 1991; Van Ments, 1990).

Reflection in the upgrading of learning might seem to describe a central activity of adult education – that, with the support of appropriate facilitation, adult learning relies on reflective processes to develop deeper meaning from learning and 'knowing' that initially might have been somewhat superficial, of a surface nature. Mezirow (1990) has stressed the importance of reflection in facilitating this process to the stage of 'transformative learning'.

Reflection and learning in a wider context

The map of learning and the representation of learning suggested roles that reflection might play in the process of learning and the representation of learning. Returning to the definition of reflection at the beginning of the chapter, it would seem that the consideration of reflection in relation to the hypothesized process of learning enables a restatement of the definition. This would be that reflection is 'a mental process with purpose and/or outcome in which manipulation of meaning is applied to relatively complicated or unstructured ideas in learning or to problems for which there is no obvious solution'.

The apparent diversity of applications of the idea of reflection is really about how this relatively simple process is used and guided rather than about the process itself. The forms of reflection – such as reflection in experiential learning, reflective practice and self-development – can differ as well because they exploit reflection at different stages in learning and the representation of learning with the objective of reaching appropriate outcomes for the matter in hand. In effect, reflection makes deeper and better considered knowledge available to us.

Table 12.1 *Input–outcome model of reflection revisited*

Inputs to reflection	Outcomes of/purposes for reflection
⇒ ⇒ **reflection** ⇒ ⇒	
Theories, constructed knowledge or feelings	learning/material for further reflection; action or other representation of learning; critical review; reflection on the process of learning; the building of theory; self-development; decisions/resolutions of uncertainty; empowerment and emancipation; other outcomes that are unexpected – eg images or ideas that might be solutions; ??emotion

There is also the capacity to 'be reflective', which seems to be an orientation to the activities of life rather than a mental process as such.

It was suggested in Chapter 8 that the analysis of reflection in learning might provide more information about the nature of reflection in other contexts in which it is applied, such as experiential learning, professional development, personal development and decision making. The inputs and outcomes or purposes of reflection mentioned in the literature were summarized in Table 8.1. The model is revisited in Table 12.1 and now can be associated with the different roles of reflection suggested from the map of learning in order to elucidate the manner in which reflection is employed in situations not directly associated with learning.

The analysis that follows relates the suggested outcomes of reflection to the roles of reflection in learning. To reiterate, the roles suggested for reflection in learning are:

- reflection in initial learning;
- reflection in the process of representation of learning;
- reflection in the upgrading of learning.

The purpose or outcome of reflection is learning or the production of further material for reflection

This purpose of reflection, in the sense that it directly relates to learning, encompasses all three of the suggested roles of reflection in learning. Later in this chapter this is discussed further in reference to the experiential learning cycle of Kolb (1984).

The purpose or outcome of reflection is action or other representation of learning

This involves reflection in initial learning. To reflect on action is to reflect on an event in the past, reprocessing or reorganizing the meaning that has been made of that event with the possibility of improving future performance. Future performance could be said to be the representation of that learning that emerges from the process and this is likely to involve the stages of 'working with meaning' or 'transformative learning'.

The purpose or outcome of reflection is reflection on the process of learning

This involves reflection in initial learning and perhaps reflection in the representation of learning. Reflection on the process of learning emerges from the overview function of 'transformative learning'.

The purpose or outcome of reflection is the building of theory

Some professionals have consciously used reflection as a means of building theory (see Chapter 6) and the relationship between espoused theory and theory in practice is central to much of Schön's work on reflection. The process of building theory or meaning involves reflection in the upgrading of learning or reflection in initial learning ('working with meaning') – the development of more, deeper or more generalizable meaning from actions interpreted at different stages of learning. The development of sophisticated theory would imply reflection in initial learning ('transformative learning').

The purpose or outcome of reflection is self-development

In its most sophisticated form, self-development is aimed towards emancipation of the self from the constraints of social and personal histories. As in emancipation, this involves reflection in initial learning where the learning is 'transformative learning'. Self-development may otherwise involve 'making sense' or 'making meaning' from more superficially learned material (reflection in the upgrading of learning). Journal writing is an important tool in self-development. It involves reflection in initial learning and in the representation of learning.

The purpose or outcome of reflection is decisions/resolutions of uncertainty

Decision making implies the use of reflection in the initial learning ('working with meaning'). The discussion of a decision involves the representation of learning. Techniques such as 'playing devil's advocate' encourage reflection in the representation of learning.

The purpose or outcome of reflection is empowerment and emancipation

Emancipation is the result of taking a critical overview of the self, one's own mental processes, the social or political contexts and so on in order to develop new situations. Reflection in initial learning, where the learning is 'transformative learning' is basic to this reflective process.

The purpose or outcome of reflection is other outcomes that are unexpected

Apart from the possibility of unconscious motivation leading to apparently unexpected outcomes, ideas that emerge could involve 'working with meaning' at a more profound level, 'transformative learning' in reflection in initial learning. New meanings may also emerge when learning is being represented (reflection in the representation of learning).

The purpose or outcome of reflection is emotion(?)

The role of emotion in reflection is uncertain. It certainly accompanies reflection and can be the subject matter for it. If reflection can be a direct outcome of reflection in a similar way to the other outcomes, then it might emerge from reflection in any of its roles.

'Being reflective'

'Being reflective' is a meaning of reflection that is applied particularly in the literature of professional practice. 'Being reflective' is interpreted as an orientation to practice or other aspects of life and it seems to imply a quality in a person who uses reflection frequently, 'comfortably' and – perhaps by implication – publicly, and who demonstrates that it has value for their work. Rather than suggesting that a person uses particular forms of reflection, it implies that reflecting is habitual – perhaps as a learning style (Kolb, 1984; Honey and Mumford, 1986) – and that the person concerned could use any or all forms of reflection effectively and with ease.

A reconsideration of experiential learning

This book has prompted many questions about the nature of reflection. One in particular needs to be looked at again because it is fundamental to the definition of reflection. It arises in the context of reflection in experiential learning (see Chapter 3). The Kolb cycle (Kolb, 1984) suggests that reflection can act on experience in the form of perceptions of raw experience or on already learnt material. These different situations arise in the initial cycle and then subsequent cycles when the experience has been generated as a result of the first cycle and the material of learning is material that is already familiar or learnt. The query is whether both of these operations, as Kolb and others say, concern reflection or reflection only occurs on already learnt – or secondary – material. If the latter is true, then the processing of raw experience would not actually entail the process of reflection.

One factor that supports the notion of reflection as a secondary action on already learnt material has been stated – that the prefix 're' itself suggests that it is a secondary action. However, further speculation can be made on the basis of the map of learning and the representation of learning (Figure 11.1, page 138). If reflection does act on raw experience, then, in terms of the map, it is used in the stages of 'noticing' and 'making sense', and is part of the processing of the material of learning towards the point where it is 'making meaning'. When experience is the material of learning that has already been learnt, such as ideas or concepts, the term reflection implies that the person reflecting makes secondary considerations as they do so. This – as reflection is suggested to operate in the map – is involved in the more sophisticated stages of learning, namely 'making meaning', 'working with meaning' and 'transformative learning'.

The interpretation of reflection as secondary is supported by several writers who describe reflection as being, or imply it to be, a meta-cognitive process, and ' meta-cognitive processes mediate other forms of knowledge' (James, 1993). The meta-cognitive view of reflection is similarly illustrated in publications about the use of learning logs, such as Morrison (1990).

The suggestion that reflection might only act on material that has already been learnt implies that the use of the word 'reflection' in the Kolb cycle might need to be reinterpreted where it is applied directly to raw experience. In terms of the map of learning, the material is simply undergoing a process of being learnt. If the learning is later tested in experimentation or processed into action, generating new experiences, then, in the second and subsequent cycles, the word 'reflection' would be appropriate.

If what Kolb calls 'reflection' differs according to whether the processing is of raw experience or already learnt material, the implication is that learners may need to be guided differently when they are initially assimilating the material of learning from raw data than later when they have involved the meta-cognitive processes of reflecting on material already learnt (or processed). As was said earlier, in many situations it might be difficult to distinguish between raw experience and the already processed material of learning. However, where reflective techniques are being deliberately employed to enhance a particular area of learning, the distinction may be helpful. For example, Wildman and Niles (1987) illustrate the two processes of initial experiential learning based on raw data and the subsequent cycles where the teachers taking part in the study reflected on the meanings of their learnt observations. Wildman and Niles note specifically the difficulty of enabling the teachers to observe teaching events – the raw experience – in an objective manner in order that they could subsequently reflect on them

On another point, the map of learning and the representation of learning provides a basis for reasoning why the use of the experiential learning cycle facilitates effective learning and is worthy of the exaltations of its benefits. The map relates experiential learning to the notions of deep and surface approaches to learning. Action is an outcome in the experiential learning cycle. Acting will normally be underpinned by understanding. Similarly, the provision of an explanation has a basis in understanding. In terms of the map, this implies that the learner reaches the stage of 'working with meaning' in order to act, do or experiment. The learner is, by implication, drawn through the stages of 'noticing' and 'making sense' to 'making meaning' and 'working with meaning' in order to fulfil the action required. The learner must therefore be taking a deep approach to the learning. In other words, the requirement for action drives the quality of the learning in the whole cycle and prevents it from stalling at a surface learning stage. At that stage ('making sense', say), the learner would not have a sufficiently coherent grasp of the material to put it into action.

Conclusion

In this chapter, first an overview of the map of learning and the representation of learning was given, then it was looked at in greater detail when the relationships between the stages of learning and the forms of representation of learning were explored. The concept of limiting factors from ecology is useful in suggesting that the stage of learning may usually set an upper limit on the possible form of representation of the learning, though other factors in the learning environment may intervene to reduce the quality of learning. Deep/surface learning is crucial in the structuring of the map of learning and the representation of learning, suggesting the identities of not only the stages of learning, but also the ways in which these relate to the forms of representation of the learning.

The contention of this book is that reflection is closely related to learning. The map of learning and its representation has been developed in order, speculatively, to provide a means of locating reflection in the learning process. The map also provides a more general means of speculating on the role of reflection in cognitive processing. Reflection seems to operate mainly in three areas of learning and the representation of learning. They are reflection in initial learning, reflection in the process of representation and reflection in the upgrading of learning.

With reflection located in the process of learning and the representation of learning, the purposes or outcomes of reflection were matched to the locations of reflection in learning and the representation of learning as above. While most of the purposes for reflection called on several reflective locations, there was no difficulty in linking the purposes of reflection with the roles demonstrated in the map of learning.

The greater insight into the process of reflection that has emerged in analysing it in relation to learning suggests a modification to the definition. This is that reflection is a mental process with purpose and/or outcome in which manipulation of meaning is applied to relatively complicated or unstructured ideas in learning or to problems for which there is no obvious solution'. The apparent differences in the literature of reflection relate not to the process itself but to its different applications and the framework of guidance that shape these.

Part III

Using reflection to improve learning and practice

Chapter 13

The conditions for reflection

Introduction

This is the first of four chapters with a more practical orientation to the notion of reflection. The important role of reflection in learning has been established, and these chapters are concerned with the enhancement of learning and professional practice by working with reflection in real situations. In general, the material of these chapters relates to adult and higher education or professional development, but does not need to be related only to classroom learning (Strange, 1992).

The four chapters work on the premise that reflection does not necessarily just happen but that conditions can be structured to encourage it to happen. In my work with teachers, I have noted the observation by Wildman and Niles (1987) to be true that 'teacher-as-reflective-practitioner will not just happen simply because it is a good or even compelling idea'. The chapters on reflection in learning suggest that most adults reflect in the process of some of their learning, but most do not do so in a deliberate manner to progress in their thinking or action and, even in structured settings, reflection can be a circular process (Harvey and Knight, 1996). The conditions that foster progression in the thinking or development of the learner (Francis, 1995) are the focus of this chapter.

While there are many observations in the literature that suggest that reflection is better nurtured under particular conditions, references to what these conditions are tend to be brief. Thus, this chapter represents a collation of the ideas that can be gleaned, grouped appropriately. They are intended to be of practical value and to underpin the tasks and strategies to promote reflection described in the last two chapters.

This chapter is organized under a series of headings for convenience, but there is not always clear distinction between them. Because the chapters in this part of the book have a practical character, while it is appropriate to begin them with a summary, they do not end with a conclusion.

The conditions for reflection – the learning environment

The learning environment was considered in Chapter 9. Here, the focus is on the significant qualities of the environment that affect reflection. It is important to reiterate that the significant aspects of the environment are those perceived by the learner, and these may be quite different from those perceived to be important by an observer.

Time and space

Learners need time in order to reflect (Walker, 1985), as well as time and opportunities to learn to reflect as it is unlikely that they will be fully able to use their ability to reflect straight away, even as trained professionals (Hatton and Smith, 1995; Francis, 1995). There have been several references to the difficulty experienced by learners in using the time allocated for reflective work. Wildman and Niles (1987) observe that 'Teacher after teacher related accounts of how project time [that is, for learning to reflect on practice] . . . evaporated under pressure to attend to specific needs of students [and so on]' and a number expressed the 'sense of guilt at spending time thinking on themselves . . .'. On the same lines, Barnett (1994) refers to the psychological time needed for reflection and Thorpe (1993) refers to the need to give back time and space to students for reflection in their curriculum.

Not only is separate time needed for specific activities of reflection, but time is needed for more interaction within periods of teaching or lectures (Meyers, 1986). An overfilled curriculum is one of the greatest disincentives for teachers to give time for reflection and for learner to take time to reflect. From a slightly different point of view, Meyers decries the inability of many teachers to tolerate what he calls creative silence – 'the time when ideas can "simmer" or "cook" awhile in learner's minds before opening one's mouth'. Reference has been made earlier to studies of 'wait time' that suggest that similar reasoning applies to the time given in pauses during speech, which have been found to aid learning by providing time for reflection (Tobin, 1987).

The facilitators of reflection

A facilitator is both a part of the learning environment and will influence other aspects of the learning environment. They will understand the nature of reflection, how it relates to the qualities of learning (deep and surface learning) and will be clear about what they are attempting to achieve in the learners. There will be different reasons for working with reflection and they will be clear what the overt reasons are and interested in the personal interpretations of these reasons by the learners. They should particularly be aware of the role of reflection as a means of upgrading learning and enable more mature learners to become aware of how they can use reflective techniques to upgrade their previous less organized but valid levels of knowledge and understanding. Similarly, they will understand how reflection in the representation of learning can enhance the quality of learning as well as deepen its meaning.

The good facilitator is likely to have an understanding of reflection because it is a valued personal experience. They should understand, for example, how reflection can play a role in self-development and emancipation. Several writers have pointed out the significance of the facilitator's 'being reflective', providing a model of reflective practice (Barnett, 1992). Knowles (1993), for example, engages in the sharing of reflections on his autobiography in the context of encouraging student teachers to learn to reflect. There are some anomalies here, however. While the educators of professionals promote reflective activities, such as journal writing, there are relatively few reports of them practising what they preach.

Taking it that facilitators may help learners by modelling reflection, Gibbs (1988) describes how learners are asked to watch the operation of a model of a reflective conversation by facilitators in order that the learners can see what they are trying to achieve in reflecting on an experience. Gibbs indicates that the crucial features of such a conversation should be:

- a stage of description of events, of looking for details, being objective, questioning how knowing has occurred and how the experience is similar to, or different from, others;
- a stage entailing judgements about the quality of the experience ('good' or 'bad'), the best and worst features and what went well or badly in it;
- a stage of analysis in which there is deeper questioning of what happened ('why?'), making sense of it and how such occurrences might be explained.

Many of the qualities of a facilitator of reflection will coincide with those of a good counsellor (Dryden and Feltham, 1994) – in particular in respect of the ability to listen and attend well to what is being said (Boud, Keogh and Walker, 1985; Knights, 1985). Possibly contradicting this model is Taylor's view (1997), which questions how much the facilitator should be supportive, instead asking how much they should be critically reflexive, challenging the learners to deepen their reflective processes. The resolution to these two views probably lies in facilitators having a sensitive flexibility to act in both ways. Indeed, the role of the facilitator might change over a period of working with students as initially they may require an emotionally supportive and 'guiding' approach, but later, as they become more able to reflect, they may want the facilitator to withdraw (Heron, 1989). This mirrors the notion of teacher as midwife in the process of 'connected teaching' where 'the cycle is one of confirmation–evocation–confirmation. Midwife teachers help students to deliver their words to the world and they use their own knowledge to put the students into conversation with other voices – past and present – in the culture' (Belenky, Clinchy, Goldberger and Tarule, 1986).

Somewhat similarly, Brookfield (1993) talks of facilitating critical thinking in students by using the metaphor of a conversation in learning, the qualities of which are reciprocal and involving – a recognition that the course of a good conversation is unpredictable and that it entails diversity and disagreement. The qualities of reciprocal interaction, unpredictability and challenge are features of many of the other conditions for reflection described below.

The above suggests that there are decisions to be made about the role that the facilitator of reflection might adopt.

The curricular or institutional environment

Students may learn to improve their learning or become reflective practitioners within the context of one class or module, but facilitation will be more effective if it is supported throughout a curriculum (King and Kitchener, 1994). Zeichner and Liston (1987) describe the manner in which a programme was modified in order comprehensively to encourage reflection and reflective practice among teaching students (see Chapter 6). Taking a broader view still, Strange (1992) describes a campus-wide initiative to promote reflective learning:

> No one argues that reflective thinking should not be the domain of traditional faculty members in traditional classrooms, but the potential for encouraging reflective thinking as a goal for students' out-of-class experiences is untapped on most campuses, where lines are drawn between 'academics' and 'everything else'. Why not consider reflective thinking as an outcome of a total learning effort that is richly addressed in a variety of ways throughout the college experience?

In terms of the wider involvement of staff, Wildman and Niles' comment on the importance of involving administrative staff as well as other staff when they introduced reflective activities among a group of teaching staff (1987), is useful: 'In our view, systematic reflection is primarily driven by the individual but we have found that collegial groups provide both the emotional and technical support that is often necessary for professionals reflecting about their practice'.

An environment that will encourage reflection is one in which students are challenged by the environment or rewarded by it for reflection in initial learning, the representation of the learning and the upgrading of their learning.

An emotionally supportive environment

The expression of personal material in reflection can be threatening. Knights (1985) comments that her experience suggests that 'very few people, however highly qualified academically, have confidence in their capacity to think. The fear of being "knocked back or laughed at" is very widespread. This certainly inhibits participation in group discussion and, in my view, also discourages private reflection'.

An emotionally supportive environment will have, at least, the following qualities:

- it will be a good learning environment socially for that individual;
- it will be an environment in which learners feel safe to take risks in their cognitive explorations;
- it will be an environment in which there is understanding of the emotional concomitants of reflection – and one in which these can be supported;
- it will contain and help those who react negatively to counselling perhaps because, initially, reflection is an alien activity for them and they have difficulties with the task.

As has been observed earlier, while the references to the emotional aspects of reflection tend to be sketchy in theoretical writing, these aspects become obvious in practical situations (Boud, Keogh and Walker, 1985; Pearson and Smith, 1985). Reflection can lead to catharsis (Calderhead and James, 1992) or, in a less dramatic manner, cause personal issues to be unearthed in the learner that may seem to be unrelated to the task in hand. Such an unearthing process is not necessarily negative and can contribute to self-development, although counselling skills may be needed to provide the necessary support. The literature on co-counselling provides ideas for working with the emotional concomitants of reflection (Jakins, 1970; Evison and Horobin, 1983).

If reflection is being used to promote self-development or attitude or behaviour change, it should involve risk as taking risks is where growth can occur. In their study of teachers, Wildman and Niles (1987) report that 'basic beliefs and personal dilemmas . . . are often laid bare as teachers reflect about what goes on in their classrooms'. They describe the role conflicts that were generated in the process of their work with teachers and a system that was set up so that mutual support could be given. While Wildman and Niles were concerned with trained teachers, Francis (1995) has examined the anxieties and role conflicts that may arise in educational situations where students have been socialized to expect that ' they will be graded and valued according to the degree of "fit" of their ideas to those of the "expert" lecturer'. Francis goes on to recommend 'the affirmation of tentative risk taking and to balance acceptance with a demand for rigour based on careful observation and analysis of events and the meaning-making that these provoke'. It is also important to recognize, probably overtly, that what is risky ground for one person may be safe ground for another because of differences in personal or professional experience. The differences will need to be recognized by facilitators and in the participating group.

School staffrooms, or their equivalent for other professions, may or may not be suitable places for reflection. Wildman and Niles (1987) found that the atmosphere of the place for reflection mattered to the teachers in their study, but, in the end, it is the individual's perception of 'right environment' in that moment that matters. Some of the ideas for creating positive environments in training and particular environments used to promote 'accelerated learning' are conducive to a reflective environment (Lawlor and Handley, 1996, for example).

A sensitive approach will be required for learners whose process of reflection appears to be stalled by emotional barriers (Boud and Walker, 1993). Barriers result in learners avoiding reflection that is difficult, but also deter them from facing issues that they may gain most from reflecting on (Thorpe, 1993). Again, counselling skills may be necessary, but mutual support of learners can be helpful. Techniques in co-counselling can also be useful.

The 'hidden agendas' of the environment

There are many factors in the learning environment that are 'hidden' and unpredictable but can be highly significant in their effect on reflection. Power relationships between staff and learners can inhibit reflection and there may be gender, racial or social class issues. In a similar way, a learner may skew their reflective activity to fit what they imagine is expected of them or because of a fear of self-revelation. There are still strong social norms that militate against 'self-analysis'. Some of these effects are likely to be exacerbated where external assessment is involved.

The conditions for reflection – management issues

The management of reflection enables the value of reflection to be realized in learning or other developments. The following represent some generalizations about managing reflective exercises so that learning or development can best be achieved.

The purpose and outcome of reflection

The definition of reflection adopted in this book suggests that reflection has purpose and/or outcomes. As has been suggested earlier, there is a possibility that reflection can be a circular process within which development then does not occur. It is necessary to be clear about why reflection is being encouraged beyond passing on what is known about its role in learning and the kinds of outcomes that might result. The purpose will point in the direction of development and the expected outcomes will anticipate growth in capacity in some area or other. There is a possibility in a formal educational situation that while purpose and outcome might be known to the teaching team, they may not adequately be transmitted to learners. The reasons for reflecting need to be particularly clear when reflection is a task for learners for whom the idea is unfamiliar. Too often, as has been indicated, assumptions are made about the nature of reflective activity.

Strategies for guiding reflection

There are four general points to be made here. First, if reflection is to be guided, the structure of a task provides the best guide for reflection. Hoover (1994) found that giving the general prompt to teaching students to write reflectively without a predetermined focus 'frequently led to an outpouring of complaints and survival concerns about . . . teachers [in the schools], curricular demands and moving from a university setting into the reality of the public schools'. On the other hand, the provision of structure – in this case, videotaped lessons – enabled the students to focus their reflection more progressively in terms of their teaching practice. However, there is value in the venting of feelings via unfocused writing.

Second, different types of reflective exercise will generate different types of reflection. One interesting difference is the type of structure that taps into less conscious or tacit areas of knowing (James, 1997; Korthagen, 1993). Examples of such structures are art, drama or poetry. The introduction of such forms of guidance for reflection will demand more thought as to how the results are used to enable progress or practice and as to the form of their introduction to learners. Such exercises can arouse a sense of threat if they are unfamiliar and this aspect needs to be handled appropriately.

Third, reflection may be guided in an organized sequence. In the sequence of guidance that I used (Moon, 1996a) in short professional development courses, reflection was used to increase the impact of the course on work practice. This was achieved by focusing initially on current behaviour, next on what had been learnt and then on how behaviour in practice can be different. In this way, progression is built into the structure of reflection (see Chapter 14). John's structure for reflection is another example (Johns, 1994; see also Chapter 6).

Fourth, although structure for a task needs to be provided, more support in the beginning can give way to less structure later. For example, Morrison (1996) describes how his students are given a range of areas on which they can reflect to help them initially. Later they become more self-directed.

Some advocates of reflective techniques propose the use of several different structures of reflection in order to ensure that the purposes are best achieved. In teacher education, Knowles (1993), for example, uses a life history account technique to begin with and finds that 'Insights gained from writing a personal history account provide starting points for further and deeper examination'. He also suggests that dialogue journals (see Chapter 16) offer an opportunity 'for continuing the conversation begun in the life history account'. Dialogue journals enable the critical review of personal attitudes (of teachers). A simpler example of using different structures for reflection is where the learner is encouraged to use a combination of unfocused reflection, which is subject to no tutor review, and focused reflection, which is assessed in some way. Morrison's students use a journal format that is seen by tutors and they are asked to apply what they have learnt in the course of their reflection to a problem. This second-order reflection is then assessed (Morrison, 1996). In these examples, reflection in the representation of learning is being used to facilitate more reflection in initial learning or else it is a process of upgrading learning.

The dangers of adherence to recipes for reflection

The structuring of material to guide learners into reflection can easily turn into a situation akin to responding to a questionnaire or following a recipe. If the responses can be made rapidly and do not challenge the learner, then they may not be engendering reflection. This proviso applies to any activity designed to promote reflection.

The issue of public and private material in reflection

Another issue that requires advance planning is that of the public or private domains of reflection. The material of reflection that is to be seen by teachers or peers will be different from that which remains in the hands of the learner. What is made public will be produced with an eye to the potential audience and may not enable the learner to learn as much from the process of reflection as would be the case if the process was a private one. On the other hand, private reflections cannot be subject to guidance.

It is worth noting that there are 'degrees of publicity' of reflective material. Sharing ideas with another learner is less threatening than sharing in a peer group, and these are both different again to situations in which reflective material is subject to being seen by a teacher and/or assessed. Morrison's use of a task that is second-order reflection circumvents some of the issues relating to assessment. Whatever is decided, the publicity or privacy of the material of reflection needs careful consideration or balancing in a formal situation.

Group or individual work on reflection

The benefits of reflection are to the individual in a traditional learning situation, but working with others can facilitate learning to reflect and can deepen and broaden the quality of the reflection so long as all the learners are engaged in the process. Another person can provide the free attention that facilitates reflection, ask challenging questions, notice and challenge blocks and emotional barriers in reflection (Knights, 1985; Eastcott and Farmer, 1992). It is important to recognize that learning to be helpfully supportive to another person's reflective processes can be a learning process just as much as learning to reflect itself, though the two areas of learning can occur alongside each other. The support role for reflection has been described as that of a 'critical friend' (Francis, 1995; Hatton and Smith, 1995). Hatton and Smith describe the role as 'a technique . . . which creates an opportunity for giving voice to one's own thinking while at the same time being heard in a sympathetic, but constructively critical way'. The idea of 'critical friendship' seems to be similar to the co-counselling relationship that is described by Knights (1985), although the emphasis of co-counselling might be on facilitation of reflection and that of critical friendship more on challenge and critique.

It is worth remembering that group work sessions can be good hiding places for those who want to avoid engagement with learning or reflection. For this reason, and because it is the individual's capacity for reflection that will enhance that individual's learning or practice, a mix of working with others and working alone is likely to bring about the best progress in learning.

Understanding of the different states of epistemological understanding

Throughout this book there have been many references to the fact that the reflective capacity of an individual depends on the stage of epistemological understanding that the person has reached. The research of Perry (1970), Belenky, et al. (1986), and King and Kitchener (1994) has indicated that the process of reflection differs in its level of sophistication, culminating, in the most effective reflectors, with meta-cognitive reflection, which can explore the nature of the reflection process and the assumptions on which knowledge is based. The implication of the stage approaches to reflection and the research that is associated with them is that individuals, even in one educational level, may vary in the way in which they deal with the same task or structure. The further implication of this is that the guidance for reflection may need to take into account the different stages. Usher (1985) illustrates this problem with references to his experiences of working with adult students who, on the theory of adult education, are expected to function as autonomous learners, preferring experiential learning methods. He finds that they are unable to extract appropriate material from learning from experience because of their level of understanding of the nature of knowledge.

Help for learners in learning to reflect

On the basis that not everyone finds reflection an easy manner of working, it can be important to introduce reflective tasks gradually rather than, for example, expecting learners to work on the clean white page of a new learning journal without practice (Rainer, 1978; Walker, 1985). In the early stages of working with reflection, learners will often ask if they 'are doing it right' and express dissatisfaction at the deliberately non-directive responses that they often receive.

Starting with short exercises on which feedback is given from a tutor, mentor or peers will circumvent some of the insecurities (Knights, 1985) and it can be valuable for a learner if they can be helped to see the advantages or benefits of reflection at an early stage (Strange, 1992). Eastcott and Farmer (1992) provide some useful exercises that can generate oral skills of reflection.

There is a broad literature on learning styles that suggests that different people find different learning styles easier or more difficult (Kolb, 1984; Honey and Mumford, 1986). Strange suggests that particular forms of stimulation may be appropriate for learners who are not that oriented towards the reflective mode. She suggests that a range of out-of-class activities that stimulate reflection can be helpful.

As reflection is inextricably linked with learning, it may not be helpful to learners if they feel that they are learning a new and different skill when they reflect, but it can help to see it as part of learning. The encouragement of reflection may be more a matter of planning class activities that encourage reflection than treating it as an isolated capacity. Using learners' own learning skills and abilities as the subject matter for reflection provides a method of doing this. It can seem odd that the research on student learning and/or the use of reflection is not passed on to those who are in a position to utilize the results, but this is often the case. Self-assessment is one applied form of passing on the information (Boud and Knights, 1994; Stephani, 1997). Classroom evaluation techniques (CATS) are short exercises that reflect and provide feedback on teaching and learning during or after a class, and usually tax reflective capacities of learners (Angelo and Cross, 1990). In a similar way, reflection on strengths and weaknesses in study promotes reflection (Main, 1980; Gibbs, 1981).

Sometimes it is not so much a matter of encouraging reflection, but removing barriers to reflection. Hatton and Smith (1995) observed:

> that students saw the academic context and expectations of essay writing established within the wider institution as inhibiting their ability and willingness to reflect in an assessable piece of work. The traditional genre is characterized by features that are in many ways the antithesis of the personal, tentative exploratory, and at times, indecisive style of writing which would be identified as reflective.

A curriculum that encourages reflection

The point made above reinforces the need to manage the encouragement of reflection so that learners are not put into a situation where demands for specific styles of writing are in conflict. In this respect, reflection in a programme of learning is best set into the context of a curriculum in which reflection is valued. The work of Zeichner and Liston (1987) is a good example (see Chapter 6).

Mechanisms to facilitate the transfer of habits of reflection

The purposes and outcomes of reflection were mentioned earlier. If it is the intention that reflection in a classroom situation should be later applied in, for example a professional situation or autonomous learning, the process of transfer needs to be considered in advance (Harvey and Knight, 1996). How will reflection be applied in this later stage, and what will facilitate the maintenance at the stage of transfer? Knowles (1993) considers some of the issues involved in teacher education.

The conditions for reflection – the qualities of tasks that encourage reflection

Examples of actual tasks that encourage reflection are the subject of the next three chapters, but there are some generalizations that can be made here. Tasks that encourage reflection will exploit reflection in initial learning, in representation of learning or provide situations in which learning can be upgraded by means of reflective activity.

The task may use 'messy' or ill-structured material of learning

Reflection on real-life situations is likely to involve ill-structured data. As the growth of the ability to reflect or make reflective judgements develops partly as a result of contact with ill-structured material of learning (King and Kitchener, 1994), exposure to such material is important. The reproduction of lecture notes on Internet or intranet systems, for example, could easily discourage reflection.

Asking the 'right' kinds of questions encourages reflection

Similarly to the points made above, reflection can be generated by asking the kinds of questions that do not have clear-cut answers. Morgan and Saxon (1991) have produced a classification of questions, from low-order questions where factual responses are required, to questions that promote analysis, synthesis or reasoning. They note that there are practical classroom management reasons for the tendency of teachers to rely on questions of a lower order nature and, therefore, this is a manner in which teachers do not promote reflection. Morgan and Saxon do provide many examples of questions that promote reflection in any age group.

Setting challenges can promote reflection

Challenges may be set by asking questions, within the nature of a task or by the unstructured nature of the material of reflection. Examples of challenges are given in Chapter 16.

Tasks that challenge learners to integrate new learning into previous learning

There have been references previously to the integration of new learning into what is already known by the learner. Use is made of this kind of task when, for example, teaching students are required to reflect on their previous conceptions of teaching, learning and schools, and to relate the new, more theoretical understandings to their previous knowledge. The integration of new and earlier understandings is a manner in which learning can be truly owned and made meaningful to the learner (Boud, Keogh and Walker, 1985).

Tasks that demand the ordering of thoughts

The ordering of thoughts may seem to be a stage of reflection that follows exposure to disorganized data such as that described previously. Reflection may entail periods of divergent and convergent processing of ideas as there is focus on and then the assimilation of new ideas (Heron, 1985).

Tasks that require evaluation

Evaluation is both a task that utilizes reflection and an activity in its own right that can involve the making of judgements based on reflection. In either case, evaluation represents a special example of the ordering and focusing of attention.

Chapter 14

Reflection in professional situations – two case studies

Introduction

This chapter consists of two case studies in which reflection is consciously involved in processes occurring in professional situations in order to improve the outcomes of those processes. The first case study describes the use of reflection to enhance the outcomes of a short course in continuing professional development. In the second case study, reflection is employed in several ways to ensure an efficient outcome to a national decision-making meeting. In both of the case studies, the professionals involved were health promotion specialists or those with a health promotion remit, but the principles are amenable to application in many other situations.

Increasing the impact of short courses

There are problems with many short courses in ensuring that they are worth while. The impact of a course is a measure of the difference that the course makes to the practice of the participant after they have been on the course, which will usually be demonstrated in improved or changed behaviour in practice. There is little in the literature on the use of reflection in short courses to enhance the impact of courses, though many activities used in short courses do encourage reflection.

It is important not to divorce the description of reflection in the context of a short course from the implications of the work for other contexts. As in previous chapters, the aim of the reflective activity here is to improve the quality of the learning and the practical outcomes of that learning in a practice situation. The main difference between this scenario and others described in chapters on professional development is the brevity of the contact between the facilitator and the learners or participants. The training context may also have a different 'feel' to that of other learning situations.

The background to this case study was a UK-wide project that aimed to improve the ability of non-specialists in health promotion to better promote and educate for health within their own settings (HEA, HEBS, HPW, HPANI, 1995). 'Non-specialists' have opportunities to promote health, but no dedicated training in health promotion. They include nurses, teachers, police, youth workers, community workers, social workers, dentists, medical staff and others, with nurses tending to predominate. Health promotion specialists have traditionally had a considerable role in training these groups using short courses. There was concern at national level, both about the diverse content of the courses and their effectiveness (HPW, 1994).

This situation is not unusual. For many professionals, continuing professional development opportunities are provided by very short courses because managers cannot afford the loss of staff time. This sort of training is not always efficient, with many participants evaluating the training in terms of 'going on the course' or of sitting through the training when the fundamental issue is whether or not they are able to change their practice as a result of the learning. It was evident in this case that participants on health promotion courses would frequently return to their work situations to be confronted with a backlog of the work missed and sometimes a sense from their colleagues that 'well, you've had your time off now'. The time when they have just arrived back from a course with enthusiasm for change and ideas fresh in their minds is critical for the possibility of new practice being implemented. Participants need time to reflect on what they have learnt and how change can occur. Their new ideas need to be actioned, they need support from their managers and colleagues and lower-than-usual workloads rather than backlogs (HEA, et al., 1995; Moon, 1996a).

One way of making short courses in continuing professional development more efficient is to specify the improvement of (identified) practice as a clear expectation to which the content of the course is directly related. In other words, it is not specified only in an aim – a hope that the trainer's input will result in change – but is stated clearly in learning outcomes that are intended to be obtained and are couched in terms of a definite change in work practice. The aim may be helpful as a general indication of course coverage, but the learning outcomes are an essential expression of the learning that must occur as a result of the course.

If the learning outcomes are expressed in terms of change in work practice, this implies that the participants in the training need to be thinking about the implications for their work practice from the start of their training – perhaps before it begins – and the key to this is the use of reflection. The lack of opportunity to reflect on learning as it occurs is probably one of the greatest omissions from training courses (Boud, Keogh and Walker, 1985), if not of learning in many formal situations. To justify the omission by saying that people reflect on the learning after the event is optimistic but unrealistic.

Reflection can be supported in the training process by a direct consideration of how present practice is accommodated to the new learning. In the current example, this means consideration of the manner in which the change in practice is more effective in promoting health in the clients of the participants on the course. In terms of learning, the new learning needs to cause a restructuring of the existing understandings about working in the cognitive structure in order to lead to a change of practice at work.

A change in practice implies a conscious shift in behaviour. One of the theoretical problems that arises when people are required to modify their practice in a short period of time is that it tends to be tacit knowledge (Schön, 1983) and therefore not easily available for expression, let alone modification. That people are required to change something for which they may have no coherent concept might be seen as naive. This is an issue of importance for the development of effective short courses. On a longer course, with a longer period of consideration, participants can learn to frame their current practice in such a way that they can talk about it and then envisage change (Garrett, 1983; Burnard, 1991; HEA, et al. 1995; Moon, 1996a). Candy, Harri-Augstein and Thomas (1985) describe this: 'the learner has access to a behavioural record – a sort of reflected image – on which to base future improvement . . . if people are aware of what they are presently doing, and can be encouraged to reflect on it and to consider alternatives, they are in an excellent position to change and to try out new ways of behaving'.

Simply telling people how to behave differently is too superficial and, unless it makes immediate and deep sense to them, this will not enable them to change their behaviour. On a short course, with no time for the awareness of practice to emerge gradually, there needs to be guidance and support in the appropriate directions. With these issues in mind, I (Moon, 1994 and 1996a) suggest a sequence of guided phases for the facilitation of reflective activities. The first involves the proper assimilation of new learning, the second involves the active integration of that new learning within the participant's past patterns of knowledge and skills (practice) and the third stage involves the anticipation of how work practice will be different in the light of the new learning. Going through these processes will involve, in different parts, reflection on initial learning, reflection in the representation of learning (in the written work – see below) and reflection in the upgrading of learning as the old ideas are brought into a more meaningful order in relation to the new learning. The sequence is expanded and put in terms of questions in Figure 14.1.

The sequence of phases of reflective activities shown in Figure 14.1 is retrospective but also involves the process of anticipation. The suggestion has

---

Phase 1 Develop awareness of the nature of current practice

- What is your current work practice with reference to this subject matter or these skills? (For example, how do you currently promote or educate for health?)

Phase 2 Clarify the new learning and how it relates to current understanding

- What is it that you have learned here/on this course that can improve your practice? (For example, what have you learned that is useful to you for the promotion of health?)

Phase 3 Integrate new learning and current practice

- How does this new learning relate to what you knew and did before? (For example, what are the general implications of the new knowledge/skills for your practice?)

Phase 4 Anticipate or imagine the nature of improved practice

- How will you act in such a way that your practice is improved (as a result of the learning)? (For example, what will you do that represents improvement in your promotion of and education for health – what will you do differently?)

Figure 14.1 *Schema to guide reflective activity in professional development towards improvement of professional practice*

been made previously that anticipation has components of reflection-on-practice and the understanding of previous habits of practice together with imagination of the change of practice in the future. In this sequence, the understanding of previous practice is integrated with the new learning in order to allow imagination of future practice. A large part of this guided process does involve reflective activities. The fact that much practice is tacit makes the process more difficult to achieve quickly, and this argues for particularly clear and considered guidance being applied to reflective processes. This, in turn, suggests that the activities that carry the reflection will need to be properly integrated into the course to maximize their effect.

On a longer course, the sequence of the stages of reflective activities might operate for each new block of learning as well as forming a thread throughout the course, so their expression in each block might not need to be so explicit. However, it is important for participants to be aware of this thread of reflective activity in order to understand its purpose and how it relates to the anticipated outcomes of improved practice (Moon, 1996a). Particularly on a longer course, a workbook or learning journal is a useful vehicle for the process of reflecting (see Chapter 15).

Many short courses last just one day and this may appear to preclude the use of a workbook to underpin the stages of reflection. One way round this is to split the one day into two half-day sessions. The gap between the two halves can then be considered to be part of the course and, under guidance, participants can be required to observe and reflect on their current and improving practice in a workbook. The second session is then valuable as an opportunity for evaluation and consolidation as well as further learning. When the process of reflection underpins the learning on a course, splitting any course into several sessions extends the period of potential learning to include the span between the sessions.

If there is no possibility of splitting a short course into sessions, under comprehensive guidance, the participants can be required to engage in some reflective activity in advance of the course. An example of such an activity might be that they reflect on the nature of their current practice with reference to the subject matter of the anticipated course. The requirement for structured reflection before a course can provide an advance organizer so that new learning can be linked to concepts already in mind (Ausubel and Robinson, 1969). The use of reflective pre-course work is illustrated in the second part of this chapter (and in Moon and England, 1994).

A further possibility for increasing the impact of a day course is to require, as a condition of 'passing' the course, that some form of assignment be completed in the workplace after the course itself. There are difficulties here in ensuring that the work is done, and the value of it can be lessened by the lack of opportunity for discussion or reflection.

The sequence of stages for reflective activity (see Figure 14.1) was applied in the development of two health promotion programmes, one used now across Scotland (HEBS, 1997). These courses involve around a full week of attendance – usually in several sessions – and a number of months during which participants continue to reflect on and monitor their practice and complete a written assignment. The assignment is designed to encompass the understanding of current practice and the assimilation of new learning towards change in practice. This process is supported by reading or the gathering of further information.

As has been indicated in previous chapters on reflective practice in teacher and nurse education, there is a need for those who run courses to at least understand the processes of reflection if not to be role models in this respect for their students. Those who run short courses need to be properly equipped and, towards that end, a course in training trainers to run courses, such as those described above, is developed alongside both of the courses.

Another such course was also developed and piloted by myself as part of a Master's degree programme (in Health Promotion) at the University of Central England in 1994 (Moon, 1994). In order to develop trainers who could understand and run health promotion courses with an underpinning of reflection, reflective activity explicitly underpinned the training for trainers course. Reflection was specifically built into the course in two ways, the first of which was by means of ongoing workbook activities. Participants used a loose-leaf format to write in response to guidance questions and statements given before the course or in note form on the events of the day. There was encouragement for more private reflection, but while it was a course requirement that the workbooks should be reviewed by staff, the private sections could be removed. An example of the guidance was 'How does [what you have learned today] tie up so far with your previous knowledge of training?' This was presented as a class activity to be written in note form, to be produced in more detail later.

Reflective activity was built into the course in a second way within the class. Students were given time in dedicated sessions after topics had been covered to reflect on the topic and its implication for them. Again, the material was put into the workbooks either at the time or later.

The evaluation of the course for trainers indicated that the students appreciated the reflective content, particularly because this contrasted with the rest of their postgraduate course, which was not reflective. An observation the trainers made was that when time was pressing, it was very easy for them to allow the sessions on reflection to be squeezed out. The manner in which reflective activity is squeezed out is of significance in many other situations of formal education. Time allocated to thinking or reflection is easily lost when there is active teaching competing with it.

The use of reflection in group decision making

Enabling meetings to come to decisions in a quick and efficient manner is an art, but it requires effort and forethought. The case study on which the following discussion is based was a meeting that brought together 12 participants from all over the UK for a period of two days. It was necessary that a clear set of decisions should emerge from the meeting. As above, the subject matter was the training of specialists in educating for and promoting health, but, in this case, the aim of the meeting was to review the forms of training that were being used locally by health promotion units to train non-specialist health promoters. Many units were known to be running what were termed 'foundation courses in health promotion', but the spread of these, their form, length and quality were variable.

The aims of the meeting were to come to an understanding of the type of health promotion training that is useful for non-specialist health promoters and reach a conclusion on a means of improving the training situation. A contentious possibility for the latter was the development of a nationally based curriculum for foundation courses. The subject matter was therefore ill-structured and messy and there were sensitive political issues in the relationship between the national and local health promotion agencies. Some of the participants were already running local training initiatives. The meeting demanded well-considered reflection leading to a conclusion. The time period for reaching conclusions was short and money and reputation were staked on the effectiveness of the process, particularly as disquiet had been publicly expressed about the ineffectiveness of previous meetings of this type. It was far from an unusual situation in professional or business life. In essence, it mirrored situations described as tasks of reflective judgement by King and Kitchener (1994), and to reach effective conclusions, at least some of the participants needed to be enabled to function at high levels of reflective judgement.

The previous experience suggested that simply asking a group of articulate and highly professional individuals to come together in a pleasant setting was not going to produce the result that was required. An observation made of previous meetings was that:

> there is often conscientious planning of how information is to be gathered from participants (e.g., brainstorming, small group work, etc.), however, less time is given to the planning of the more difficult process of achieving consensus and making a clear conclusion. This may result in a series of half-considered statements. At the worst, workshop reports are derived from unprocessed flipchart jottings (and at the very worst these jottings are written up by someone who has not even attended the workshop).

> (Moon and England, 1994)

In this context, mediocre and contentless conclusions may result with the better quality or more creative thinking being disregarded.

Some of these problems in reaching conclusions seemed to arise from a myth perhaps – particularly among this group of health professionals – that putting people into a highly structured work situation in a meeting or workshop is dictatorial. The planning of the workshop was done on the premise that it is possible to ask people to work in a structured setting that is designed to reach a conclusion, while retaining a friendly atmosphere that is conducive to reaching the appropriate end result.

While most of the workshop was designed to be interactive, there were two issues on which it was considered that further input would be useful for participants – university accreditation and competences and NVQs. Expert speakers were selected and asked to be concise and provide a one-sided sheet of information as a handout. The other planning of the workshop structure was very precisely controlled by the aim and a series of eight objectives that were derived from the aim. The objectives were designed to provide a structure to the workshop by virtue of the sequence of decisions that they anticipated. The aim and objectives and the structure of the workshop were communicated to all participants in advance. Most of the objectives signalled the requirement that decisions needed to be reached on the basis of group reflection. The last of the objectives concerned the intention to conduct a thorough evaluation of the whole process. Alongside the objectives were statements of expected outcomes. There was also, built into the initial session, the opportunity for participants to specify personal objectives – an expression of what they themselves wanted to get out of the time in the meeting.

The evaluation of the workshop indicated that the most successful element of it in contributing to the outcome was the use of 'pre-work'. The idea of pre-work was obtained from discussions with professionals from a management training unit where efficiency in decision-making is driven more overtly by financial pressures. Pre-work is a reflective task sent out in advance to participants, which may need to be completed and sent back before the event or brought to the event. In this case, it needed to be returned before the event and the contents of the material returned was used in the first sessions of the workshop. The pre-work consisted of four questions. The advice had been that there should be no more than five questions and, on a matter of change such as this, they should follow this pattern:

- one should refer to the current state of the subject of change;
- one or more should refer to the anticipated ideal;
- one or more should refer to hindrances to the passage from the present state to the attainment of the ideal state.

In many ways, these questions are reminiscent of the structure of reflection set out in Figure 14.1 earlier in the chapter, in similar ways calling on the different roles of reflection in learning. Three questions followed those lines exactly and one asked for a definition of a foundation course (the subject of one of the objectives). The content of the responses to the pre-work questions was directly related to the working session (see below). The responses proved valuable in reducing the vital, but messy, phases of brainstorming because ideas had been produced by participants in peace, at home, and were the more fruitful for this. They initiated an easy flow of further ideas and reflection in the small groups.

While the value of the pre-work may have resided largely in the quality of the reflection that it encouraged by being done in advance, another function that it may have performed is similar to that of advance organizers (Ausubel and Robinson, 1969). In these, a 'sketch' of material relevant to a task is provided in advance of the task and serves to bring to mind what is already known, but also provides a means of structuring the understanding of new material learnt subsequently.

The structure of the meeting consisted of an introductory and 'warm-up' session, the two speaker sessions and a concluding session with four small group working sessions in between these. Each working session focused on one or more of the objectives, associated outcomes and the material from the associated pre-work. The notion of consensus was explicitly introduced to support the reflective discussion towards reaching a conclusion. A definition of the word 'consensus' was provided in the material that was sent out in advance:

A condition of affairs where communications have been sufficiently open and the group has been sufficiently supportive to make everyone in the group feel that he has had his fair chance to influence the decision . . . . If there is a clear [position or statement] that most people subscribe to and if those who oppose it feel they have had their chance to influence the decision, then a consensus exits.

(Schein, 1988)

The results of the working group discussions were to be presented on a flipchart sheet in their final form. This was stressed because of the poor legibility of material that often appears on flipcharts in these situations because it has been scribbled at the last moment.

The last (plenary) session was a review and evaluation of the whole workshop, both verbally and on paper, and a separate consideration of the attainment of personal objectives. A second evaluation was conducted by mail a month after the workshop. This elicited particularly useful and reflective evaluation.

The material on the flipcharts was written up in a short report by an 'outside' report writer who had attended the sessions as an observer. The structure of the report was pre-arranged and it was produced within four days of the meeting so that the participants could receive it in draft form very soon after the event. Corrections and modifications were made by them and a final report was issued within a month of the event to around 200 interested parties across the UK.

Most of the processes of the workshop consisted of reflections on the practices and knowledge of the participants. There were relatively few 'facts' with which to work, and many uncertainties in terms of sensitivities. Most of the working sessions of the workshop were based jointly on the processes of the guiding and focusing of reflection towards responses to predetermined questions that, in turn, provided the information needed for the national training initiative that followed. In contrast to the myth mentioned above, the participants did not resent the structures that were imposed in order to reach the desired end and, according to all of the evaluations, they found the progress made and outcome satisfying and enjoyable. The opportunity to consider and work on their own objectives was appreciated.

Chapter 15

Learning through reflection – the use of learning journals

Introduction

Probably all of us reflect. For those who do, being reflective can be an orientation to their everyday lives. For others, reflection comes about when the conditions in the learning environment are appropriate – when there is an incentive or some guidance (the conditions that favour reflection have been discussed in Chapter 13). This chapter, together with the next, focuses on the practical activities that will provide a context in which reflection can be encouraged. The activities are mostly no more than situations in which various conditions that favour reflection are accentuated or harnessed in a formalized manner, as they are, for example, in a learning journal. The activities are grouped for convenience according to these 'accentuated conditions'– though there will be much overlap.

Because the use of journals as a vehicle for reflection in educational situations is becoming common, and because the literature on writing journals is relatively abundant, the use of journals to enhance learning and practice warrants this subject being covered in a chapter on its own. There is a form of journal called a 'dialogue' journal and because this differs, in that it involves written conversation between two or more people, reference is made to it in the next chapter.

Writing in a journal as a means to reflection

There are various words used in the literature in a synonymous manner to 'journal', such as log, diary, dialectical notebook, workbook and autobiographical and reflective writing. Sometimes it is called a profile and a 'progress file' (NCIHE, 1997). Precisely defining words seems to be fairly unhelpful here so by 'journal' is meant predominately written material that is based on reflection and is relatively free writing, though it may be written within a given structure. A journal is written regularly over a period of time rather than in a single session. Within this generalized form there are many variations, and this chapter is an attempt to capture the essence of the activity in its relation to reflection in order that it can be applied elsewhere. It 'imposes form on experience' (Grumet, 1989).

Journal writing in education and professional development is not restricted to the disciplines for which writing is the main representation of learning (Young and Fulwiler, 1986; Fulwiler, 1987). Some of the more unusual descriptions of how journals are used come from the quantitative disciplines, such as engineering (Gibbs, 1988), maths (Selfe, Petersen and Nahrgang, 1986; Korthagen, 1988), physics (Grumbacher, 1987; Jensen, 1987). Journals are used in English and the humanities (Belanoff, 1987), philosophy (Kent, 1987), professional education and development – for example, Wolf (1980), James (1992, 1993), Knowles (1993), Johns (1994), Hoover (1994), Hatton and Smith (1995), HEBS (1997) and Handley (1998). Walker (1985) describes the use of journals in religious contexts, and Christensen (1981) and Redwine (1989) describe journal use in general adult education.

In terms of the manner in which reflection functions in relation to learning in journal writing, the reflection is primarily in a represented form on paper, though it may be electronic or spoken into an audio-recorder, and the learning comes from the process of representing and reading back. Journal writing also provides a means by which learning can be upgraded – where unconnected areas of meaning cohere and a deeper meaning emerges. These processes can be directed towards a wide range of outcomes or purposes in improvement of the learning itself practice.

Like so much of the literature on reflection in education, assessment of the value of the reflective process is difficult. Even more than in most literature on reflection, the accounts of journal writing tend to be written by enthusiasts, often journal writers themselves, and it is likely that few who do not feel at ease with reflective writing would encourage others to try it. There are a few evaluative studies (see later), but while hard evidence is hard to quantify, many reports convey enthusiasm and expression of value in learners (Selfe, Petersen and Nahrgang, 1986; Morrison, 1996, for example).

The nature of the outcome of journal writing will depend on the prior structuring of the whole exercise, but then the same structure may be used to fulfil a number of different aims, hence the notion of a unified outcome is problematical. For example, for Rainer (1978), one of the main writers on journal writing, a journal is a means of learning to free with oneself. Cooper (1991) sees it as attending to one's immediate needs, providing a sense of nurturing. For Progoff (1975), it is finding one's voice. It can be therapeutic – Holly (1991) says 'Just writing makes me feel better', or it is seen as a method of fostering creativity (Christensen, 1981). For Berthoff (1987), it is the 'language of speculation' and a form of 'learning how to think', of keeping things 'tentative' and a means 'to forestall closure'.

Holly (1989) refers to the meta-cognitive effect of journal writing in the way that it 'facilitates consciousness of consciousness which enables critical self-enquiry'. Such reflection might require a particular form of guidance and structure to ensure that both of the stages of initial observation and later reflection on reflection can occur. Wolf (1980) stresses the initial stage of this as the 'snaring [of] moments of experience for later analysis'. It tends to be the potential for self-criticism of journal writing and the development of understanding of the personal construction of knowledge that are rationales for the use of journal writing in professional contexts (Bruner, 1990). For example, Calderhead and James (1992) describe their use of 'recording and profiling' as a means of enabling student teachers to conceptualize the nature of their own professional development, understanding their prior educational experiences in relation to their current re-evaluation of these experiences.

The purposes of writing journals

In terms of journals in formal education, Stephani (1997) suggests that this method is more suitable for courses where there are 'smaller numbers of mature learners who have a clearer sense of their own goals' than for the traditional higher education situation where traditional patterns of expectation of teaching, learning and assessment may cause difficulties. These are, however, only the same problems that occur for any unusual self-managed form of learning in higher education, and some of these rigid expectations need to be overcome in any degree studies in the development towards being functional employees in the future.

There are many purposes for which writing journals is cited, or more often implied, in the literature as being helpful. Some of the purposes relate to personally initiated writing, and some to formal educational situations. In the latter cases, in particular, a clear statement of purpose for the learners can be important for the success of the activity. Most initiators of journal writing would identify several of the purposes below as being achievable by writing a journal. The following is a description of various purposes that journal writing could serve.

To record experience

The primary purpose of journal writing may be to record experience, with the emphasis initially being put on the recording (Wolfe, 1980) rather than the reflective activity, although this may come later. Recording experiences may entail long- or short-term recording. For example, it may last for the duration of a piece of research, recording the decision making and thinking that precedes it, as well as the events of the research (Holly, 1989; Stephani, 1997). The record of achievement or the development of a progress file (NCIHE, 1997) is an example of a longer-term record that may rely largely on the recording of events rather than reflective material. The development of professional portfolios to enable promotion or assessment on the job usually entails some reflective overview written at the time or later (James, 1993).

To develop learning in ways that enhances other learning

This represents a group of purposes generally specified in formal learning situations. Writing a journal can, for example, encourage the valuing of personal observation and knowledge.

To deepen the quality of learning, in the form of critical thinking or developing a questioning attitude

Mortimer (1998) describes the use of portfolio development with reflective commentary as a means of increasing critical ability and encouraging the adoption of a deep approach to . . . learning' in a group of undergraduates in their first year. Her evaluation study suggested that, for many students, this was successful and enhanced their motivation to learn. In another of the few evaluated studies of the use of journals, Selfe, Petersen and Nahrgang (1986) demonstrated that the purpose of enhancement of thinking and learning was fulfilled as the journal writing helped mathematics students to understand concepts that they had learned in class. In a physics class, Jensen (1987) describes a journal structure in which freshmen were asked to explain physics concepts as if to a sympathetic listener in order to improve their physics learning. However, for Berthoff (1987), the technique that is crucial for developing critical approaches to learning is the initial noting of detail – the 'look' – and the 'look again' – returning to the material to reflect on it in a double-entry journal (see later).

To enable the learner to understand their own learning process

The examples of the use of journals that conform to this purpose tend to be from situations where a group of individuals is being taught to teach or train another group of learners. Morrison (1996) suggests that a journal helps students to 'self-direct and gain control of their own cognitive processes . . . e.g., using preferred learning styles in organizing tasks'. Handley (1998) uses a journal to enable IT trainers to understand the limitations of their own learning styles, which are presumed to affect their teaching style. In this way, they can be better facilitators of the learning of others.

To facilitate learning from experience

Journal writing is about learning from experience of events, but some writers have been clearer in their specification of this purpose. For example, Wolf (1980) designed a journal so that the sequence of recording takes account of the cycle of experiential learning, with the initial recording of an event, then reflection, an account of the subjective inner experience and further reflection and generalization. On a broader basis, journals that accompany field work or work experience provide a method of developing the meaning of experiences so that the learner can relate their unique experience to established theory or develop their own theory.

Walker (1985) describes the use of a portfolio to support the learning on a course for those who would be leaders of religious communities. All of the teaching staff encouraged the use of the portfolio, the aim of which was to record their learning experiences and, in the process, reflect on their implications for personal development.

To increase active involvement in learning and personal ownership of learning

Writing a journal involves working with meanings and 'It thrusts the student into an active role in the classroom' (Jensen, 1987).

To increase the ability to reflect and improve the quality of learning

For most writers, reflection is a means of supporting other learning. Chapter 12 suggested that it is fundamental to good-quality (deep) learning and Stephani (1997) justifies the use of journals on the basis that they deepen learning.

To enhance problem-solving skills

There are examples of the use of journals to support students in engineering, physics and mathematics and, in several of these, students are asked to record their processes of problem solving. The explicit description of a process while writing a journal appears to transfer to later problem-solving situations or to aid them in giving explanations to others (Jensen, 1987; Grumbacher, 1987; Korthagan, 1988).

As a means of assessment in formal education

Journals may be used as a form of assessment. Their use will be enhanced in terms of learning if the appropriate assessment criteria can be identified in advance between the staff and the learners. Redwine (1989) describes the use of an autobiographical journal to accompany a submission for the assessment of prior experiential learning, which gives returning (to learning) adult students exemption from parts of a programme of learning. As was noted in Chapter 13, prior knowledge that material will be scrutinized can affect the writing of journals or any other reflective writing.

To enhance professional practice or the professional self in practice

A common purpose for journal writing is to encourage the development of what is called reflective practice, although, as earlier chapters have indicated, reflective practice has many identities. This use is often in the professional development context, but, increasingly, there is a more generalized application of the term. The central issue in improving practice might seem to be the translation of the products of reflection into the real world of action so that they affect practice and something is done differently. Some journal structures seem to aim towards this objective more clearly than others – requiring the learners to think about what they will do that is actually different (Moon, 1996a; HEBS, 1997). The issue of the transfer of ideas into practice is a problematical one where initial education is concerned as a journal can only facilitate appropriate attitudes towards practice and perhaps encourage the habits of reflection.

In the context of professional development, there are examples of e-mail journal writing as a means of communication between students on teaching practice when they are at a distance from their tutors.

To explore the self, personal constructs of meaning and understand one's view of the world

The reflexive nature of journal writing means that exploration of the self and personal constructs that influence how one views the world is implicit in most effective journal writing (Christensen, 1981; Walker, 1985; Grumet, 1989; Morrison, 1996). Progoff's structured journal (1975) is, perhaps, the most comprehensive tool for exploration of the self, but it is particularly important in the professional contexts where the implications of the individuals' construing of their prior experience can distort their perceptions of new experience (Holly, 1989, and 1991; Calderhead and James, 1992; Knowles, 1993).

To enhance the personal valuing of the self towards self-empowerment

Hallberg (1987) suggests that the use of journals (such as that of Progoff) 'is far more powerful and far-reaching in its effects than is generally recognized. [It is] . . . working to change that student's enduring attitudes, values and sense of personal identity'. He considers that there should be greater acceptance of the effect of journal writing in enhancing this 'person making' process. Cooper (1991) talks of journals as 'a way to tell our own story, a way to learn who we have been, who we are and who we are becoming. We literally become teachers and researchers in our own lives, empowering ourselves in the process'. In a professional context, empowerment is seen as the 'integration of . . . own needs, values and desires with the often conflicting views of society' or the workplace (Cooper, 1987). Morrison (1996) uses questions inspired by the work of Prawat (1991) to prompt teaching students to address questions concerning 'self and settings'.

For therapeutic purposes or as means of supporting behaviour change

The origins of Progoff's developments were in psychotherapy where he asked patients to keep a notebook of the 'events of their inner life' prompted by the therapy sessions. He describes this procedure as having 'a very favourable effect therapeutically', and he extended it by 'drawing forward the inner processes' by means of questions and discussion (Progoff, 1975). Used in another way, a journal can be an 'emotional dumping ground', a location for writing through unpleasant feelings, letters that are not designed to be sent, clarifying conflicts and working out guilt (Cooper, 1991). Journals can also be used to identify behaviours that might be irritating or ineffective in particular circumstances, such as a propensity to have a negative attitude. Notes can be made of when and under what circumstances the behaviour occurs, bringing it to consciousness so that change is made possible. This use of journals has value in situations of training or teacher education when habits can interfere with learning to practice.

As a means of slowing down learning, taking more thorough account of a situation or situations

Several writers talk of using journal writing to change the pace of learning (Jensen, 1987, for example) or to take time in order to become more sensitive observers (Holly, 1991). Christensen (1981) considers that journal writing is a means of safeguarding learners from the push towards expectations of greater volumes of learning to be achieved more and more quickly.

To enhance creativity by making better use of intuitive understanding

By slowing and taking better account of the 'inner movement of our lives', Christensen (1981) suggests that intuitive elements of the self can 'break through' and give rise to creative insight.

To free-up writing and the representation of learning

Jensen (1987) found that one of the effects of journal writing for physics students was that they came to write essays more fluently. With a focus on improving writing in English classes, D'Arcy (1987) describes how 'I also came more and more to encourage my students to use journal writing as a kind of running commentary on the other work – a way of thinking onto paper'. However, in journal writing, 'fluency can . . . become gush' – Berthoff (1987) points out the importance of maintaining fluency within the bounds of a structure that makes it productive.

To provide an alternative 'voice' for those not good at expressing themselves

There are different ways of learning and expressing that learning. Some have much to express, but are either not in suitable social or emotional situations for that expression. Journal writing is an alternative form of expression.

To foster reflective and creative interaction in a group

Many talk about the use of interaction as a means of facilitating journal writing for individuals, but one of the purposes for which Walker (1985) used journals with his students was to generate material in individuals that would contribute towards reflective and creative discussion in groups.

The outcomes of journal writing

There are a few experimental studies that have attempted to evaluate journal writing. Perhaps the precision required to enable the collection of meaningful results is counteractive to the reflective writing of a journal (Selfe, Petersen and Nahrgang, 1986). Adding to the difficulties of measurement are the different purposes journal writing is used for and the different ways in which students might learn or benefit from the exercise, some of which may not be demonstrable in the short term (Jensen, 1987). In general, students involved in experimental studies usually find journal writing useful, though they have difficulties to start with (Morrison, 1996). Even in single studies, different students benefited from, or liked, writing in journals for different reasons (Selfe, *et al.*, 1986).

Two of the most useful experimental studies of journal writing were concerned with the quality of the actual writing of the learners and not so much its generalized benefits. Wedman and Martin (1986) used Van Manen's concepts of levels of reflection (see Chapter 6) as a theoretical framework for assessing reflectivity. In the student teacher group with which they worked they found that their students were able to reflect, although some were fairly inadequate at it. There also appeared to be a progression.

Hatton and Smith (1995) also considered that students learn to reflect. They developed criteria that enable categorization of different types of reflective writing. The development of such a schema allows the results of methods to increase reflectivity to be measured. They found that some of the students in their study were producing writing that could not be categorized as being reflective.

The forms of journal writing

Journals come in a range of shapes and forms and many consist of several different types of writing, some being more personal and others more structured. The provision of structures in journal writing seems to have several purposes. Structure can help learners starting reflective writing. It can ensure that they reflect on the appropriate issues and help them 'move on' in their thinking and learn from the reflective processes. In this connection, it is worth noting the distinctions between those forms of writing that are 'one-off' recording and those to which the writer returns for further reflection. The differences between structured and unstructured forms of journals is somewhat arbitrary.

Unstructured forms

Free writing and reflecting
This form is usually chronological, though may not involve writing every day.

Recording relating to an ongoing event or issue
There is some element of record-keeping here.

Double-entry journals
The initial recording of the experience is made on one part of the journal, for example on one side of a page and this may be factual. At a later time, the writer reflects further on the written account of the experience and writes their thought on the other side. The writing in this second session may be designed to reach conclusions about action.

Structured forms

Autobiographical writing

There is an autobiographical element to journal writing. It may not be chrono-logical and may be related in some way to the current time, such as relating a previous experience that is similar to one in the present (as in Progoff, 1975). Autobiographical writing may accompany a portfolio, making sense of the materials in terms of personal development.

Structure is given in the form of exercises

The exercises may be the same at each writing session or different (examples of exercises are given later in this chapter).

Structure is given in the form of questions to answer or guidance about issues to be covered

The questions might ensure that the appropriate areas of material are covered.

The journal is used to accompany other learning and the structure is determined by that learning

The intention is that the writer thinks again about the initial experience and draws conclusions from the second 'look'. A journal might accompany work on a dissertation or a research project. Recording the reflective processes that occur during the selection of a topic on which to work can be helpful.

Structure is provided within the journal itself and the writer chooses where to write

Progoff's 'intensive journal' is an example of this structure. The writer moves about within the sections of the journal according to the content of their writing or what they want to work on. There are many sections with associated methods of working. Dream, fantasy and image, current and past experiences, and summaries of life periods are among the areas of functioning that are covered in this way (Progoff, 1975; Hallberg, 1987; Lukinsky, 1990).

Profiles or portfolios

There is another group of 'life accounts' that are not usually called 'journals', but can have the same effect. Portfolios tend to include other documents alongside reflective writing that summarize and interrelate the content. The content may be other than written accounts, such as graphic material, stories or poetry.

Practical issues in journal writing – some considerations

Again, the practical issues covered here tend to be viewed in the context of the classroom or formal education setting. There are a number of decisions to make that are likely to influence the quality of the learning that results from the process, and the motivation with which learners engage in writing. Different purposes to which writing journals are put have been demonstrated. Writing in a journal is alien for many learners, and it will help to 'sell' the idea if the purpose behind it and the anticipated learning that should result is clearly articulated.

The purpose for which a journal is to be written is likely to determine its design and structure. There may be writing tasks that are given regularly or periodically, such as reflection on teaching practice each week or on events or books read, and there may be the encouragement for free personal reflection as well. A loose-leaf arrangement will encompass all possibilities and can enable a learner to sequence the material in an order that is appropriate for them. Personalizing a journal provides a sense of ownership of it and dissociates it from more formal learning materials. It will help learners to identify this task as one that requires a different orientation to that more usually adopted in learning situations (Francis, 1995).

A statement of the purpose will also suggest criteria on which any assessment will be based. Several different methods for grading or marking this sort of material are illustrated in the literature. The journal itself may be assessed or a question set where the response requires learners to use the material of their journals (Morrison, 1996). Where the journal itself is assessed, a competence-based assessment – 'competent', on the basis of known criteria, or 'not yet competent' – may be more appropriate than grading. A variation on this is to guarantee a basic mark for an adequate journal and to give additional marks for evidence of particular qualities of reflection or learning (Kent, 1986).

Most journal designs allow the possibility of some free or personal writing. If the journal is to be assessed, there is the issue of the privacy of the free writing to be considered. Material will be written differently if it is to be seen – and the learning from it will be different – than if it is purely private. Loose-leaf arrangements mean that private reflections can be removed before a journal is assessed or, alternatively, private pages can be stapled.

Privacy in the form of confidentiality of material is an issue if learners are encouraged to work with peers on reflecting or to share the products of it. It is widely accepted in the literature that there is much to be gained by learners if they work with others or in groups. 'Critical friends' (Hoover, 1994; Francis, 1995) or co-counselling arrangements can maintain the learning process from a journal, and can prevent the learner from avoiding material or 'going around in circles (see Chapter 14). The availability of emotional support can help those who find themselves in areas of emotional discomfort. Systems of peer support may suffice. Francis suggests that structured writing is less likely to generate such discomfort, but, equally, does not necessarily provide the psychological space in which emotional matters can be worked through.

Another consideration that may emerge from the nature of the journal is how often or how much writing should be done and this may be guided by assessment criteria. Extensive 'rambling' may be both a problem for marking and an excuse of avoiding meaning and learning. On the other hand, very brief writing may not go beyond description of events. Allied to the matter of how much to write is the location for the writing. Reflective writing takes time and adding it to normal study time after class may be unfair on learners (Thorpe, 1993), but then class situations may not be conducive to reflection. One approach to this is to ask learners to jot down notes and ideas in class to be pursued later.

In terms of the learning to be achieved from journal writing, it is important to build into the process some situations in which learners are required to re-read their material. Discussions or assignments on matters that have been recorded can encourage this process, though Walker (1985) suggests that a re-reading of the whole out of the context of assessment enables the learner to get a sense of the development that has taken place.

Getting started

The fact that not everyone finds reflection or reflective writing easy has been pointed out a number of times and the implication of this is that journal writing needs to be introduced carefully. Knowles (1993) describes the ways in which he gently encourages teaching students to write their personal history accounts. He talks of the development of 'open, safe and respectful learning environments' and the acceptance of personal experience as having value for learning to teach. He shares his own experiences and talks about the task with the learners, allowing them to 'complete the assignment in almost any way that promotes the growth of individuals' professional knowledge and skills and their satisfaction with the completed account and process'. Francis (1985) and Walker (1985) describe how they use a series of exercises in reflective writing to introduce the idea before they talk about the journal itself.

A particularly helpful idea for the introduction of journal use that is reported by Gibbs (1988) from Garry and Cowan (1986) is that students who have participated in the experience of journal writing one year should write guidance notes for the students who will be doing so in the following year. The notes produced by a group of engineering students include the following suggestions for starting to write:

- start with 'what is on top' at that time or by writing down an anecdote;
- or start by thinking about the quality of ideas and experiences – for example, the strengths or weaknesses of them;

- or start with the previous entry or, where appropriate, previous comments of the tutor.

The students say that it is helpful to consider who the writing is intended for and keep exploring and probing to get at the deep meanings with efforts being made to work towards truths uncovered in experience. The writing is a process of seeking advice from the self for imminent action and of seeking the next questions that require responses.

Working in the context of the professional training of trainers with an educationally mixed group of adults, Handley (1998) initiates the use of a learning journal by discussing learning styles. Participants pair off and each describes to the other a significant learning experience and, from the manner of the description, they decide their preferred manner of learning. They use a learning styles questionnaire (Honey and Mumford, 1986) to determine learning style, then discuss their styles and the implications of them for their teaching and learning. In their role of trainers (and this would apply to any educators), they need to recognize that their manner of teaching is likely to be derived from the manner of their own learning. The writing of a journal is initiated in a detailed recording of a significant learning event of the day that is described as it happened. The learners then read it over, reflecting on it and its implications for learning and action. The writing is discussed in a short, small group session the next morning. This exercise is completed on the first day of a course that lasts several weeks. Also, on each of the subsequent four residential days, an incident in the day is written up in the same way. On the last evening, they summarize their reflections of the whole week, looking at the implications of this for their workplace practice. There are assignments to be completed over the whole of the six-month course (with two other residential components) and the learning journal is used as a reflective tool to accompany other elements of the assignment. While the material of the first week of the journal is not assessed, the other journal sections accompany the assignments as part of the assessed work. Judgement is on a competency basis.

Exercises for use in journals

The exercises and activities described below are particularly suited to forming part of the structure of journal writing, though they can be used independently, as can those in the next chapter. They may used as 'one-off' exercises in the process of journal writing or as a regular element of its structure. The purpose of the exercises can usefully be seen as means by which the process of reflecting is facilitated, sometimes deepened or directed, rather like loosening the soil (Progoff, 1975). The best sources of exercises and activities for journal writing are in Rainer (1978) and Progoff, though the latter is a somewhat inaccessible book, designed to be read alongside attendance at a workshop on using the journal.

Writing from different angles

Writing in the present tense can increase the intensity of a described event, which may mean that more understanding is derived from the experience. An altered point of view of the self may be gained by writing about the self in the third person or as if it was at a different stage of life (older and younger).

Metaphor

Finding a metaphor for a person or an experience can enable the subject matter to be explored in a new way. Metaphor has, for example, been used as a means of exploring the concepts of teaching and learning by students in teacher education (Francis, 1995).

Unsent letters

Cooper (1991) suggests writing 'unsent letters' as a journal exercise. The writer chooses a person they keep in mind on the occasion of writing and writes them a letter 'honestly and deeply', but keeps the letter in the journal, using it to communicate with themselves rather than the other. The content of the letter may be emotional or could be directed to a prominent theoretician in the learner's discipline, with the content being academic reflection.

Reflection on a book or reading assignment

Learners may reflect on a book or media presentation that has some relevance to the writer's life or studies. Kent (1987) describes her use of this exercise with philosophy students and D'Arcy (1987) describes the use of journal writing 'as a kind of running commentary' on the reading and writing tasks of her students. She comments that the freedom of the journal writing 'enabled the students' own voices to be heard in their writing'. An example is given of the thoughts of a 14-year-old student on the opening of Shakespeare's Romeo and Juliet.

A critical friend

A critical friend might read the journal entry and make comments deliberately to promote deepening of the reflection (see Chapter 13).

Responding to questions

The questions might be set in advance by a teacher or could be posed in a peer support situation. A group might take turns in setting questions for themselves. Examples of frameworks of questions are given in earlier chapters (see Chapter 6). Morrison (1996) suggests a useful framework of questions for the personal, professional, academic and evaluative areas of development.

Describing the process of solving of problems

Korthagan (1988) and Selfe, Petersen and Nahrgang (1987) ask their mathematics students to describe the processes of solving a mathematical problem.

Focusing on a past experience that has relevance for current learning

The experience might be a period of learning, schooling, being nursed and so on. Writing this material in the present tense will make it easier to examine attitudes prevailing at the time and to relate them to understandings in the present.

Lists

Rainer (1978) suggests that a list can generate an unexpected topic for reflection or enable learners to focus on a particular topic prior to writing. A list might be written on 'things I am good at' or 'things I would like to change in the way I . . .' (think, act and so on), for example.

Stepping stones

Stepping stones is an exercise modified from Progoff (1975) and is a very effective way of loosening memory. Doing the exercise usually has the effect of generating surprise in the writer as to the range of memories they have on a particular topic or person or issue in their life.

The writer starts with a topic in mind – education, learning experiences, a person, a religious belief – anything. In chronological order, they list their first memory of that topic in terms of a word or short phrase, then a second, a third and so on coming towards the present time, maintaining the order and not reaching more than eight to ten items. By the time the most recent event has been written, other examples that occur chronologically earlier in the sequence will have arisen in the mind and a new sequence from earliest to the present (eight to ten) can be written to include them and so on. Some of the memories may be obvious candidates for more detailed reflection.

If this exercise is run in a group situation where everyone is working on lists of the same topic, a round of sharing one or two memories each is likely to spark off more memories and therefore more sequences to be written.

The stepping stones exercise is a valuable means of finding significant but maybe unexpected material on which to reflect further. It is interesting, too, that the stepping stones listed for a particular topic on one day will differ considerably from the list generated on another day and that in itself is worth exploring.

Period reflections

This is also an exercise modified from Progoff (1975). Looking back over a year or two, most people can discern that their lives can be divided into periods of time, with each period of time having a theme. The theme may be expressed as an idea, a title or even an image. Once the identity of the theme has been made, the period of time may be the subject of review and Progoff suggests that the 'feeling' about the period is collected in an image for the period.

Dialogues with people

Both Rainer and Progoff describe the use of imaginary dialogues with other people. The 'other' is likely to be significant person in the writer's life in the present or past, but not necessarily someone they know personally. The person may, for example, be a mentor, 'wisdom figure', spiritual leader or a dead or absent parent.

Progoff suggests that the writer 'gets in touch' with the other by means of several techniques, such as a stepping stones exercise (see above) in which the stepping stones of the writer's knowledge or acquaintance with the other are written before the dialogue is begun.

Dialogues with events and projects

A very useful series of sections in Progoff's book (1975) deal with dialogues with different elements of a person's life. One that is particularly significant in an educational situation is a dialogue with work, where the imaginary dialogue with work with which the writer is engaged is written out. In the formal learning situation, this might be a project or essay or, on a larger scale, a career and so on. The dialogue addresses the 'work' as if it is a person, and there is likely to be a specific topic that is the subject of the dialogue. The writing of an essay, for example, might seem to be 'blocked' or a career not progressing and so on.

Progoff suggests that all of the dialogues are set up in a similar manner to the dialogues with people, using the stepping stones technique to engage with the subject. Other areas for dialogue work are society, the body, events, situations and circumstances.

Working with dreams and imagery

Working in a journal with dreams and imagery is as legitimate as working with conscious thoughts and feelings. They are just as much products of the brain and can bring interesting and useful new areas of content to a journal. Working in this way may usefully circumvent emotional blocks. There are many different ways of working with dreams and images (see Shohet, 1985; Reed, 1985).

Past, present and future

This technique can bring unexpected considerations to bear on an area of life. Around 10 minutes is spent reflecting and writing on a past occurrence. In the professional context, it might be a period of practice or learning or an event. There is no interpretation, just a description. The next 10 to 15 minutes are spent writing down future associations and anticipations that arise in free association from the description of the past material. This is then brought into the current time in an integrated account that includes consideration of the meanings and its implications for the present.

SWOT analysis

A SWOT analysis is a commonly used tool that facilitates thinking about some issue or event. It may be used in an evaluative manner or as a prelude to change. In either case, such an analysis can provide useful material for further reflection and can 'move thinking on'. A SWOT analysis can be performed on an event, an ongoing situation or organization. It involves the separate noting of issues under the four words that make up the acronym – strengths, weaknesses, opportunities and threats.

Chapter 16

Learning through reflection – more ways and means

Introduction

The previous chapter focused on a particular method of encouraging reflection – the writing of journals. This chapter is a compilation of other ways and means of encouraging reflection to enhance the processes of learning and practice. As in the previous chapter, the 'means of encouraging reflection' are mostly what have been identified as the conditions that favour reflection, accentuated or harnessed as a specific activity. The divisions of activities are more convenience and are not mutually exclusive. The first group consists of activities that encourage reflection by developing the use of dialogue.

As in the writing of journals, the reflection engendered in most of these exercises is in a represented form – either oral or written. Reflection in initial learning occurs in those examples where the learner is presented with difficult material and is forced to undergo reflective activity in order to produce a reasonable response. In the same way as journal writing, there will be occasions when the material of learning that has been learnt superficially becomes linked into meanings and that learning is then upgraded.

It is important to remember to ensure that exercises do not become simply recipes to be followed – that, rather, they are used with awareness and concern that they do, indeed, generate reflective activity.

Encouraging reflection by developing dialogue

Dialogue journals

Dialogue journals are written reflective dialogues between two or more people who take turns to make an entry on a paper that passes between them. Dialogue journals originated in the school setting in the 1980s, but the idea has been applied at other educational levels, as well as among professionals themselves. Roderick (1986) describes a situation in which teachers reflect in this way on their practice and, in another situation, there is a written dialogue between researchers engaged in enquiry about the process of writing a dialogue (Roderick and Berman, 1984). The technique has been used to generate reflective discussion between teachers and teaching students (Staton, et al., 1988). The most usual pattern of dialogue described in the literature, though, is that between a teacher and a pupil. It may be initiated by either and passes back and forth over a period of time, with each responding or bringing new ideas or comment into the situation. The frequency of comment may be daily or over a longer period (Roderick and Berman, 1984).

In the literature, there are many claims of advantage for the system of dialogue journals, for example, that it improves writing skills and personalizes education in the unique nature of the dialogue between teacher and student (Staton, et al., 1988). The written dialogue form can generate a slow-paced reflective conversation in which both participants have time to respond in a considered manner to each other's material. The slow pace, itself, may have the effect of deepening the level of learning or this process can deliberately be facilitated by one of the parties. The opportunity to steer the dialogue into more valuable reflection is a particular advantage of the method as the process provides a means of deepening the reflection and introducing critique.

The disadvantage of dialogue journals in the traditional form between teacher and student is the time it takes for the teacher to work with all students in the class. However, there are many ways of applying the idea, particularly when use is made of e-mail. The greatest challenge is in maintaining the quality and depth of the discussion when there is no teacher input. Setting criteria for the assessment of the quality of dialogues between students would be an interesting possibility.

Training students to ask questions that facilitate reflection

Asking any question may stimulate reflection in another person, but Chapter 13 suggested that there are particular types of questions that enforce reflection. Morgan and Saxon (1991) suggest that what characterizes these questions is that they:

- develop supposition and hypothesis – such as 'I wonder what the effects of the millennium bug will be?';

- focus on personal feelings – for example, 'What were your thoughts when you read this passage?';
- focus on future action or projection – say, 'If you were in that situation, what would you be feeling?';
- develop critical assessment or value judgements – for example, 'Can we justify spending a vast sum on the opera house when five streets away, people are sleeping in cardboard boxes?'

Students can be taught to probe for meaning by using a series of questions – to chase meaning. If students are taught to use appropriate questions, they can make better use of dialogue among peers to facilitate reflection, whether orally or in written or electronic form.

Pugach and Johnson (1990) describe a particular format of written dialogue that helps teachers to deal comprehensively with problems in practice. In peer collaboration, one teacher takes the role of facilitator and one of initiator. In the first stage of reframing the issue by asking clarifying questions, the initiator is helped to question aspects of the situation and clarify the factors involved. In this way, they explore new perspectives on the problem. In the second stage of summarizing the problem, the initiating teacher defines the situation again, identifying the pattern of behaviour, the teacher's affective response and noting the variables over which they have control. At the third stage, the initiator identifies three possible plans of action, explores the anticipated outcomes and selects one for implementation. The last stage is the development of the plan for evaluation of the action to be taken. The value of this systematic guidance for reflection on practice has been supported in research over a period of three years.

Generating reflection by using non-verbal techniques

Most of the forms of reflection to which reference has been made in this book are verbal and sequential. There are several calls in the literature for use of techniques – sometimes termed 'right hemisphere techniques' (Korthagen, 1993) – that generate different forms of reflection and may bypass the resistances that can block normal reflective processes or else introduce new perspectives for reflection. Korthagen suggests that these techniques tap a non-rational process that is influential in guiding action.

Activities described below can be useful to individuals or in group situations where 'sharing' of the content of the representation may or may not be appropriate. Personal meaning can be sensitive and following up with reflective writing is an alternative possibility. One of the problems with this kind of activity is that skill or talent can obstruct meaning. For example, those who cannot draw worry about their lack of talent and those who can worry about the quality of what they produce. Drawing skill simply gets in the way of this kind of expression.

Poetry, drawing, sculpting, narrative and other forms of representation of meaning

Clarke, James and Kelly (1996) suggest that these 'aesthetic' forms 'make possible unique forms of understanding'. Learners may, for example, be asked to depict a particular situation in learning or practice or abstract concepts, such as 'draw a picture of education' (Korthagan, 1993) or 'draw how it feels to be a social worker'.

Role play simulations and drama

Re-enacting events or incidents makes it possible to analyse actions taken and experiment with actions that might have been taken. This is an effective manner of recalling and reflecting on feelings that have been evident in the real situation.

Drawing exercises

There are many graphical exercises that are reflective and can generate learning. James (1993) suggests the drawing of a life line as a means of plotting a life history. A more creative version is the 'route map' of life in which a learner depicts their life as a route across a map – difficult times being displayed, for example, as mountainous regions. This exercise could be adapted to cover 'your school years' or focus on particular experiences, such as 'myself as a learner' or biologist or parent and so on. It is interesting to note that the same activity enacted on different days can generate completely different reflections. The nature of 'today' determines what is 'picked up' in reflection on the past.

Projective techniques

The use of materials on to which meaning can be projected can be less threatening than direct work and, therefore, useful for introducing such reflective activities. Korthagan (1993) and James (2993) suggest the use of photographs or pictures as a means of stimulating meanings. Korthagen suggests that pictures are used alongside word cards. The words are emotive or evaluative words that can be used to illuminate meanings in the picture cards.

Repertory grid techniques

Korthagan (1993) describes the use of some of the ideas of the repertory grid (Kelly, 1955) to elicit personal constructs about particular issues. In the initial grid process, a learner is given three cards with words, ideas or names on them and is asked in what way two of the items on the cards are the same and different from the third. After a relatively few repeats of this process, the constructs that distinguish 'same' from 'different' run out. The learner is then confronted with the identity of the constructs they use to view a part of their world.

Guided fantasy

States of fantasy and imagination can be facilitated under conditions of relaxation by a 'leader' drawing the participants into a scene or story by using words that represent sensory imagery. The scene or story might be real or imaginary or real with some details changed. For example, learners might be led to imagine themselves performing effectively in a situation that they fear, such as examinations or a difficult professional situation.

Concept maps and other spatial representations of ideas

A concept map is a graphical method of representing a concept. Concept maps encapsulate the whole idea or concept with the main themes radiating from the central concept and subdividing in a hierarchical arrangement. In this way, they can depict the relationships between the elements of the idea (Deshler, 1990; Buzan, 1993). This arrangement of knowledge seems to suit some learners more than others.

There are many ways of using concept maps. They are a useful means of reflecting on the ideas that we take for granted and their underlying values (Deshler 1990). They can also be used to provide a summary of information and a means of monitoring personal meanings over a period of time, or comparing them with the personal meanings of others. On a similar basis, maps can be used to compare the meaning and connotations of one idea or term with another. As a map can reflect back to the learner their view of something, they open up the possibility of change. In an example, Deshler demonstrates how he discovered that his annoyance with squirrels emanates from their stealing of birdfood from a birdfeeder By changing his concept of 'birdfeeder' to 'bird and squirrel feeder', he could come to welcome the squirrel's feeding activities. Buzan promotes the use of concept maps as a means of retaining material and a potential facilitator of creativity.

Concept maps can be developed over time because the information is not sequential. Looking back at a concept map may reveal areas that are missing, duplication, more accurate ways in which the elements of the map could be organized, new links or assumptions that underlie the ideas and their linkage (Deshler, 1990). Deshler provides the following examples of activities based on the drawing of concept maps:

- one person explains their map to another and so tests their own understanding of it;
- individuals listen to explanations as above, and ask probing questions;
- a map is constructed with another to provide a focus for joint reflective activities and explore the mutuality of ideas.

Generating reflection by reviewing and revisiting the material of learning

The opportunity to revisit the material of learning is an opportunity to reflect on it, so long as the revisiting involves some restructuring and is more than just a 'looking over'. There can be different objectives for the reflective activities described below. The same activity can be introduced for different reasons, but it is helpful to learners to know why they are being asked to function in a particular manner.

Summarizing material

Hullfish and Smith (1961) describe oral or written summarizing as an 'effective tool for building a continuing reflective atmosphere'. They suggest that summaries can be done by individual students or small groups or developed by the whole class. Hullfish and Smith suggest that the teacher's summary may be valuable, but that 'a summary is the student's opportunity to be the interpreter and organizer of his own experience'. The restructuring should at least involve a discrimination of main points from lesser points. An exercise that enforces such discrimination is that of précis writing. Condensing information while retaining the sense of the whole with appropriate emphasis is the essence of good note-taking, but it is rarely considered as a useful study skill in its own right.

Hullfish and Smith also suggest that a reflective atmosphere can be produced if the summarizing can be linked back to an outline that has been given at the start of a class. Outlining may be an opportunity to remind students of how the new material relates to what they know already – in the manner of an advance organizer (Ausubel and Robinson, 1969).

Some other quick reflective classroom activities have been mentioned earlier (Chapter 13). These are developments of 'classroom assessment techniques' – CATS (Angelo and Cross, 1993). Here are some examples.

- Students summarize the content of a class, lecture or topic in one sentence, phrase or even a word, then write a brief account of the choice of words in the summary.
- Students pair up and one explains the important issues of a topic to another in five minutes. The speaker may be allowed an initial two minutes to organize their thoughts before the explanation. The other of the pair then provides feedback, adds points or disagrees for three minutes. The process is then reversed, with another topic being explained by the student who gave feedback before.
- A topic is explained in writing for a named target audience.
- Individually or in groups, students make or plan a poster display on a particular topic.

- A conflict is identified in the material and learners summarize the issues on either side – perhaps in a chart form.
- Learners are asked to prepare a glossary of terms involved in a particular topic. The discussion of meanings that would be involved in group work on this would be valuable. Defining simple terms that are constantly used in teaching and learning can be challenging.
- Learners develop questions that would probe deep learning of a particular topic. These could be used with other learners.

There are many variations on these sorts of activities. Where the activity is individual, there is further value to be gained in asking learners to compare their work with that of others, consider how it differs and perhaps then integrate their work to create a joint response.

Activities designed to integrate learning

Hullfish and Smith (1961) say 'No effort should be spared in challenging students to seek out the relationships of what is learned in one class to what is learned in another'. If this assertion is maintained, then recent tendencies, particularly in higher education, towards the 'packaging of learning' into modules or topic resource materials create a need for integrating learning by reflecting on how one area of learning relates to another and to previous knowledge. 'Progress files' or records of achievement in higher education (NCIHE, 1997) can provide a mechanism or place in the curriculum for such activities. Some examples of activities that actively encourage integration of learning follow. Most can be done either in groups or alone.

- Learners are asked to list ideas that two or more areas of learning have in common.
- Learners identify problems or issues of concern that would require knowledge gained from two or more areas of learning.
- There may be distinct differences between the methods used or nature or organization of the knowledge in areas of learning that learners could be asked to identify.

Analysing critical incidents

Critical incident analysis is a specialized form of 'revisiting' of previous learning or experience in which 'individuals or groups unpick a significant event or an incident and reflect upon it to come to understand what they have learned from it' (James, 1993). More specifically, an aim of critical incident analysis can be to uncover the network of personal assumptions that have informed an individual's understanding, interpretation and action with regard to the situation.

Brookfield (1990) describes uses of critical incident analysis with professionals looking at their practice, but also with groups interested in their personal relationships and political assumptions. Each person writes a vivid description of a recent incident that has had an impact on them. Triads are formed and, in turn, the incidents are read out. After each, the other two try to identify assumptions that are embedded in the description. The assumptions are analysed in two ways. First, in the manner in which they guided which particular incident they chose to describe. Second, in their relationship to the actions that the person took. Brookfield suggests that the participants think of assumptions as 'rules of thumb' – they might be beliefs, ideas, theories, intuitions or personal understandings. Requests for additional information by the listeners are indicators to the whole triad of what they perceive as significant in the incident described.

Brookfield suggests that a useful introductory activity for the session is for the facilitator to describe an incident of their own that the participants, in small groups, then analyse for assumptions. He also uses a debriefing session as a means of closing the workshop.

In a variation on the use of critical incident analysis, Kennedy (1990) describes similar patterns of activity that are used to uncover understandings of a person's social ideology. A situation is described in which a person first becomes aware of the social or cultural 'cocoon' in which they have been existing. This is shared in groups and the person then analyses the forces that tend to maintain the status quo and those that operated towards a 'breakthrough' in order to understand the nature of curtailment and emancipation. James suggests a further variant – successful events are celebrated as a 'positive vehicle' for reflecting on practice.

Action learning sets

Action learning sets represent another specialized form of review or revisiting that, in turn, generates reflection and learning, though in this case the learning is drawn further into action rather than reflection. Beaty, Jaques and McGill (1997) describe a relatively formalized version of action learning sets and illustrate their value in education and professional development settings. However, their nature can be varied considerably.

Action learning is a means by which an individual can use the reflective processes of a group to bear on a problem or an issue that they have at the time. The group may be self-led or facilitated. Participants agree to bring to the meeting the details of an issue or problem that will be resolved in some form of action. Examples might be a change in professional practice, an area of teaching that they feel they would like to run differently, a project that needs action, a personal need to improve study skills or areas of learning with action implications and so on. The issue may or may not be within the realm of expertise of the other members of the group.

The meetings for action learning may be one-off or ongoing. In each meeting, time is shared between participants after a period of time has been allocated for opening and closing. When it is their turn, an individual (initiator) describes the issue and the surrounding circumstances. The others ask questions to clarify the issue, facilitate the reflection of the initiator and support their movement towards resolution and action. If there is a series of meetings, there will be opportunities to support the initiator in their progress towards resolution and later during the action phase.

Generating reflection by means of evaluative techniques

Situations of assessment or evaluation are specialized forms of review (as above). However, the review is channelled via criteria of judgement and any learning that results from reflection may be about the techniques of learning and the representing learning instead of, or as well as, learning about the content.

Formal assessment

In many conventional situations of assessment, the learner learns nothing more than that a mark has been attributed to their work on the basis of criteria about which they may not be entirely clear. The real chances of useful learning come from collaborative approaches when the learner is involved in the development of some or all of the assessment criteria (Race, 1991) and when peer or self-assessment is used. In these situations, the whole act of representing learning is immediately more reflective, moving between the requirements of the task laid down in the criteria and in the processes of review. Much has been written about peer and self-assessment (Brown and Dove, 1991; Brown and Knight, 1994; Boud, 1995, for example).

Informal peer and self-assessment

A learner's ability to assess or evaluate their own work is an important skill to be gained in higher level learning. The conduct of peer and self-assessment does not have to contribute to grades or the accumulation of marks, and reflection on personal performance makes a productive break in normal classroom activity.

Feedback

Feedback on work can be a red slash or a helpful comment that demonstrates empathy with the work and its producer. Plenty has been written about this, but the quality of feedback is in danger of degradation in the face of burgeoning student numbers. A form of feedback that is not exploited in the UK – possibly because of a competitive ethos among students – is the development of formal or informal systems of peer feedback. In some countries, learners would not expect to hand in an essay without giving it to a colleague for comments. Reflection as a result of peer feedback can be enhanced if it is incorporated into assessment. For example, on completion of an essay, learners can be asked to review and provide feedback on each other's work in the form of half a sheet of written comment. The writer does or does not modify the work on the basis of the feedback, but hands the feedback sheet, with considerations of the value of the feedback, in with the essay. A proportion of the marks is allocated to this reflective work (Emig, 1997).

Generating reflection by using ill-structured material

In mass higher education, teachers can feel compelled to 'tidy up' learning. In the absence of enough books, material is printed out as handouts or from the Internet, discussion in tutorial groups gives way to more lectures and learning is packaged in study guides and computer programs. Resources such as these can still provide learners with ill-structured learning materials, but, in reformul-ating the material of teaching, tidying up is a great temptation. Many references have been made to the value of ill-structured material of learning in promoting reflection. Perhaps the important point here is that tidied-up learning can reduce reflective activity and reduce the potential effectiveness of learning.

The use of pre-prepared overhead projector slides is another example of the manner in which delivery is 'tidied up'. It is understandable that teachers should want prepare as much as possible in advance of teaching when they will face a class of several hundred and, in effect, be required to put on a 'performance'. However, 'chalk and talk' may be a mode of delivery that is more conducive to reflection on the part of learners – and perhaps teachers as well as the time taken to write provides natural pauses for reflection.

Exposure to 'real-life' situations

Reflection on real-life situations is likely to involve ill-structured data and problems with no 'right' or 'wrong' answers.

Exposure to the ill-structured issues that characterize a discipline

Meyers (1986) suggests that students should be made aware of the characteristic ill-structured issues within their disciplines as well as the wonders and mysteries from early in the study of a discipline. Instead of just the successful experimental work of a discipline being described to learners, the dead end and the unsuccess-ful work is also valuable material. Learners are asked 'What if . . . ?' questions. They are asked to consider alternative views on a topic.

In a similar way, Riddle (1997) suggests that the raw material of argument about a topic should be presented and that we should not 'tidy up arguments and stack them on the shelves as pre-packaged thinking'.

Situations that challenge initial thinking on an issue

An example here is in the arrangement of a secondary experience that causes the learner to think again about an experience they have previously undergone and initially reviewed (Boud and Knights, 1994). Problem solving as a learning method incorporates such methodology (Boud and Feletti, 1991).

Situations that challenge assumptions

Examples have been given earlier of techniques that involve methods such as critical incident analysis or well-structured questioning.

Situations in which learners are challenged to commit themselves to judgements or choices

When learners are pressed to make a difficult choice, they are forced to work across and between ideas and make assessments of evidence – a situation that they are likely to perceive as consisting of ill-structured information. An example of this type of situation is in peer or self-assessment, to which reference has been made earlier.

Situations where learners must integrate new learning into previous learning

There have been several previous references to the integration of new learning into what is already known. Use is made of this kind of task when, for example, teaching students are required to reflect on their previous conceptions of teaching, learning and schools, and to relate the new, more theoretical understandings to previous knowledge. The integration of new and earlier understandings is a manner in which learning can be truly owned and become meaningful to the learner (Boud, Keogh and Walker, 1985).

Situations that demand the ordering of thoughts

The ordering of thoughts may seem to be a stage of reflection that follows exposure to disorganized data, such as that engendered in the activities and so on described earlier. Many processes of reflection will entail periods of divergence of processing followed by convergence.

Generating reflection by learners reflecting on their own learning

Any technique that enables a learner to understand more about their own learning behaviour is likely to enhance reflection in learning and offer the possibility of improvement of technique. A number of the methods by which a learner may learn about their processes are mentioned in the literature – some have been mentioned elsewhere in this book. Main (1985) describes how he enables learners to understand their difficulties by means of counselling, Gibbs (1981) advocates group work as a means of generating awareness of study habits for the improvement of study skills, but there are also study inventories that provide the learner with feedback information on their learning. Candy, Harri-Augstein and Thomas (1985) mention the reading recorder and some less sophisticated ways of researching personal reading.

In their further development of work on enabling learners to understand their processes in order to improve learning, Harri-Augstein and Webb (1985) describe the 'morphology' of the 'learning conversation'. The learning conversation enables the learner to reflect on what is involved in learning for them, what works and what does not work. The conversation may utilize the support of a coach, who guides the learner through the stages, and, while it starts in the description of a real experience, it progresses to consideration of the learning process itself and how improvement might be achieved. This pattern is evident in most of the approaches described above.

Generating reflection by teaching critical thinking and philosophy

Reflection is part of learning itself. Methods of reviewing learning should therefore include the review of reflective processes. As critical thinking is very close to, or an aspect of, reflection, techniques of teaching critical thinking and philosophy generate more reflection. They do so by reiterating many of the kinds of techniques mentioned above – for example, by good questioning and confronting the learner with ill-structured material of learning (Meyers, 1986; Lipman, 1991; Brookfield, 1993). Teaching critical thinking in the context of philosophy teaching has been found to benefit other learning (Resnick, 1987). Following a course in philosophy legitimizes and enables practice in the questioning of assumptions that underpin any other learning – the process of reflection.

References

Angelo, T and Cross, K (1990) *Classroom Assessment Techniques,* Jossey-Bass, San Francisco

Argyris, C and Schön, D (1974) *Theory into Practice,* Jossey-Bass, San Francisco

Arlin, P (1990) 'Wisdom, the art of problem solving', in *Wisdom, its Nature, Origins and Development*, ed R Sternberg, Cambridge University Press, Cambridge

Atkins, S and Murphy, K (1993) 'Reflection: a review of the literature', *Journal of Advanced Nursing*, **18**, pp 1188–92

Ausubel, D and Robinson, F (1969) *School Learning,* Holt, Rhinehart and Winston, London

Balkan, D (1966) *The Duality of Human Existence,* Beacon Press, Boston, MA

Bandler, R and Grindler, J (1979) *Frogs into Princes*, Real People Press, Moab, UT

Bannister, D and Fransella, F (1974) *Inquiring Man*, Penguin, Harmondsworth

Barnett, R (ed) (1992) *Improving Higher Education*, SRHE/OUP, Buckingham

Barnett, R (1994) *The Limits of Competence*, SRHE/OUP, Buckingham

Barnett, R (1997) *Higher Education, a Critical Business*, SRHE/OUP, Buckingham

Beaty, L, Gibbs, G and Morgan, A (1997) 'Learning orientations and study contracts' in *The Experience of Learning*, eds F Marton, D Hounsell and N Entwistle, Scottish Academic Press, Edinburgh

Beaty, L, Jaques, D and McGill, I (1997) 'Action learning in higher education' I and II, UCoSDA Briefing Papers 43 and 44, February and March 1997

Belanoff, P (1987) 'The role of journals in the interpretive community' in *The Journal Book*, ed T Fulwiler, Heinemann, Portsmouth, New Hampshire

Belenky, M, Clinchy, B, Goldberger, R and Tarule, J (1986) *Women's Ways of Knowing*, Basic Books, New York

Bercholez, S and Chodzin Kohn, S (1994) *Entering the Stream*, Random House, London

Berthoff, A (1987) 'Dialectical notebooks and the audit of meaning', in *The Journal Book*, T Fulwiler, Boynton/Cook Publishers, Heinemann, Portsmouth, New Hampshire

Biggs, J (1988) 'Approaches to essay writing' in *Learning Strategies and Learning Styles*, ed R Schmeck, Plenum Press, New York

Biggs, J (1993) 'From theory to practice: A cognitive systems approach', *HE Research and Development*, **12**, pp 73–85

Biggs, J and Collis, K (1982) *Evaluating the Quality of Learning*, Academic Press, New York

Birren, J and Fisher, L (1990) 'The elements of wisdom: overview and integration' in *Wisdom, its Nature, Origins and Development*, ed R Sternberg, Cambridge University Press, Cambridge

Boud, D (1989) 'Some competing traditions in experiential learning' in (1989), *Making Sense of Experiential Learning*, S Warner Weil and I McGill, SRHE/OUP, Buckingham

Boud, D (1995) *Enhancing Learning Through Self-assessment*, Kogan Page, London

Boud, D and Feletti, G (1991) *The Problem of Problem-based Learning*, Kogan Page, London

Boud, D, Keogh, R and Walker, D (eds) (1985) *Reflection: Turning experience into learning*, Kogan Page, London

Boud, D and Knights, S (1994) 'Designing courses to promote reflective practice', *Research and Development in HE*, **16**, pp 229–34

Boud, D and Miller, N (1996) *Working with Experience*, Routledge, London

Boud, D and Walker, D (1990) 'Making the most of experience', *Studies in Continuing Education*, **12**, (2), pp 61–80

Boud, D and Walker, D (1993) 'Barriers to reflection on experience' in *Using Experience for Learning*, eds D Boud, R Cohen and D Walker, SRHE/OUP, Buckingham

Boyd, E and Fales, A (1983) 'Reflective learning: key to learning from experience', *Journal of Human Psychology*, **23**, (2), pp 94–117

Brammer, L, Schostrom, E and Abrego, P (1989) *Therapeutic Psychology*, Prentice Hall, Englewood Cliffs, New Jersey

Bright, B (1993) 'What is reflective practice?', *Curriculum*, **16**, pp 69–81

Brookfield, S (1983) 'Using critical incidents to explore learners' assumptions', in *Education for Adults*, Vol. 1, ed M Tight, Croom Helm, London

Brookfield, S (1987) *Developing Critical Thinkers: Challenging adults to explore alternative ways of thinking and acting*, Jossey-Bass, San Francisco

Brookfield, S (1990) 'Using critical incidents to explore assumptions' in *Fostering Critical Reflection in Adulthood,* ed J Mezirow, Jossey-Bass, San Francisco

Brookfield, S (1993) *Developing Critical Thinkers*, OUP, Oxford

Brown, S and Dove, P (January 1991) 'Self and peer assessment', Paper 63, SCED, Birmingham

Brown, S and Knight, P (1994) *Assessing Learning in Higher Education*, Kogan Page, London

Bruner, J (1966) *Towards a Theory of Instruction*, Harvard University Press, Cambridge, MA

Bruner, J (1990) *Acts of Meaning*, Harvard University Press, Cambridge, MA

Burnard, P (1991) *Experiential Learning in Action*, Avebury Press, Aldershot

Buzan, T (1993) *The Mind Map Book*, BBC Books, London

Calderhead, J and Gates, P (eds) (1993) *Conceptualising Reflection in Teacher Development*, Falmer Press, London

Calderhead, J and James, C (1992) 'Recording student teachers' learning experiences', *Journal of Further and Higher Education*, **16**, (1), pp 3–12

Candy, P, Harri-Augstein, S and Thomas, L (1985) 'Reflection and the self-organised learner: A model of learning conversations' in *Reflection: Turning experience into learning*, D Boud, R Keogh and D Walker, Kogan Page, London

Carr, W and Kemmis, S (1986) *Becoming Critical*, Falmer Press, London

Christensen, R (1981) ' "Dear diary": a learning tool for adults', *Lifelong learning: the adult years*, October

Clarke, B, James, C and Kelly, J (1996) 'Reflective practice: reviewing the issues and refocusing the debate', *Inst. J. Nursing Studies*, **33**, (2), pp 171–80

Clift, R, Houston, W and Pugach, M (1990) *Encouraging Reflective Practice*, Teachers College Press, New York

Cooper, J (1991) 'Telling our own stories' in *Stories Lives Tell: Narrative and dialogue in education*, C Whitehead and N Noddings, Teachers College Press, New York

Copeland, W, Birmingham, C and Lewin, B (1993) 'The reflective practitioner in teaching: towards a research agenda', *Teaching and Teacher Education*, **9**, (4), pp 247–59 de Corte, E (1996) 'New perspectives of learning and teaching in higher education' in *Goals and Purposes of Higher Education in the 21st Century*, ed A Burgen, Jessica Kingsley, London

Cox, H, Hickson, P and Taylor, B (1991) 'Exploring reflection, knowing and constructing practice' in *Towards a Discipline of Nursing*, eds G Gray and R Pratt, Churchill Livingstone, Melbourne

Court, D (1988) 'Reflection in action: some definitional problems' in *Reflection in Teacher Education*, P Grimmett and G Erikson, Teachers College Press, New York

Cunningham, P (1983) 'Helping students to extract meaning from experience' in *Helping Adults to Learn How to Learn: New Directions for Continuing Education*, No. 19, R Smith, Jossey-Bass, San Francisco

Dahlgren, L (1997) 'Learning conceptions and outcomes' in *The Experience of Learning*, eds F Marton, D Hounsell and N Entwistle, Scottish Academic Press, Edinburgh

Daloz, L (1986) *Effective Teaching and Mentoring*, Jossey-Bass, San Francisco

D'Arcy, P (1987) 'Writing to learn' in *The Journal Book*, ed T Fulwiler, Heinemann, Portsmouth, New Hampshire

Dennison, B, and Kirk, R (1990) *Do, Review, Learn, Apply*, Blackwell, Oxford

Deshler, D (1990) 'Conceptual mapping: drawing charts of the mind' in *Fostering Critical Reflection in Adulthood*, ed J Mezirow, Jossey-Bass, San Francisco

Dewey, J (1933) *How We Think*, D C Heath and Co, Boston, MA

Dryden, W and Feltham, C (1992) *Brief Counselling*, OUP, Oxford

Dryden, W and Feltham, C (1994) *Developing the Practice of Counselling*, Sage, London

Eastcott, D and Farmer, R (1992) *Planning Teaching for Active Learning*, CVCP/USDTU, Sheffield

Egan, G (1990) *The Skilled Helper*, Brooks and Cole, Pacific Grove, California

Eisner, E (1982) *Cognition and Curriculum: A basis for deciding what to teach*, Longman, New York

Eisner, E (1991) 'Forms of understanding and the future of education', *Educational Researcher*, **22**, pp 5–11

Eizenberg, N (1988) 'Approaches to learning anatomy: developing a programme for medical students' in *Improving Learning*, ed P Ramsden, Kogan Page, London

Emden, C (1991) 'Becoming a reflective practitioner' in *Towards a Discipline of Nursing*, eds J Gray and R Pratt, Churchill Livingstone, Melbourne

Emig, R (1997) personal communication

Entwistle, N (1988) *Styles of Learning*, David Fulton, Edinburgh

Entwistle, N (1992) *The Impact of Teaching on Learning Outcomes*, USDU, Sheffield

Entwistle, N (1996) 'Recent research on student learning and the learning environment' in *The Management of Independent Learning*, eds J Tait and P Knight, SEDA/Kogan Page, London

Entwistle, N (1997) 'Contrasting perspectives on learning' in *The Experience of Learning*, eds F Marton, D Hounsell and N Entwistle, Scottish Academic Press, Edinburgh

Entwistle, A and Entwistle, N (1992) 'Experience of understanding in revising for degree examinations', *Learning and Instruction*, **2**, pp 1–22

Entwistle, N and Entwistle, A (1997) 'Revision and the experience of understanding' in *The Experience of Learning*, eds F Marton, D Hounsell and N Entwistle, Scottish Academic Press, Edinburgh

Eraut, M (1992) 'Developing the knowledge base: A process perspective on professional education' in *Learning to Effect*, ed R Barnett, SRHE/OUP, Buckingham

Eraut, M (1994) *Developing Professional Knowledge and Competence*, Falmer Press, London

Erdos, G (1990) 'Teaching thinking skills' in *Lines of Thinking: Reflections on the psychology of thought*, Vol. 2, eds K Gilhooly, M Keane, R Logie and G Erdos, John Wiley and Sons, Chichester

Evison, R and Horobin, R (1983) *How to Change Yourself and Your World: A manual of co-counselling theory and practice*, Co-Counselling Phoenix, Sheffield

Eysenck, M and Keane, M (1995) *Cognitive Psychology*, 3rd edn, Erlbaum, Hove

Fenstermacher, G (1988) 'The place of science and epistemology in Schön's conception of reflective practice' in *Reflection in Teacher Education*, eds P Grimmett and G Erikson, Teachers College Press, New York

Fitzgerald, M (1994) 'Theories of reflection for learning' in *Reflective Practice in Nursing*, A Palmer, S Burns and C Bulmer, Blackwell, Oxford

Francis, D (1995) 'Reflective journal: a window to preservice teachers' practical knowledge', *Teaching and Teacher Education*, **11**, (3), pp 229–41

Fransella, F and Dalton, P (1995) *Personal Construct Counselling in Action*, Sage, London

Friere, P (1970) *Pedagogy of the Oppressed*, Penguin, Harmondsworth

Fulwiler, T (1987) *The Journal Book*, Heineman, Portsmouth, New Hampshire

Garrett, R (1983) *The Power of Action Learning in Practice*, Gower, Aldershot

Garry, A and Cowan, J (1986) 'To each according to his need', *Aspects of Educational Technology*, Vol. XXI, Kogan Page, London

Gibbs, G (1981) *Teaching Students to Learn*, OUP, Oxford

Gibbs, G (1988) *Learning by Doing: A guide to teaching and learning methods*, SCED, Birmingham

Gilbert, J, Watts, M and Osborne, R (1985) 'Eliciting student views using an interview about instances technique' in (1995), *Cognitive Structure and Conceptual Change*, H West and A Pines, Academic Press, New York

Gilhooly, K, Keane, M, Logie, R and Erdos, G (1990) *Lines of Thinking: Reflections on the psychology of thought*, Vol, 2, John Wiley and Sons, Chichester

Goodman, J (1984) 'Reflection and teacher education: A case study and theoretical analysis', *Interchanges*, **15**, p 39

Gore, J (1993) *The Struggle for Pedagogies*, Routledge, London

Gray, J and Forström, S (1991) 'Generating theory from practice and the reflective technique' in *Towards a Discipline of Nursing*, G Gray and R Pratt, Churchill Livingstone, Melbourne

Gray, J and Pratt, R (1991) *Towards a Discipline of Nursing*, Churchill Livingstone, Melbourne

Greenwood, J (1993) 'Reflective practice: a critique of the work of Argyris and Schön', *J. Adv. Nursing*, **18**, pp 1183–87

Gregorc, A (1973) 'Developing plans for professional growth', NASSP Bulletin, December 1993, pp 1–8

Grimmett, P (1988) 'The nature of reflection and Schön's conception in perpective' in *Reflection in Teacher Education*, eds P Grimmett and G Erikson, Teachers College Press, New York

Grimmett, P and Erikson, G (1988) *Reflection in Teacher Education*, Teachers College Press, New York

Grimmett, P, McKinnon, A, Erikson, G and Riecken, T (1990) 'Reflective practice in teacher education' in *Encouraging Reflective Practice in Education*, eds R Clift, W Houston and M Pugach, Teachers College Press, New York

Grumbacher, J (1987) 'How writing helps physics students become better problem solvers' in *The Journal Book*, ed T Fulwiler, Heinemann, Portsmouth, New Hampshire

Grumet, M (1989) 'Generations: reconceptualist curriculum theory and teacher education', *Journal of Teacher Education*, **40**, pp 13–17

Habermas, J (1971) *Knowledge and Human Interests*, Heineman, London

Hallberg, F (1987) 'Journal writing as person making' in *The Journal Book*, ed T Fulwiler, Heinemann, Portsmouth, New Hampshire

Handley, P (1998) personal communication

Harri-Augstein, S and Thomas, L (1991) *Learning Conversations*, Routledge, London

Harri-Augstein, S and Webb, I (1995) *Learning to Change*, McGraw-Hill, Maidenhead

Hart, M (1990) 'Liberation through consciousness-raising' in *Fostering Critical Reflection in Adulthood: A guide to transformative and emancipatory learning*, ed J Mezirow, Jossey-Bass, San Francisco

Harvey, L, and Knight, P (1996) *Transforming Higher Education*, SRHE/OUP, Buckingham

Hatton, N, and Smith, D (1995) 'Reflection in teacher education – towards definition and implementation', *Teaching and Teacher Education*, **11**, (1), pp 33–49

HEA, HEBS, HPW and HPANI (1995) *Handbook on the Development of Foundation Courses in Health Promotion*, Health Promotion Wales, Cardiff

Head, J, and Sutton, C (1985) 'Language understanding and commitment' in *Cognitive Structure and Conceptual Change*, eds L West and A Pines, Academic Press, New York

HEBS (1997) *Promoting Health: A short course in developing effective practice*, Health Education Board for Scotland, Edinburgh

HECIW (1996) *Welsh Higher Education Credit Framework Handbook*, Wales Access Unit, Cardiff

HEQC (1997) *Graduate Standards Programme: Final Report*, HEQC, London

Heron, J (1985) 'The role of reflection in a co-operative enquiry' in *Reflection: Turning experience into learning*, eds D Boud, R Keogh and D Walker, Kogan Page, London

Heron, J (1989) *The Facilitator's Handbook*, Kogan Page, London

Holly, M (1989) 'Reflective working and the spirit of enquiry', *Cambridge Journal of Education*, **19**, pp 71–80

Holly, M (1991) *Keeping a Personal–Professional Journal*, Deakin University Press, Victoria

Holm, D and Stephenson, S (1994) 'Reflection – a student's perspective' in *Reflective Practice in Nursing*, eds A Palmer, S Burns and C Bulmer, Blackwell, London

Honey, P and Mumford, A (1986) *Using Our Learning Styles*, Honey Publications, London

Hoover, L (1994) 'Reflective writing as a window on preservice teachers' thought processes', *Teaching and Teacher Education*, **10**, pp 83–93

Hounsell, D (1997) 'Contrasting conceptions of essay writing' in *The Experience of Learning*, eds F Marton, D Hounsell and N Entwistle, Scottish Academic Press, Edinburgh

Houston, W and Clift, R (1990) 'The potential for research contributions to reflective practice' in *Encouraging Reflective Practice in Education*, eds R Clift, W Houston and M Pugach, Teachers College Press, New York

HPW and other health promotion agencies (1994) *Report of a National Workshop on Health Promotion Foundation Courses*, Health Promotion Wales, Cardiff

Hullfish, H, and Smith, P (1961) *Reflective Thinking: The method for education*, Dodd, Mead and Co, New York

Jakins, H (1970) *Fundamentals of Co-counselling Manual*, revised ed, Rational Island, Washington

James, C (1992) *The Personal Professional Profile: A rationale for practice*, School of Education, University of Bath, Bath

James, C (12 November 1993) 'Developing reflective practice skills –' the potential', paper presented to 'The Power of the Portfolio' national conference

James, C (1997) 'How do you do? An introduction to professional knowledge and its development', inaugural professorial lecture, University of Glamorgan Business School, Pontypridd, Mid Glamorgan

James, C and Clarke, B (1994) 'Reflective practice in nursing: issues and implications for nurse education', *Nurse Education Today*, **14**, pp 82–90

Jaworski, B (1993) 'Professional development of teachers – the potential of critical reflection', *British Journal of Inservice Education*, **19**, pp 37–42

Jensen, V (1987) 'Writing in college physics' in *The Journal Book*, ed T Fulwiler, Heinemann, Portsmouth, New Hampshire

Johns, C (1994) 'Nuances of reflection', *Journal of Clinical Nursing*, **3**, pp 71–75

Jones, S, and Joss, R (1995) 'Models of professionalism' in *Learning and Teaching in Social Work*, M Yelloly and M Henkel, Jessica Kingsley, London

Kelly, G (1955) *The Psychology of Personal Construct Theory*, Vols 1 and 2, Norton, New York

Kelly, J (1994) 'On reflection', *Practice Nurse*, **8**, (11), pp 188–92

Kemmis, S (1985) 'Action research and the politics of reflection' in *Reflection: Turning experience into learning*, eds D Boud, R Keogh and D Walker, Kogan Page, London

Kennedy, W (1990) 'Integrating personal and social ideologies' in *Fostering Critical Reflection in Adulthood*, ed J Mezirow, Jossey-Bass, San Francisco

Kent, O (1987) 'Student journals and the goals of philosophy' in *The Journal Book*, ed T Fulwiler, Heinemann, Portsmouth, New Hampshire

Kenworthy, N (1986) 'Taking the pilot on board', *Senior Nurse*, **4**, (1), pp 17–20

King, P and Kitchener, K (1994) *Developing Reflective Judgement*, Jossey-Bass, San Francisco

Kirby, P and Teddlie, P (1989) 'Development of the reflective teaching instrument', *Journal of Research and Development in Education*, **22**, (4), pp 45–51

Kitchener, K (1983) 'Educational goals and reflective thinking', *Educational Forum*, **48**, (1), pp 75–95

Kitchener, K, and Brenner, H (1990) 'Wisdom and reflective judgement' in *Wisdom, its Nature, Origins and Development*, ed R Sternberg, Cambridge University Press, Cambridge

Kneale, P (1997) 'The rise of the "strategic student": how can we adapt to cope?' in *Facing Up to Radical Changes in Universities and Colleges*, eds M Armstrong, G Thompson and S Brown, SEDA/Kogan Page, London

Knights, S (1985) 'Reflection and learning: the importance of a listener' in *Reflection: Turning experience into learning*, eds D Boud, R Keogh and D Walker, Kogan Page, London

Knowles, J (1993) 'Life history accounts as mirrors: a practical avenue for the conceptualization of reflection in teacher education' in *Conceptualizing Reflection in Teacher Development*, eds J Calderhead and P Gates, Falmer Press, London

Kohlberg, L (1963) 'The development of children's orientations towards moral order: One sequence in the development of moral thought', *Vita Humana*, **6**, (11), pp 333–93

Kolb, D (1984) *Experiential Learning as the Science of Learning and Development*, Prentice Hall, Englewood Cliffs, New Jersey

Kolb, D, and Fry, D (1975) 'Towards an applied theory of experiential learning' in *Theories of Group Processes*, ed C Cooper, Wiley, London

Korthagen, F (1988) 'The influence of learning orientations on the development of reflective teaching' in *Teachers' Professional Learning*, ed J Calderhead, Falmer Press, London

Korthagen, F (1993) Two modes of reflection, *Teacher and Teacher Education*, **9**, (3), pp 317–25

LaBoskey, V (1993) 'A conceptual framework for reflection in preservice teacher education' in *Conceptualizing Reflection in Teacher Development*, eds J Calderhead and P Gates, Falmer Press, London

Lauder, W (1994) Beyond reflection: practical wisdom and the practical syllogism, *Nurse Edn Today*, **14**, pp 91–98

Laurillard, D (1993) *Rethinking University Teaching*, Routledge, London

Lawlor, M, and Handley, P (1996) *The Creative Trainer*, McGraw-Hill, Maidenhead

Lipman, M (1991) *Thinking in Education*, CUP, Cambridge

Main, A (1980) *Encouraging Effective Learning*, Scottish Academic Press, Edinburgh

Main, A (1985) 'Reflection and the development of learning skills' in *Reflection: Turning experience into learning*, eds D Boud, R Keogh and D Walker, Kogan Page, London

Marton, F and Entwistle N (1988) 'What does it take to improve learning?' in *Learning to Teach in Higher Education*, ed P Ramsden, Routledge, London

Marton, F, Hounsell, D, and Entwistle, N (1984) *The Experience of Learning*, 1st edn, Scottish Academic Press, Edinburgh

Marton, F, Hounsell, D, and Entwistle, N (1997) *The Experience of Learning*, 2nd edn, Scottish Academic Press, Edinburgh

Marton, F and Ramsden, P (1988) What does it take to improve learning?, *in Improving Learrning: New perspectives*, Kogan Page, London

Marton, F and Saljö, R (1997) 'Approaches to learning' in *The Experience of Learning*, eds F Marton, D Hounsell and N Entwistle, Scottish Academic Press, Edinburgh

McIntyre, D (1993) 'Theory, theorizing and reflection in initial teacher education' in *Conceptualizing Reflection in Teacher Education*, eds J Calderhead and P Gates, Falmer Press, London

McKinnon, A, and Erikson, G (1988) 'Taking Schön's ideas to a science teaching practicum' in *Reflection in Teacher Education*, eds P Grimmett and G Erikson, Teachers College Press, New York

Meacham, J (1990) 'The loss of wisdom' in *Wisdom, its Nature, Origins and Development*, ed R Sternberg, CUP, Cambridge

Meyers, C (1986) *Teaching Students to Think Critically*, Jossey-Bass, San Francisco

Mezirow, J (1983) 'Critical theory of adult learning and education' in *Education for Adults*, Vol. 1, ed M Tight, Croom Helm, London

Mezirow, J and associates (1990) *Fostering Critical Reflection in Adulthood*, Jossey-Bass, San Francisco

Miller, J (1990) *Creating Spaces and Finding Voices*, State University of New York

Moon, J (1975) 'Some Factors Involved in Learning from Textual Material', dissertation for M.Ed (Psych), University of Glasgow

Moon, J (3 December 1976) Some thoughts on study skills, *Reading*, **10**, pp 24–34

Moon, J (1994) 'Advanced Training Skills Project: Report on initial stages in the project', UK Professional Development Project/University of Central England, Birmingham

Moon, J (December 1995) *Levels in Higher Education*, UCoSDA Briefing Paper 27, Dec 1995.

Moon, J (1996a) 'What can you do in a day? Advice on developing short training courses on promoting health', *Journal of Inst Health Education*, **34**, (1), pp 20–3

Moon, J (Autumn 1996b) 'Generic level descriptors and their place in the standards debate', *In Focus*, HEQC, London

Moon, J (1997) 'Higher education under pressure: what are we in danger of losing?', Italic No. 3 Learning Support Project, University of Wales, Cardiff

Moon, J (1998) 'Higher education under pressure', Italic No. 3 Learning Support Project, University of Wales, Cardiff

Moon, J and England, P (1994) 'The development of a highly structured workshop in health promotion', *Journal of Inst Health Education*, **32**, (2), pp 41–4

Morgan, N and Saxon, S (1991) *Teaching Questioning and Learning*, Routledge, London

Morrison, K (1990) *Learning Logs*, University of Durham, Durham

Morrison, K (1995) 'Dewey, Habermas and reflective practice', *Curriculum*, **16**, pp 82–94

Morrison, K (1996) 'Developing reflective practice in higher degree students through a learning journal', *Studies in HE*, **21**, (3), pp 317–32

Mortimer, J (1998) 'Motivating student learning through facilitating independence: self and peer assessment of reflective practice – an action research project' in *Motivating Students*, S Brown, S Armstrong and G Thompson, SEDA/Kogan Page, London

NCIHE (1997) *Report of the National Committee of Inquiry into Higher Education* (the Dearing Report), NCIHE, London

Newell, R (1994) 'Reflection: art, science or pseudoscience?', *Nurse Education Today*, **14**, pp 49–81

Nichol, D (April 1997) *Research on Learning and Higher Education Teaching*, UCoSDA Briefing Paper 45

Novak, J (1985) 'Metalearning and metaknowledge – strategies to help students to learn how to learn' in *Cognitive Structure and Conceptual Change*, eds H West and A Pines, Academic Press, New York

Nyatanga, L (1989) 'Experiential taxonomy and experiential learning', *Senior Nurse*, **9**, (8), pp 24–27

Oates, L and Watson, L (1996) 'Providing the instructional infrastructure to support flexible learning' in *Enabling Student Learning: Systems and strategies*, eds G Wisker and S Brown, SEDA/Kogan Page, London

O'Connell Killin, P de, and Beer, J (1994) *The Art of Theological Reflection*, Crosshead, New York

Odum, E (1968) *Ecolog*, Holt, Rhinehart and Winston, New York

Palmer, A, Burns, S and Bulman, C (1994) *Reflective Practice in Nursing*, Blackwell, Oxford

Pask, G (1976) 'Styles and strategies of learning', *British Journal of Educational Psychology*, **46**, pp 4–11

Pearson, M, and Smith, D (1985) 'Debriefing in experientially-based learning' in *Reflection: Turning experience into learning*, eds D Boud, R Keogh and D Walker, Kogan Page, London

Perls, F, Hefferline, R and Goodman, P (1951) *Gestalt Therapy*, Dell Publishing, New York

Perry, W (1970) *Forms of Intellectual and Academic Developments in the College Years*, Holt, Rhinehart and Winston, New York

Piaget, J (1971) *Biology and Knowledge*, Edinburgh University Press, Edinburgh

Pines, A, Fensham, P and Garrard, J (1985) 'Describing the cognitive structure of learners' in *Cognitive Structure and Conceptual Change*, eds L West and A Pines, Academic Press, New York

Polyani, M (1966) *The Tacit Dimension*, Doubleday, New York

Prawat, R (1991) Conversations with self and conversations with settings, *American Educational Research Journal*, **28**, pp 737–57

Proctor, K (1993) 'Tutors' professional knowledge of supervision and the implications for supervision practice' in *Conceptualizing Reflection in Teacher Development*, eds J Calderhead and P Gates, Falmer Press London

Progoff, I (1975) *At a Journal Workshop*, Dialogue House Library, New York

Progoff, I (1980) *The Practice of Process Meditation*, Dialogue House Library, New York

Prosser, M (1987) 'The effects of cognitive structure and learning strategy on student achievement' in *Student Learning: Research in education and cognitive psychology*, eds J Richardson, M Eysenck and D Warren Piper, SRHE/OUP, Buckingham

Prosser, M and Miller, R (1989) 'The how and what of learning physics', *European Journal of the Psychology of Education*, 4, pp 513–28

Pugach, M and Johnson, L (1990) 'Reflective practice through structured dialogue' in *Encouraging Reflective Practice in Education*, eds R Clift, W Houston and M Pugach, Teachers College Press, New York

Race, P (1991) 'Learning through assessing' in *Self and Peer Assessment*, eds S Brown and P Dove, SCED Paper 63, Birmingham

Rainer, T (1978) *The New Diary*, J P Tarcher Inc, Los Angeles

Ramsden, P (ed) (1988) *Improving Learning*, Kogan Page, London

Ramsden, P (1992) *Learning to Teach in Higher Education*, Routledge, London

Redwine, M (1989) 'The autobiography as a motivational factor for students' in *Making Sense of Experiential Learning*, eds S Warner Weil and I McGill, SRHE/OUP, Buckingham

Reed, H (1985) *Getting Help from your Dreams*, Inner Vision, Virginia Beach, Virginia

Reid, B (1994) 'The mentor's experience' in *Reflective Practice in Nursing*, eds A Palmer, S Burns and C Bulmer, Blackwell, Oxford

Resnick, L (1987) *Education and Learning to Think*, National Academy Press, Washington DC

Richardson, J, Eysenck, M and Warren Piper, D (1987) *Student Learning: Research in education and cognitive psychology*, SRHE/OUP, Buckingham

Richardson, V (1990) 'The evolution of reflective teaching and teacher education' in *Encouraging Reflective Practice in Education*, eds R Clift, W Houston and M Pugach, Teachers College Press, New York

Riddle, M (1997) 'Literacy through written argument' in *The Quality of Argument: A colloquium on issues of teaching and learning in higher education*, M. Riddle, School of Lifelong Learning, University of Middlesex, London

Roderick, J (1986) 'Dialogue writing: context for reflecting on self as teacher and researcher', *J. Curr. and Supervision*, **1**, (4), pp 305–15

Roderick, J, and Berman, L (1984) 'Dialoguing and dialogue journals', *Language Arts*, **61**, (7), pp 686–92

Rogers, C (1961) *On Becoming a Person*, 9th ed, Sentry Houghton Mifflin, Boston

Russell, T (1993) 'Critical attributes of a reflective teacher' in *Conceptualizing Reflection in Teacher Development*, eds J Calderhead and P Gates, Falmer Press, London

Salmon, P (1989) 'Personal stances in learning' in *Making Sense of Experiential Learning*, eds S Warner Weil and I McGill, SRHE/OUP, Buckingham

Schein, E (1988) *Process Consultation*, Vol. 1, Addison Wesley, Reading, MA

Schmeck, R (1988) *Learning Strategies and Learning Styles*, Plenum Press, New York

Schön, D (1983) *The Reflective Practitioner*, Jossey-Bass, San Francisco

Schön, D (1987) *Educating the Reflective Practitioner*, Jossey-Bass, San Francisco

Schön, D (1992) 'The crisis of professional knowledge and the pursuit of an epistemology of practice', *J. Interprofessional Care*, **6**, (1), pp 49–63

Schulman, B (1988) 'Schön's gate is square but is it art?' in *Reflection in Teacher Education*, eds P Grimmett and G Erikson, Teachers College Press, New York

Selfe, C, Petersen, B, and Nahrgang, C (1986) 'Journal writing in mathematics' in *Writing Across the Disciplines*, eds A Young and T Fulwiler, Boynton/Cook, Upper Montclair, New Jersey

Selman, H (1988) 'The dangers of dichotomous thinking in education' in *Reflection in Teacher Education*, eds P Grimmett and G Erikson, Teachers College Press, New York

Shohet, R (1985) *Dream Sharing*, Turnstone Press, Wellingborough, Northamptonshire

Smith, F (1988) *Understanding Reading*, Holt, Rhinehart and Winston, New York

Smyth, J (1987) *Rationale for Teacher's Critical Pedagogy: A handbook*, Deakin University Press, Geelong

Smyth, J (1989) 'Developing and sustaining critical reflection in teacher education', *Journal of Teacher Education*, **40**, (2), pp 2–9

Staton, J, Shuy, R, Peyton, S, and Reed, L (1988) *Dialogue Journal Communication*, Ablex, Norwood, New Jersey

Steinaker, N, and Bell, R (1979) *The Experiential Taxonomy: A new approach to teaching and learning*, Academic Press, New York

Stephani, L (1997) *Reflective Teaching in Higher Education*, UCoSDA Briefing Paper 42

Sternberg, R (ed) (1990) Wisdom, its Nature, Origins and Development, CUP, Cambridge

Strange, C (1992) 'Beyond the classroom', *Liberal Education*, **78**, pp 28–32

Strike, K and Postner, G (1985) 'A conceptual change view of learning and understanding' in *Cognitive Structure and Conceptual Change*, eds L West and A Pines, Academic Press, New York

Svensson, L (1984) 'Learning and organising knowledge' in *The Experience of Learning*, F Marton, D Hounsell and N Entwistle, Scottish Academic Press, Edinburgh

Svensson, L (1997) 'Skill in learning and organising knowledge', in *The Experience of Learning*, F Marton, D Hounsell, N Entwistle, 2nd edn, Scottish Academic Press, Edinburgh

Swartz, R (1989) 'Making good thinking stick: the role of meta-cognition, extended practice, and teacher modeling in the teaching of thinking' in *Thinking Across Cultures*, eds D Topping, D Crowell, V Kobayashi, Lawrence Erlbaum Association, Hillsdale, New Jersey

Tait, J and Knight, P (1996) *The Management of Independent Learning*, SEDA/Kogan Page, London

Thorpe, M (1993) 'Experiential learning at a distance' in *Using Experience for Learning*, eds D Boud, R Cohen and D Walker, SRHE/OUP, Buckingham

Tobin, K (1987) 'The role of wait time in higher cognitive learning', *Rev. Ed Res.*, **57**, (1), pp 69– 75

Trigwell, K and Prosser, M (1991) 'Improving the quality of student learning: the influence of the learning context and the student approaches to learning on learning outcomes', *H.E.*, **22**, pp 251–66

Usher, R (1985) 'Beyond the anecdotal: adult learning and the use of experience', *Studies in the Edn. of Adults*, **17**, (1), pp 59–74

Usher, R (1993) 'Experiential learning or learning from experience; does it make a difference?' in *Using experience for Learning*, D Boud and R Cohen, SRHE/OUP, Buckingham

Valli, L (1993) 'Reflection in Teacher Education Programmes' in *Conceptualizing Reflection in Teacher Education*, eds J Calderhead and P Gates, Falmer Press, London

Van Manen, M (1977) 'Linking ways of knowing ways of being', *Curriculum Inquiry*, **6**, pp 205–08

Van Manen, M (1991) *The Tact of Teaching*, The State of New York Press, New York

Van Ments, M (1990) *Active Talk*, Kogan Page, London

Van Rossum, E and Schenck, S (1984) 'The relationship between learning conception, study strategy and learning outcome', *British Journal of Educational Psychology*, **54**, pp 73–83

Vaughn, J (1990) 'Encouraging reflective practice in education' in *Encouraging Reflective Practice*, eds R Clift, W Houston M and Pugach, Teachers College Press

Walker, D (1985) Writing, reflection, in *Reflection: Turning Experience into Learning*, R Keogh and D Walker (eds) Kogan Page, London

Warner Weil, S and McGill, I (1989) *Making Sense of Experiential Learning*, SRHE/OUP, Buckingham

Warner Weil, S and McGill, I (1989) 'A framework for making sense of experiential learning' in *Making Sense of Experiential Learning*, eds S Warner Weil and I McGill, SRHE/OUP, Buckingham

Wedman, J and Martin, M (1986) 'Exploring the development of reflective thinking through journal writing', *Reading Improvement*, **23**, (1), pp 68–71

West, H and Pines, A (1985) *Cognitive Structure and Conceptual Change*, Academic Press, New York

White, R (1985) 'Interview protocols and dimensions of cognitive structure' in *Cognitive Structure and Conceptual Change*, eds L West and A Pines, Academic Press, New York

Wildman, T and Niles, J (1987) 'Reflective teachers: tensions between abstractions and realities', *Journal of Teacher Education*, **3**, pp 25–31

Winter, R. (1995) 'The assessment of professional competences: the importance of general criiteria' in *The Assessment of Competence in Higher Education*, eds A Edwards and P Knight, Kogan Page, London

Witherell, C, and Noddings, N (1991) *Stories Lives Tell: Narrative and dialogue in education*, Teachers College Press, New York

Wolf, J (1988) Experiential learning in professional education: concepts and tools, *New Directions for Experiential Learning*, **8**, p 17

Young, A, and Fulwiler, T (1986) *Writing Across the Disciplines*, Boynton/Cook, Upper Montclair, New Jersey

Zeichner, K, and Liston, D (1987) 'Teaching student teachers to reflect', *Harvard Educational Review*, pp 23–48

Index

accommodation 25, 106, 109–111, 123, 134, 137–46
action learning sets 210
action research 35–37, 50
administrators 68, 72, 118
advance organizers 111, 121, 184
anticipation 97, 109
approaches to learning 105, 120–36
assessment 114, 127–28, 130–31, 139, 191, 211
assimilation 25, 106, 109–111, 123, 137–46
attainment 127
autobiographical writing *see* life history

Barnett, R viii, 5, 9, 14, 15–16, 30, 42, 47, 67, 88, 102, 166–67
Boud, D 13, 21, 24, 28, 29, 30, 31, 32, 70, 85, 93–95, 97, 102, 141, 169 170, 176, 213

client 78, 79
client-centred approach 80
co-counselling 169, 196
cognition 94, 133
cognitive structure 83, 105–112, 134–46, 151
collaborative enquiry 87
concept maps 207
conscientization 86
consciousness raising 87
consensus 184–85
constructivist view of learning 82, 105–108, 114, 117
counselling 78–88, 133, 167
critical incident analysis 209

curricular environment 168

dance 61, 80
decisions *see* decision making
decision making 77, 100, 157–58, 177, 182
deep approach to learning *see* approaches to learning
Dewey, J viii, 3, 11–19, 20, 27, 44, 61, 91, 92–94, 96, 99
dialogue journals 186, 204
diary *see* journal
drama 61, 80, 206
drawing 206
dreams 201

educational programmes 67
emotion 26, 29, 61, 72, 94–95, 99, 100, 132–33, 133, 137, 150 157–58, 169 170
emotional barriers 97
emotional block *see* emotional barriers
empowerment 77, 82, 86, 100, 157–58 192
emancipation *see* empowerment
essay writing 125, 131, 212
evaluation of reflective activity 75
experienced practitioners 68
experiential learning 20–38, 50, 98, 100, 103, 159–60

feelings *see* emotion
folk psychology 104
Friere, P 86

gestalt therapy 80

227

Visit Kogan Page on-line

Comprehensive information on
Kogan Page titles

Features include

- complete catalogue listings,
  including book reviews and
  descriptions

- special monthly promotions

- information on NEW titles and
  BESTSELLING titles

- a secure shopping basket facility
  for on-line ordering

PLUS everything you need to know
about KOGAN PAGE

http://www.kogan-page.co.uk